D1596483

FOUCAULT'S CRITICAL ETHICS

just ideas

transformative ideals of justice in ethical and political thought

series editors

Drucilla Cornell

Roger Berkowitz

FOUCAULT'S CRITICAL ETHICS

Richard A. Lynch

FORDHAM UNIVERSITY PRESS

NEW YORK 2016

Copyright © 2016 Fordham University Press

All rights reserved. No part of this publication may be reproduced, stored in a retrieval system, or transmitted in any form or by any means—electronic, mechanical, photocopy, recording, or any other—except for brief quotations in printed reviews, without the prior permission of the publisher.

Fordham University Press has no responsibility for the persistence or accuracy of URLs for external or third-party Internet websites referred to in this publication and does not guarantee that any content on such websites is, or will remain, accurate or appropriate.

Fordham University Press also publishes its books in a variety of electronic formats. Some content that appears in print may not be available in electronic books.

Visit us online at www.fordhampress.com.

Library of Congress Cataloging-in-Publication Data

Names: Lynch, Richard A., 1967– author.
Title: Foucault's critical ethics / Richard A. Lynch.
Description: First edition. | New York, NY : Fordham University Press, 2016.
   | Series: Just ideas | Includes bibliographical references and index.
Identifiers: LCCN 2015042263 (print) | LCCN 2016013129 (ebook) |
   ISBN 9780823271252 (cloth : alk. paper) | ISBN 9780823271269 (ePub)
Subjects: LCSH: Foucault, Michel, 1926–1984. | Ethics. | Power (Philosophy)
Classification: LCC B2430.F724 L96 2016 (print) | LCC B2430.F724 (ebook) |
   DDC 170.92—dc23
LC record available at https://lccn.loc.gov/2015042263

Printed and bound in Great Britain by
Marston Book Services Ltd, Oxfordshire

18 17 16   5 4 3 2 1

First edition

GARY PUBLIC LIBRARY

for Stacy

Contents

3 9222 03231 8136

All I have managed here, and it is more than I intended, is to give a confused statement of an intention which presumes itself to be good: the mere attempt to examine my own confusion would consume volumes. But let what I have tried to suggest amount to this alone: that not only within present reach of human intelligence, but even within reach of mine as it stands today, it would be possible that young human beings should rise onto their feet a great deal less dreadfully crippled than they are, a great deal more nearly capable of living well, a great deal more nearly well, each of them, of their own dignity in existence, a great deal better qualified, each within his limits, to live and to take part toward the creation of a world in which good living will be possible without guilt toward every neighbor: and that teaching at present, such as it is, is almost entirely either irrelevant to these possibilities or destructive of them, and is, indeed, all but entirely unsuccessful even within its own "scales" of "value."

—James Agee

Mais qu'est-ce donc que la philosophie aujourd'hui—je veux dire l'activité philosophique—si elle n'est pas le travail critique de la pensée sur elle-même?

But, then, what is philosophy today—philosophical activity, I mean—if it is not the critical work that thought brings to bear on itself?

—Michel Foucault

Michel Foucault as Critical Theorist

"Foucault disconcerts," as Charles Taylor memorably put it (Taylor 1984, 152).[1] The opening image of *Discipline and Punish*, for example, in which eyewitness accounts retell in graphic detail the difficult and violent 1757 execution of the regicide Damiens, jars readers, piquing our attention if we are not entirely repulsed. Perhaps more profoundly disconcerting than this initial description, however, is Foucault's suggestion that beneath the apparent humanization of punishment since the eighteenth century there is a transformation in the mechanisms of social control, mechanisms that now subject each and every member of society to a constricting web of observation and normalization. The operation of modern power, which Foucault describes in rich detail, is itself disconcerting. The fact that we are disconcerted by Foucault's work, however, tells us something about our own values and normative standpoints and is itself, I would like to suggest, a positive thing.

For Foucault inspires. Many groups, causes, and individuals have been sparked—empowered—by Foucault's works and life to take action in positive and important ways. First among the most notable examples would be the AIDS action group ACT-UP (the AIDS Coalition to Unleash Power), founded in March 1987. ACT-UP played a key role in initiating the medical, political, and personal responses to the crisis of AIDS in the 1980s and 1990s. It contributed to a transformed cultural and political landscape in which AIDS and homosexuality have lost much of their stigma and in which new medical research has produced treatments that make HIV a manageable condition, and it gave many individuals new reasons to fight for their rights and lives rather than resigning themselves to neglect and death.[2] (The 2003 U.S. Supreme Court decision that antisodomy laws are unconstitutional and the subsequent legalization of gay marriage first in Massachusetts and eventually nationwide are just two prominent indications of the transformations that ACT-UP helped initiate.)

In the academy, too, Foucault's influence runs deep and wide. A number of feminist theorists, to take just one field as an example, have used Foucault's work to develop new understandings of social relationships and more subtle accounts of gender discrimination.[3] The impact of his ideas can be felt in fields ranging from history, philosophy, and sociology to geography, education, and psychiatry.

Individuals, too, have taken inspiration from Foucault's work and life. David Halperin even dubbed him "Saint Foucault" and identifies himself as among those for whom "Foucault's life—as much or perhaps even more than his work—continues to serve as a compelling model for an entire generation of scholars, critics, and activists" (Halperin 1995, 6, 7). Particularly notable among that generation is Ladelle McWhorter, who observed, "Michel Foucault's work . . . embodied a philosophical promise nothing else I had ever studied before had ever held out to me" (McWhorter 1999, xiii). If we listen well to Foucault, we cannot help but hear a hope, perhaps even a vision, that moves his pen. My own hope is that this work will help in some small way make that vision more explicit.

So Foucault inspires, and he does so in part because he disconcerts. This disconcert—the discomfort that a reader experiences when she reads of Damien's execution, or when she recognizes the hidden social dynamics that Foucault brings to light—this disconcert forces us to reflect upon the values that prompted it and to evaluate more carefully our own values as well as the social situations that Foucault has described. Michel Foucault thus raises challenges and questions for his readers, questions that simultaneously cut in two directions—outward toward social structures and inward toward one's own beliefs. Foucault challenges, questions, criticizes, and "dereifies" social norms, structures, and institutions; he calls into question our pre-suppositions about society and individuals, including ourselves. Foucault disconcerts us in much the same way as Socrates disconcerted his fellow Athenians in the agora 2,400 years ago.[4]

This double-edged critique—both disconcerting *and* inspiring, of the so-cial *and* individual, aimed outward *and* inward—is expressed in Foucault's adage that "everything is dangerous." He notes in "On the Genealogy of Ethics," an interview with Paul Rabinow and Bert Dreyfus: "My point is not that everything is bad, but that everything is dangerous, which is not exactly the same as bad. If everything is dangerous, then we always have something to do" (DE326.1, 231–232). He continues, "I think that the ethico-political choice we have to make every day is to determine which is the main dan-ger" (DE326.1, 232). To face a constant choice as to what is the most im-portant danger now—a choice that Foucault's analyses of modern society thrust upon us—is disconcerting. But it is also liberating: in facing this choice, we are given the opportunity to assess and address new problems in new ways. And so, precisely because we have a certain kind of freedom—precisely because not only our actions but our interpretations as well are subject to challenge and revision[5]—we can be inspired to grapple with these new problems. In Foucault's ubiquitous ability to disconcert we can already recognize the two central themes of his work that I will take up: power and ethics. Foucault's example in this interview is the antipsychiatry movement. This movement identified many problems with mental hospitals, but once those hospitals were abolished in Italy, new problems emerged within the free clinics that took their place. Ethically motivated resistance to an estab-lished power that exercised considerable control over people's lives (mental hospitals) produced new institutions, giving those affected some new free-doms but also new restraints and difficulties.

Foucault's remarkable ability to disconcert, then, prompts us to a critical examination of both social contexts and norms and values. Thus, Foucault gives us—or at least demands of us—a critical theory and, in particular, a critical ethics. It is a presupposition of my reading of his work that Foucault is best understood as a critical theorist. In the next sections of this introduc-tion, I will try to make the argument that Foucault is a critical theorist, like thinkers in the Marxian and Frankfurt School traditions. This argument will in turn provide the frameworks within which we can identify and articulate the central concerns and arguments that follow.

II

Nancy Fraser observes: "To my mind, no one has yet improved on Marx's 1843 definition of critical theory as 'the self-clarification of the struggles and wishes of the age'" (Fraser 1989, 113).[6] Marx's work is one of the essential starting points for critical theory. There are a number of important features in the passage that Fraser has highlighted. First, critical theory is an activity of "self-clarification": it aims at understanding one's own situation and circumstances. Second, what is to be clarified includes both struggles and wishes—social and political activity as well as hopes, needs, and desires. Finally, these are struggles "of the age," struggles in the present. Foucault expressed this sentiment in *Discipline and Punish*, when he spoke of writing a "history of the present" (1975ET, 31).

But "self-clarification of the struggles and wishes of the age" is not merely for the sake of knowledge. On the contrary, Marx expressed the motivation for critical theory in his eleventh thesis on Feuerbach: "The philosophers have only *interpreted* the world, in various ways; the point, however, is to *change* it" (Marx 1845, 145). Marx elaborates this in the 1843 letter to Arnold Ruge that Fraser cites: "we do not attempt dogmatically to prefigure the future, but want to find the new world only through criticism of the old" (Marx 1843b, 13). Another key idea is recognizable here: critical theory is not dogmatic. Such a refusal of dogmatism characterizes Foucault's own work, too. He notes in "On the Genealogy of Ethics" that "you can't find the solution of a problem in the solution of another problem raised at another moment by other people. . . . I would like to do genealogy of problems, of *problématiques*" (DE326.1, 231). Marx continues, in what could anachronistically be described as a Foucauldian vein:

> But if the designing of the future and the proclamation of ready-made
> solutions for all time is not our affair, then we realize all the more clearly
> what we have to accomplish in the present—I am speaking of a *ruthless
> criticism of everything existing*, ruthless in two senses: The criticism must
> not be afraid of its own conclusions, nor of conflict with the powers that
> be. (Marx 1843b, 13)

That Foucault's work is relevant for critical theory is not in dispute—scholars have long recognized that he has much to contribute to it. Stephen White, for example, acknowledged that "Foucault brings a number of significant insights to critical theory" (White 1986, 419). My point is stronger, however: Foucault's work is not merely relevant to but lies at the heart of critical theory—Foucault is a critical theorist. This becomes clear if we consider how Seyla Benhabib, an heir to the Frankfurt School tradition, defines critical theory.

In *Critique, Norm, and Utopia*, Benhabib identifies several key characteristics of critical theory. First, she notes, "the tradition of critical theory has rejected 'foundationalism'" (Benhabib 1986, 280). Rather than appealing to a priori bases of human nature and society, critical theory looks to the social sciences "in order to substantiate its ancient concepts like reason, freedom, and justice" (280). Foucault's work throughout his career has employed empirical social sciences in order to challenge certain philosophical givens as well as to articulate new accounts of power, subjectivity, and freedom, accounts that are not grounded in an a priori but emerge from historical practice.

Second, critical theory does not seek a monopoly of knowledge production. Rather, it works with the social sciences to go from a mere "epistemological critique" (one that criticizes the foundations of the sciences) to an "immanent critique":

> The distinction between an epistemological and an immanent critique
> is the following: whereas in the first mode, only the conceptual foundations of the sciences and their knowledge claims are analyzed, the second approach aids in the development of new scientific theories, conceptualizations, and verification procedures, thus actively collaborating with them. (280)

Her first example of this collaboration is the Frankfurt School's 1930s work, in which psychoanalysis, economics, and sociology were integrated to yield both a critique of these social sciences' methods and new empirical and theoretical insights. Foucault's work, too, offers rich illustrations of this approach: both his archaeological and genealogical work develop epistemological critique—challenges to the conceptual foundations of the human sciences and humanistic discourse about asylums and prisons—but they also clearly inaugurate what she terms "immanent critique." Foucault's analytics of power is merely the most obvious example of a new theory developed in his philosophico-historical collaboration.

Third, Benhabib continues, critical theory is necessarily self-reflexive. This self-reflexivity follows from the first two characteristics that she has identified: While critical theory refuses foundations and is committed to an immanent critique, "it cannot give up the search for criteria of valid knowledge and action altogether" (281). Only through self-reflection can a philosophy maintain standards (admittedly provisional standards) through such an immanent critique, without appealing to foundations. She observes:

> In the tradition of critical theory, such questioning means analyzing both the *context of genesis* and the *context of application* of theories. Self-reflexivity, in the sense emphasized by critical theory, entails critical awareness of the contingent conditions which make one's own standpoint possible (context of genesis), and an awareness of whom and what the knowledge one produces serves in society (context of application). (281)

Benhabib's characterization of critical-theoretical self-reflexivity could pass as a succinct summary of Foucault's work. In fact, Foucault's work consistently illustrates how these two contexts are intricately interwoven in actual practice. This is at the heart of virtually all of Foucault's books: in *History of Madness* (1961ET2), to take just one example, he elaborates the contingent emergence of a particular and historically specific conception of madness and how this conception correlates with the development of institutions like asylums. In his later work, reflection upon the ways in which these contexts of genesis and application are integrated is, if anything, more explicit—hence his emphasis upon an analysis of power and subjectivity.

Benhabib adds, "Such self-reflexivity leads us, in Horkheimer's words, to become aware of 'the motives of thought,' and is a constituent of individual and collective autonomy" (281). Foucault's work has been indisputably valuable in helping us understand the motives of our thought. And autonomy, or freedom, is an essential concept for an ethics; it should come as no surprise—as we will see in later chapters—that reflexivity is a central feature of Foucault's critical ethics. On Benhabib's definition, we have to conclude that Foucault's work is critical theory. In the first lecture of his 1983 Collège de France course, Foucault himself noted that his work should be understood within this tradition of critical theory:

> That other critical tradition poses the question: What is our present? What is the present field of possible experiences? . . . it is this form of philosophy that, from Hegel, through Nietzsche and Max Weber, to the Frankfurt School, has founded a form of reflection in which I have tried to work. (DE351.2, 95; a variant translation is at CdF83ET, 20–21)

Benhabib concludes her discussion with a final observation:

> The development of critical theory after 1941, particularly the equation of modern rationality with instrumental reason, and the unclarity of the alternative juxtaposed to such instrumental reason, meant that the connection between autonomy and self-reflection became extremely tenuous. (Benhabib 1986, 281)

The "unclear alternative" that she alludes to is the normative, ethical dimension of critical theory (cf. Benhabib 1986, 8). And if it has become "extremely tenuous," then we should expect to see that the ethical would become explicitly thematized in critical theory. This is exactly what has happened. In the Frankfurt School tradition, Jürgen Habermas's work turned to moral theory in the early 1980s as he took up themes of "discourse ethics"; Axel Honneth has continued in this direction.[7] Foucault's work paralleled this movement, as ethics became an increasingly prominent theme for him in the 1980s. And it will be a major theme in this work.[8]

III

But Benhabib simultaneously raises a second issue here when she casts the development of critical theory as "juxtaposed to instrumental reason." Thomas McCarthy echoes her characterization: "critical social theorists direct their critique against particular forms of social research while seeking to identify and develop others that are not simply extensions of instrumental rationality" (McCarthy 1990, 49).[9] By instrumental reason, they mean rationality devoted to the accomplishment of some particular goal, that is, reason as a means or instrument to an end. Instrumental reason has played a central role in modern social and political theory since its beginnings and can be recognized in the thought of both Niccolo Machiavelli and Thomas Hobbes. Let's consider the case of Hobbes.[10]

Hobbes's analyses in *Leviathan* (1651) provide a foundation for subsequent thinkers—a set of axioms to build upon or to reject—and responses to Hobbes constitute the core of the tradition of modern political theory, from Locke and Rousseau to, I would suggest, twentieth-century theorists like Max Weber and the Frankfurt School. His analysis of society is quite bleak (anticipating Weber's image of an "iron cage"), and it places instrumental reason at its center.

Instrumental reason is, on Hobbes's account, what distinguishes humans from animals. Reason, he notes, "is nothing but *reckoning* (that is, adding and subtracting) of the consequences of general names agreed upon for the *marking* and *signifying* of our thoughts" (Hobbes 1651, 22–23).

> The train of regulated thoughts is of two kinds: one, when of an effect imagined, we seek the causes, or means that produce it; and this is common to man and beast. The other is when, imagining anything whatsoever, we seek all the possible effects that can by it be produced; that is to say, we imagine what we can do with it, when we have it. Of which I have not at any time seen any sign, but in man only . . . (13)

So instrumental reason, reasoning toward achieving some particular end, is distinctively human. He continues to describe human nature as fundamentally self-interested:

> So that in the first place, I put for a general inclination of all mankind, a perpetual and restless desire of power after power, that ceaseth only in death. And the cause of this is . . . because he cannot assure the power and means to live well which he hath present, without the acquisition of more. (58)

Humans are also, on Hobbes's view, born essentially equal—even the weakest is able, through trickery or alliance, to kill the strongest (74). The combination of these traits has certain consequences:

> From this equality of ability ariseth equality of hope in the attaining of our ends. And therefore, if any two men desire the same thing, which nevertheless they cannot both enjoy, they become enemies; and in the way to their end . . . endeavour to destroy or subdue one another. (75)

Such is Hobbes's vision of humans' natural condition, in which humans, instrumentally rational and essentially equal, compete against one another for survival. He describes this as a war "of every man against every man" (76). This view of human nature is undoubtedly bleak: in this state of affairs, "the life of man [is] solitary, poor, nasty, brutish, and short" (76). This situation is untenable, and the solution is to organize society under a sovereign, each person giving up one's natural rights to exercise power freely in exchange for security. Whatever inequalities, misfortunes, or injustices that may exist under the rule of a sovereign, life would be even worse otherwise.

Self-interested instrumental rationality is at the core of Hobbes's understanding of human nature; as a result it has been taken as axiomatic in much of modern social theory. The classic response to Hobbes's pessimistic vision is Jean-Jacques Rousseau's, in his *Discourse on the Origin of Inequality* (1755). He does not see instrumental rationality as distinctly human. On the contrary, what distinguishes humans from other animals, on Rousseau's account, is precisely the freedom to choose how to act, agency:

> Man contributes, as a free agent, to his own operations. The former [an animal] chooses or rejects by instinct and the latter by an act of freedom. Hence an animal cannot deviate from the rule that is prescribed to it, even when it would be advantageous to do so, while man deviates from it, often to his own detriment. . . . Therefore it is not so much understanding which causes the specific distinction of man from all other animals as it is his being a free agent. (Rousseau 1755, 25)[11]

For Rousseau, humans distinguish themselves by the capacity to choose to act against one's own interests, the capacity to act outside the dictates of instrumental reason. He notes that he sees

> two principles in it [the human soul] that are prior to reason, of which one makes us ardently interested in our well-being and our self-preservation, and the other inspires in us a natural repugnance to seeing any sentient being, especially our fellow man, perish or suffer. (14)

This second principle is key to his response to Hobbes and is the basis for a more hopeful, less brutish view of human nature. He terms this sentiment "sympathy" or "pity," adding that Hobbes failed to notice it: "from this quality alone flow all the social virtues that he [Hobbes] wants to deny in men. . . . Benevolence and even friendship are, properly understood, the products of a constant pity fixed on a particular object" (37).[12] Unfortunately, on Rousseau's account, the rise of society puts the human condition into a downward spiral of decreasing liberty and increasing inequality, and contemporary society represents "the final stage of inequality": "And since subjects no longer have any law other than the master's will, nor the master any rule other than his passions, the notions of good and the principles of justice again vanish" (68).

A quick glance at the theory (or history) of the twentieth century suggests that modern political theory has not been able to refute Hobbes's pessimistic view. For example, Alexandre Kojève's *mis*reading of Hegel's dialectic of master and slave—which was nevertheless extremely influential on many thinkers, including Foucault—takes the struggle unto death, a "war of every man against every man," as the basic condition of human consciousness.[13] Kojève's portrait of human society leaves little room for hope.

Consider also the magnum opus of Frankfurt School theory, Max Horkheimer and Theodor Adorno's *Dialectic of Enlightenment* (1944), written in exile from Nazi Germany. From the very beginning of the work, their pessimism—or despair—for Western society, a society built upon the principles of instrumental rationality, is clear: "The program of the Enlightenment was the disenchantment of the world; the dissolution of myths and the substitution of knowledge for fancy" (Horkheimer and Adorno 1944, 3). They continue:

> The concordance between the mind of man and the nature of things
> that he had in mind is patriarchal: the human mind, which overcomes
> superstition, is to hold sway over a disenchanted nature. Knowledge,
> which is power, knows no obstacles: neither in the enslavement of men
> nor in compliance with the worlds' rulers. (4)

Enlightenment, on their view, is the trajectory of human mastery over nature and over other humans; this mastery through rationality is motivated by an instrumental desire to profit from the things mastered: "For the Enlightenment, whatever does not conform to the rule of computation and utility is suspect" (6). Their cynical, despairing account of Enlightenment shares Hobbes's presuppositions about human nature and instrumental rationality. Horkheimer and Adorno ultimately despair of escaping the trajectory of Enlightenment through its own methods; after all, "Enlightenment is totalitarian" (6). Instead, they look, futilely, to aesthetics for an alternative. This, too, fails because even culture has become an industry—a cog in the machines of mass production and mass deception. Their final hope, however faint, lies in the capacity for critical thought itself:

> The undiscerning can be permanently kept from that truth only if they
> are wholly deprived of the faculty of thought. Enlightenment which
> is in possession of itself and coming to power can break the bounds of
> enlightenment. (208)

There are striking similarities between this work and Foucault's. Both emphasize the interrelationship between knowledge and power—this is one of the central themes in *Discipline and Punish* and in most of Foucault's work in his last decade, after all. Both look to aesthetics as a possible way out of a bleak situation—for Foucault, Baudelaire's dandy illustrates modernity's aesthetic turn (cf. DE339), and aesthetics will play an important role in his ethics. And finally, the tension between despair and hope is essential to both—this tension, I think, is one of the reasons why, as Charles Taylor observed, "Foucault disconcerts."

One way to read Foucault's oeuvre is as a response to the pessimistic Hobbesian view. He suggested as much (in a different sense), in the opening lecture of his 1976 Collège de France course: "To grasp the material agency of subjugation insofar as it constitutes subjects would, if you like, be to do precisely the opposite of what Hobbes was trying to do in *Leviathan*" (CdF76ET, 28). Let us understand Foucault as proposing a kind of thought experiment, an exploration of, if you will, a "worst-case scenario." The logic of this thought experiment is essentially in the form of the modus tollens: P implies Q, not Q (~Q), therefore not P. It goes like this: Suppose that Hobbes's axioms are correct, that instrumental rationality and strategic action constitute the whole of human motivation (P). (It would be foolhardy to claim that they play no role—clearly they play at least a part.) If they tell the whole story, then we ought to be able to explain human actions in terms of the model of war (Q). (This hypothesis was Foucault's explicit theme in the 1976 course: "shouldn't we be analyzing it [power] in terms of conflict, confrontation, and war? This would give us . . . a second hypothesis: Power is war, the continuation of war by other means" [CdF76ET, 15].) Can we explain the entirety of human action in terms of power? One way to answer this question is to try to do just that. If the attempt fails, then we cannot reduce all of human action to power relations (~Q), and we can begin to articulate other sources (~P) with confidence that they are not fictional. (We may want to follow Rousseau's suggestions when we look for those other sources, and Foucault, indeed, does.)

This is, I think, a productive way to read Foucault. He himself suggested that one

> take as an entry into the question of Aufklärung, not the problem of knowledge, but that of power . . . first, to take ensembles of elements where one can detect in a first approximation, thus in a completely empirical and provisional way, connections between mechanisms of coercion and contents of knowledge. . . . One seeks to know what are the ties, what are the connections that can be marked between mechanisms of coercion and elements of knowledge, what games of dismissal and support are developed from the one to the others . . . (OT-78-01ET, 393)

Note how Foucault emphasizes that this is a provisional, empirical approximation, an entry point, not an endpoint of the investigation. And finally, we could add, this investigation will seek to determine whether the other elements, like knowledge and subjectivity, can be explained entirely in terms of power. Only when a thoroughgoing account of human behavior in terms of power relations turns out to be incomplete can one *ground* an appeal to kinds of relations that are not reducible to power. Foucault disconcerts precisely because his account in terms of power is so thoroughgoing. And many of his critics misread Foucault as overemphasizing instrumental rationality and power relations precisely because they have failed to recognize the tentative, approximate, and thought-experimental character of that emphasis. As Foucault put it in a 1978 interview,

> There have been some serious misunderstandings, or else I've explained myself badly. I've never claimed that power was going to explain everything. . . . For me, power is what needs to be explained. . . . But no one has ever accounted for it. I advance one step at a time, examining different domains in succession, to see how a general conception of the relations between the establishment of a knowledge and the exercise of power might be formulated. (DE281.2, 284)

It is only on the basis of such an analysis of power—an incomplete analysis of human action—that Foucault is able to begin to articulate an analysis of nonpower—ethical analysis.

IV

Foucault's work is often divided into three periods: the archeological (1960s), concerned with knowledge; the genealogical (1970s), addressing power; and the ethical (1980s), devoted to self-constitution. Challenging this division, Thomas Flynn proposes what he calls an "axiological approach" to reading Foucault (cf. Flynn 2005, 143ff.). His proposal is that each of Foucault's works can be read in terms of all of the three central concerns (and corresponding methods) that characterize his work. Flynn offers an important insight here: from decade to decade or period to period, Foucault did not turn from one set of problems to another, leaving the old problems behind. On the contrary, he continued to reconsider and revise his understanding of power (the central theme of his 1970s work) throughout the 1980s, and his approach to ethics (his principal preoccupation of the 1980s) is grounded in work that he did in the 1970s. In fact, while one or the other may be in the foreground, his thinking about both of these themes is tightly interwoven at each stage of his thought.

The two central themes in Foucault's critical theory—power and ethics—can be understood as two sides of a Foucauldian response to the problems we have inherited from Hobbes. Insofar as Hobbes's analysis is correct, we must recognize the intricate kinds of power relations that obtain throughout social relations. Thus the analysis of power must occupy a central role in Foucault's social theory. But, with Hobbes's critics, we must not make the mistake of thinking that all social relations can be reduced to power relations. (This mistake may lie at the heart of many misreadings of Foucault.) Those social relations that cannot be reduced to power constitute the realm of what Foucault calls "ethics."

It is, I think, an awareness of this ethical realm that underlies a sense of hope that one can hear through Foucault's writings. So what does Foucault mean by "ethics"? Perhaps Rousseau's answer to Hobbes, what he calls "pity," can begin to point us in the right direction. Foucault used a constellation of perhaps equivocal or overlapping terms—pleasure, care, friendship—and his use of these terms evolved with his approaches to ethical thinking. Feminists have been articulating some of the ethical dimensions of the second term here—care—for the past decades, although initially (though this has changed)[14] without reference to politics. Foucault's discussion of aesthetics also falls within this ethical realm. We will articulate the details in the final chapter of this work.

Another question arises here: how are we to integrate these two sides of what I've described as a "Foucauldian response to Hobbes"? The relation between power and ethics in Foucault's work can be conceptualized in several different ways. First, we could imagine the distinction as one between facts (power) and values (ethics), facticity and norms. This approach is unsatisfying, however, for a number of reasons. Not least of these is a conceptual problem within this distinction itself. Values and norms are also empirically describable, factical; power is itself inflected by, and sometimes carried out through, norms and values.

Next, we might think of power and ethics as two related vectors of analysis. Their relationship could take the form of x and y axes (with knowledge/truth perhaps the z axis). But this suggests a single point of intersection, whereas Foucault's analyses consistently bring out much more complicated relationships between social forces. Alternatively, we could conceive these vectors as parallel lines. This is Thomas Flynn's approach: he describes power, ethics, and truth as three corners of what he terms the "Foucauldian triangle" or the "Foucauldian prism" (Flynn 2005, 147, esp. fig. 1). The triangular area formed between these three lines constitutes, on Flynn's reading, Foucault's account of experience. Flynn's model is quite useful, but it still suggests that power and ethics are two distinct poles of analysis rather than interrelated threads.

A third approach is to consider Foucault's analyses of power and ethics not as intersecting or parallel vectors but as overlapping explanations that must be integrated. That is, neither the analysis of power nor the account of ethics can be considered a "complete" social analysis. Rather, only once they are interwoven can a full Foucauldian social analysis be given. An apt analogy could be to think of overlapping sound waves present in the same space but at different frequencies—creating harmonies and dissonances. This seems like the most promising alternative: the analyses of power and ethics are interconnected and mutually dependent for Foucault. Perhaps the central contribution of this book will be an elaboration of this relationship. It is an important task. For, as Arnold I. Davidson suggests, Foucault's "conceptualization of ethics . . . is as potentially transformative for writing the history of ethics as, to take the strongest comparison I can think of, John Rawls's *A Theory of Justice* is, in its cultural context, for articulating the aims of political philosophy" (Davidson 1994, 115).

v

A close analysis of Foucault's works from the last ten years of his life is particularly fruitful for this project because both power and ethics are foregrounded (and therefore most explicitly articulated) in this period. I shall therefore focus upon his works from the 1974 course at the Collège de France and *Discipline and Punish* (published in 1975) through his death in June 1984.

The first three chapters trace the articulation and development of Foucault's account of power in this decade—Foucault begins with an account of disciplinary power, soon integrating an account of biopower with it. He then begins to speak of this evolving model in terms of "governmentality," which leads him in his final years to speak of "governing oneself and others," a framework in which ethical problems explicitly arise. The fourth chapter then mirrors this trajectory, tracing the concurrent development of Foucault's ethical explorations. He begins here with resistance and with "bodies and pleasures," turning later to such themes as friendship, self-constitution, truth telling, and ethics as a critical, reflexive enterprise.

Chapter 1 will begin by arguing that Foucault's account of power is a "theory" of power, generalizable and subject to empirical confirmation. It then sets up the general principles of Foucault's theory of power through a close reading of Part 4 of *La volonté de savoir* (1976, translated as *The History of Sexuality*, vol. 1: *An Introduction*).[15] Here Foucault distinguishes his approach from other theories of power—in particular, Marxist, psychoanalytic, and liberal accounts—and then articulates several framing theoretical and methodological principles for his own account of power.

Chapter 2 accomplishes three related tasks. First, it traces the historical transformation of power from one mode or regime to another—from sovereignty as the dominant form to discipline. Second, it articulates the account of modern disciplinary power that Foucault developed in 1973 through 1976, through a close reading of *Psychiatric Power* (his 1973–1974 Collège de France course) and *Discipline and Punish* and an extended discussion of disciplinary power in a seemingly "complete and austere" institution, antebellum slavery. Third, the account of disciplinary power that emerges here highlights the dialectic of hope and despair that is so central to readers' experience of Foucault's work. However, Foucault's analysis demonstrates that disciplinary power cannot describe all of power—Foucault's analysis is not yet complete—and even within discipline, there are resources for an ethics.

Foucault's analysis of power, therefore, needed to be broadened, as we shall see in Chapter 3. Initially exploring the limitations of a model of "politics as the continuation of war" (a model at the core of his analysis of discipline), we shall see how Foucault had to situate disciplinary power as a micropower to which other macro forms cannot be reduced. Thus, in the years 1976 through 1978, Foucault will be able to describe modern forms of macropower—which he terms "biopower," a power that acts not on particular individuals but rather "populations"—and to extend his historical analysis further back to a premodern ancestor of both discipline and biopower, "pastoral power." This extended analysis gives Foucault a new frame within which to situate these modalities of power, which he calls "governmentality" or "the art of governing." It also further clarifies the resources available within this account of power for a Foucauldian ethics.

Chapter 4 thus has three tasks. First, we see how Foucault's work reframes the project of ethics (just as his analysis of power put it onto a new theoretical basis). Second, it will then articulate the trajectories and resources for ethics that emerge from Foucault's account of power—these are both specific, engaged trajectories and more general resources. Third, we will see how critique and freedom—two key concepts at the heart of Foucault's ethics within power—enable Foucault to articulate and ground a pragmatic justification of his ethical project.

Such an ethical project can never be a closed and complete system. Rather it will an ongoing, perpetual struggle of engaged critique—one that is continuously subject to revision. The conclusion reflects upon how this project is inspired by and inspirational for a profound sense of hope.

VI

The task of this work, itself inspired by the hope that speaks through Foucault's writing, is to try to make the convictions that underlie that hope explicit. As such, it will be, in a certain sense, very unfoucauldian. For Foucault himself was always reticent to speak directly or explicitly about these convictions, this vision. One of his great fears, it seems, was that if he were to spell out his vision then it would be adopted as a sort of gospel, a new rule, exempt from further criticism. As he put it in a 1982 interview, "I don't want to be a prophet" (DE362.1, 9). He was even more explicit in a 1978 interview:

> For reasons essentially having to do with my political preference in the
> broad sense of the term, I have absolutely no desire to play the role of
> a prescriber of solutions. I think that the role of the intellectual today
> is not to ordain to recommend solutions, to prophesy, because in that
> function he can only contribute to the functioning of a particular power
> situation that, in my opinion, must be criticized. (DE281.2, 287–288)

He was even more blunt in 1975: "as for saying 'Here is what you must do!,' certainly not" (DE157.1, 62).

Foucault's worry here is a fundamental problem for a liberal arts education—that is, education for freedom, for thinking on one's own (which Kant identified as the question of Enlightenment). Ursula Le Guin, in her novel *The Dispossessed*, dramatically portrays the dilemma:

> "We don't educate for freedom. Education, the most important activity
> of the social organism, has become rigid, moralistic, authoritarian. Kids

learn to parrot Odo's words as if they were *laws*—the ultimate blasphemy!" (Le Guin 1974, 168)

The speaker is describing an anarchist society, founded by Odo (a cipher for Marx), which has fallen into patterns of authority and conformity. Replace Odo's name in this quotation with Foucault's, and Le Guin's character has cogently articulated the worry that restrained Foucault from overly explicit pronouncements.

My own hope is that, as we begin to grasp fully the insights of a Foucauldian ethics, the critical attitude at its core—one that grounds freedom and that prevents this kind of reification (and beatification, à la Halperin)—will become habitual, so that the dangers of articulating a new vision will recede as it comes into practice.

1

Approaching Power from a New Theoretical Basis

It is opportune, perhaps today even mandatory, that we develop a more relevant psychology and philosophy of power relationships beyond the simple conceptual framework provided by our traditional formal politics. Indeed, it may be imperative that we give some attention to defining a theory of politics which treats of power relationships on grounds less conventional than those to which we are accustomed. (Millett 1970, 24)

To understand a Foucauldian ethics, we must situate that ethics within the frameworks in which it acts. At the heart of Michel Foucault's philosophical and historical work is an analysis of power relations and their fundamental role in society—an analysis that goes beyond "the simple conceptual framework provided by our traditional formal politics," as Kate Millett put it, and has fostered and grounded new approaches to political engagement. For Foucault, that means that ethics must emerge within a context of relations of power, which are "everywhere" and thus inescapable. (As will become clear in the course of our exposition, the claim that power is everywhere is not a condemnation to slavery, a Weberian "iron cage," or Hobbesian brutishness. Rather, it is for Foucault the condition of possibility for freedom.) To begin, then, an imperative first step is to understand Foucault's conception of power relations and their role in society.

Foucault's most explicit thinking about power is presented in the work he did in the mid- and late 1970s, particularly in his two published works, *Discipline and Punish* (1975) and *La volonté de savoir* (1976, translated as *The*

History of Sexuality, vol. 1: *An Introduction*), as well as his courses at the Collège de France between 1974 and 1979. The first chapters of this work will
present Foucault's understanding of power in these years. The initial step
is to grasp the core framework that Foucault proposed for understanding
power and its operation.

In this chapter, then, we'll look at his most condensed and generalized
presentation, in Part 4 of *La volonté de savoir*. This will allow us to accomplish four tasks. First, we will be able to present the reasons why I will call
Foucault's analyses a "theory" of power; second, we will identify the mistaken theories of power that his analysis is meant to supplant—the theories
against which he is arguing. We will next be able to see the basic characteristics of power according to Foucault's theory: a network of force relations
throughout society, relations that are characterized by resistance and that
interact by means of local tactics and larger strategies. Fourth and finally,
we will discuss the methodological guidelines that Foucault outlined for the
use of this theory.

Once we understand power as a network of force relations that infuse all
our social interactions, we will be able to trace in more detail the development of Foucault's account of power. After our initial theoretical exposition,
we shall examine three "moments" in the evolution of Foucault's theory of
power and his approach to ethics. In Chapter 2, we will address the first
moment—roughly in 1974 through 1976, especially *Discipline and Punish*.
Here, Foucault traces the emergence of a new kind of power—disciplinary
power—out of older models of sovereign right and power in the seventeenth
and eighteenth centuries. Disciplinary power is an absolutely central element of Foucault's analysis of modern power—indeed, it is what he is most
famous for. But his articulation of it, especially in *Discipline and Punish*,
makes two related mistakes: it takes disciplinary power as the *only* modality
of modern power, and it can give the impression that the omnipresence of
disciplinary power leaves us trapped in a bleak, despairing world.

The second moment (and our third chapter) focuses on how Foucault
revised and expanded his understanding of power from that point—a process that took place in 1976 through 1978. In his 1976 course at the Collège
de France, for example, Foucault uses a study of "war" as the principal or
guiding metaphor for power relations as an occasion to reflect upon his own
methodological presuppositions as well as to trace further the limits of disciplinary power. In this period, he also came to recognize that relations among
macro-level phenomena—in particular, "populations"—are not adequately

described by disciplinary power, and so his catalog of the modes of power must be broadened and supplemented.

He thus concludes both the 1976 course and *La volonté de savoir* with the introduction of a new kind of power, "biopower," a nondisciplinary power over "man as species" (CdF76ET, 242). Foucault's discussion of biopower complements that of disciplinary power, allowing for a more complete description of the contemporary regime of power relations. Much of his work at the Collège de France in 1978 and 1979 is devoted to an articulation and development of the concept of biopower and what he terms "pastoral power," (a premodern ancestor of both biopower and disciplinary power). The various modalities of modern power can then be brought together under an umbrella term, "governmentality."

Throughout this discussion, Foucault's analysis of power relations underscores two key facts. First, power relations in and of themselves are inadequate for a full analysis of society—we must speak of other kinds of relations (such as ethical relations) as well. Second, there are a number of resources for an ethics *within* the very analysis of power relations that Foucault has developed. Thus Foucault is prepared to undertake the third moment, which we will examine in Chapter 4—in which the ethical trajectories emerging from this analysis of power relations come to the foreground. Using the umbrella term "governmentality," Foucault is thus able once again to reframe his analysis of these power relations in terms of "governing oneself and others." This construction emerges from Foucault's studies of ancient Greek and Roman practices. Marked by an emphasis on the self, it yields possibilities for a richer conception of the self and of agency within a framework of power relations and a regime of power. "The notion of governmentality allows one, I believe, to set off the freedom of the subject and the relationship to others, i.e., that which constitutes the very matter of ethics" (DE356.2, 20).

A "THEORY" OF POWER

What we can call a "theory" of power emerges from Foucault's mid-1970s analyses of psychiatry, the prison, and sexuality. This theory is not restricted to descriptions of one empirical period or "regime" but describes certain general characteristics of power and its operation across historical epochs and periods.

Foucault disliked the term "theory." He noted in *La volonté de savoir* that "the aim of the inquiries that will follow is to move less toward a 'theory' of power than toward an 'analytics' of power" (1976ET, 82). Foucault emphasized analysis over theory in part because he was reluctant to make any claim to a permanent or complete understanding. In his 7 January 1976 lecture at the Collège de France, Foucault indicated at least part of his distrust for theory: "given that the question 'What is power?' is obviously a theoretical question that would provide an answer to everything, which is just what I don't want to do . . . " (CdF76ET, 13). It is only insofar as theories can be used "untheoretically" in this sense—that is, without claiming to answer everything—that they can be valuable: all-encompassing or global theories "have, I think, provided tools that can be used at the local level only when, and this is the real point, the theoretical unity of their discourse is, so to speak, suspended" (CdF76ET, 6). Nevertheless, he did refer to his own project as a theory: his task "is a question of forming a different grid of historical decipherment by *starting from a different theory of power*" (1976ET, 90–91, my italics).[1] He would again describe it as a "theoretical shift" in *The Use of Pleasure* (1984aET, 6; 1984a, 12: "déplacement theorique"). For Foucault, the term theory must be used with caution; we should embrace theory only in the sense of "a theoretical production that does not need a visa from some common regime to establish its validity" (CdF76ET, 6).

Given Foucault's reluctance about the term theory, however, we may recall Heidegger's remark in a 1924–1925 lecture course:

> For one who has learned to understand an author it is perhaps not possible to take as a foundation for the interpretation what the author himself designates as the most important. It is precisely where an author keeps silent that one has to begin in order to understand what the author himself designates as the most proper. (Heidegger 1924, 32–33)

Even if Foucault himself is silent about the theoretical significance of his analyses of power, we can take it as one of the foundations for our own reading and for his analyses of ethics.

With this terminological caution in mind, I shall use the term "theory" with respect to Foucault's work in an experimental sense: a theory is a hypothesis to organize diverse data but also to be tested and revised or abandoned in light of that data. That a theory aims to be more general than a description of a single historical period or epoch is an essential part of its value and usefulness for our understanding of the phenomena it encompasses, and it remains a useful term with respect to Foucault's analyses of power. This generalizability does not entail, however, that such a theory need "a visa from some common regime" or frame of analysis, such as Marxism or psychoanalysis, for its authority; on the contrary, a theory's warrant will come from the empirical data that it organizes and that supports it. An essential part of my project, then, is to present Foucault's theory of power as such. As we shall see in the following, Foucault continued to revise his theory in light of his ongoing empirical studies.

Foucault's theory of power encompasses a second kind of generalizability as well: power is omnipresent—that is, it can be found in all social interactions. As he put this in 1977, "it seems to me that power *is* 'always already there,' that one is never 'outside' it" (DE218.1, 141). This omnipresence has two central characteristics. First, power is coextensive with the social body, with the field of social relations. Second, it does not stand alone but is interwoven with, revealed in, other kinds of social relations.

Note that this conception of omnipresence is a restricted one.[2] First, Foucault is *not* saying that power functions as a trap or cage but rather that it is present in all of our social relations. That is to say that in any social interaction, from our most intimate and egalitarian[3] to the most hierarchical, power constitutes an at least implicit aspect of that interaction. Second, Foucault is also *not* saying that all relations reduce to power relations but simply that power is present in all social relations. This leaves open the possibility that kinds of relations other than power are also operative in particular social relations.

We can look at each of these limitations in turn. First, the claim that there is no position "outside" of power does not mean that freedom is impossible. This is because power relations always entail resistance, risks and, struggles and the possibility to change the situation and the distribution of power within it. This is indicated in the logic of power relations and resistance. Properly understood, the recognition of power relations within a situation includes recognizing the possibility of altering the situation.

> We are always in this kind of situation [inflected by power relations]. It means that we always have possibilities, there are always possibilities of changing the situation. We cannot jump *outside* the situation, and there is no point from which you are free from all power relations. But you can always change it. (DE358.1, 28)

Second, power relations' omnipresence does not entail that they are the only kind of relation in society.

The omnipresence of power: not because it has the privilege of consolidating everything under its invincible unity, but because it is produced from one moment to the next, at every point, or rather in every relation from one point to another. Power is everywhere; not because it embraces everything, but because it comes from everywhere. (1976ET, 93)

Power does not "consolidate everything" or "embrace everything"; rather, it emerges as immanent in all kinds of social relations. That social relations could not be exterior to power relations does not entail that they consist entirely or exclusively of power relations. And so power alone may not be adequate to explain all, or every aspect of, social relations.

Foucault's theory of power, then, has two kinds of generalizability: synchronic and diachronic. Power relations can be found in all of our social interactions, and the various kinds of power relations that Foucault describes, while most clearly recognizable in modern social institutions, are also present in earlier epochs.

Judith Butler, a feminist theorist profoundly influenced by Foucault, highlights both the dangers and necessity of a "theory of power":

On the one hand, any analysis which foregrounds one vector of power over another will doubtless become vulnerable to criticisms that it not only ignores or devalues the others, but that its own constructions depend on the exclusion of the others in order to proceed. On the other hand, any analysis which pretends to be able to encompass every vector of power runs the risk of a certain epistemological imperialism which consists in the presupposition that any given writer might fully stand for and explain the complexities of contemporary power . . .

This demand to think contemporary power in its complexity and interarticulations remains incontrovertibly important even in its impossibility. (Butler 1993, 18–19)

The strength of Foucault's analysis is that it allows us to recognize multiple vectors. In fact, his theory continued to evolve—for example, with the introduction of the notion of biopower—precisely because certain vectors were initially insufficiently elaborated. I think that his theory can also avoid the charge of "epistemological imperialism" because this imperialism would become an issue only if one attempted to give a "total" explanation of a particular given situation. Foucault's theory will recognize that an analysis of any particular situation will be partial and incomplete—"the 'distributions of power' . . . never represent only instantaneous slices taken from processes" (1976ET, 99)—but what his theory does offer is a toolkit that is as complete as possible for those analyses. As Butler recognizes, the task that the toolkit makes possible is "incontrovertibly important" even if such a complete description remains impossible, an ideal only to be approached asymptotically.

As I've just noted, Foucault's theory of power is not a static conception. His work focused explicitly on power in the mid-1970s, and his theory evolved, or rather was refined and specified, in Foucault's later work. (Foucault himself remarked [DE326.1, 237] that the themes he identifies in *Discipline and Punish* were in fact present at the heart of his much earlier *History of Madness*. Of course, there is a certain retrospective rereading and reinterpretation going on in this claim, but it is not entirely irrelevant. Certain problems come into focus in later work that were not yet made explicit in earlier work, and aspects of Foucault's theory of power become more sharply delineated over time, as well. Indeed, in his 1973–1974 Collège de France course he introduced this new emphasis upon power as a basis for social analysis through a critique of *History of Madness* [CdF74ET, 12–16].) We will look at each of these moments in detail in this and subsequent chapters. Our first task is to see how Foucault first articulated his understanding of power, when it became the primary object of his analyses in the mid-1970s.

Foucault's single most explicit published discussion of power in this period is given in Part 4 of *La volonté de savoir*, "The Deployment of Sexuality." The first two of four chapters in this part, "Objective" and "Method," are the most important for our purposes. He states his task clearly at the beginning of the first chapter—it is to work "toward an 'analytics' of power: that is, toward a definition of the specific domain formed by relations of power, and toward a determination of the instruments that will make possible its analysis" (1976ET, 82).

HOW *NOT* TO UNDERSTAND POWER

Foucault first distinguishes his theory from three mistaken, inadequate, or misleading conceptions (each of which corresponds to a tradition or school of social thought).

> The word *power* is apt to lead to a number of misunderstandings—
> misunderstandings with respect to its nature, its form, and its unity. By

power, I do not mean "Power" as a group of institutions and mechanisms that ensure the subservience of the citizens of a given state [such as characterize many liberal analyses]. By power, I do not mean, either, a mode of subjugation which, in contrast to violence, has the form of the rule [typical of psychoanalytic approaches]. Finally, I do not have in mind a general system of domination exerted by one group over another [i.e., class oppression], a system whose effects, through successive derivations, pervade the entire social body [as in many Marxist views]. (1976ET, 92; my comments in brackets)

Foucault's worry is not that these analyses are entirely useless but that they often mischaracterize an accidental feature of power in a particular context as an essential characteristic of power in general. "The analysis, made in terms of power, must not assume that the sovereignty of the state [liberal], the form of the law [psychoanalytic], or the over-all unity of a domination [Marxist] are given at the outset; rather, these are only the terminal forms power takes" (1976ET, 92; my comments in brackets). So each of these features may in fact be present in certain contexts as terminal forms, but none is fundamental. We must first develop a new method—based on a richer theory—that begins with the basic molecules of power relations and then builds upward to more complex forms.

The most important misconception is what he terms a "juridico-discursive" understanding of power—the bulk of the first chapter of Part 4 is devoted to a description of this "juridico-discursive" analysis. This conception, he notes, is common to many "political analyses of power, and it is deeply rooted in the history of the West" (1976ET, 83). This conception is characteristic of both psychoanalytic (Freudian and Lacanian) and critical-theoretical (Marcusean) approaches to sexuality; it is especially important therefore that we recall Foucault is not endorsing but criticizing this theory of power. His argument, in fact, is that this conception, so generally accepted, has functioned as a mask by which much of the actual operation of power is obscured, thereby making many of the actual mechanisms of power tolerable (1976ET, 86). (He pursues a similar project of unmasking power's actual modes of operation in *Discipline and Punish*.)

According to this "juridico-discursive" theory, power has five principal characteristics. First, power always operates negatively, that is, by means of interdictions. Second, power always takes the form of a rule or law. This entails a binary system of permitted and forbidden, legal and illegal. These two characteristics together constitute the third: power operates through a cycle of prohibition, a law of interdiction. Hence (and fourth), this power manifests in three forms of prohibition—"affirming that such a thing is not permitted, preventing it from being said, denying that it exists" (1976ET, 84)—which reveal a logic of censorship. Fifth and finally, the apparatus of this power is universal and uniform in its mode of operation: "From top to bottom, in its over-all decisions and its capillary interventions alike, whatever the devices or institutions on which it relies, it acts in a uniform and comprehensive manner; it operates according to the simple and endlessly reproduced mechanism of law, taboo, and censorship" (1976ET, 84).

Notice how Foucault has characterized this uniformity, "in its over-all decisions and its capillary interventions alike." Implicit in this characterization is an important distinction between macrostructures (the "over-all decisions") and micropractices ("capillary interventions")—a distinction that will be very important in the development of Foucault's own understanding of power. His analysis begins at the micro level (in *Discipline and Punish*, for example) and is modified as it encompasses the macro level (especially in the 1978 and 1979 Collège de France courses). That this distinction is not made in the "juridico-discursive" view is just another indication of how it differs from Foucault's own analysis and how it is mistaken about, and masks, the actual operation of power.

Why does Foucault term this view a "juridico-discursive" representation of power? First, it is juridical because it is modeled upon the law, upon prohibition: "it is a power [more precisely a representation of power] whose model is essentially juridical, centered on nothing more than the statement of the law and the operation of taboos" (1976ET, 85). But as Foucault makes clear, the actual operation of power cannot be reduced to one model—the law, the state, or domination—but functions in a variety of forms and with varying means or techniques.

Second, according to this view, power is in essence discursive: its prohibitions are tied together with what one can say as much as what one can do; in this way restrictions on language should also function as restrictions upon reality and action—this is the heart of the "logic of censorship."

> It links the inexistent, the illicit, and the inexpressible in such a way
> that each is at the same time the principle and the effect of the others:
> one must not talk about what is forbidden until it is annulled in reality;

> what is inexistent has no right to show itself, even in the order of speech
> where its inexistence is declared; and that which one must keep silent
> about is banished from reality as the thing that is tabooed above all else.
> (1976ET, 84)

While this view emphasizes discourse as the primary arena in which power's
effects manifest, Foucault notes that discourses are related to power in much
more complicated ways than this view would suggest:

> Discourses are not once and for all subservient to power or raised up
> against it . . . discourse can be both an instrument and an effect of
> power, but also a hindrance, a stumbling-block, a point of resistance
> and a starting point for an opposing strategy. (1976ET, 100–101)

We have here a skeletal overview of the kind of analysis that Foucault
rejects. But several of these characteristics merit more detailed comment.

First, the logic of censorship (the fourth feature of power, which we have
just seen at the heart of the "discursive" emphasis) is also the logic of repression, the principal form in which power is manifested according to this
theory—particularly in its psychoanalytic variants:

> These are the characteristic features attributed to repression, which
> serve to distinguish it from the prohibitions maintained by penal law:
> repression operated as a sentence to disappear, but also an injunction to
> silence, an affirmation of nonexistence, and, by implication, an admis-
> sion that there was nothing to say about such things, nothing to see and
> nothing to know. (1976ET, 4)

This passage comes from Part 1 of the book, "We Other Victorians." This
part of the book is frequently misunderstood by students because it is written almost entirely in an ironic voice—the views expressed therein are largely
a prose portrait of a view (including this conception of power) that Foucault
wants to throw into relief in order to criticize. (His critical distance is indicated in this passage by the phrase "attributed to.") It is interesting that
in this description, repression is distinguished from penal law since penal
practice in fact provides the empirical basis and paradigmatic example for
Foucault's own analyses of power. This distinction functions as one aspect of
the masking that this theory provides for power's actual operation.

There is also something more to be said about the universal uniformity
of power on this view (the fifth principal characteristic). The problem here

is that the model is too reductive—it collapses a variety of kinds of power to one model, the law. But it is not just that such a unidimensional analysis fails to describe adequately diverse manifestations of power. It also fails to recognize an important distinction between micro and macro forms of power—one of the key distinctions that will allow Foucault's own analysis to be much more nuanced. Microrelations occur in local interactions, between individuals and small groups such as families. Macro forms are larger, representing interactions between institutions (such as the state or the judicial system) as well as patterns formed out of many microrelations (such as cultural norms). These diverse forms may in fact operate according to very different principles and models.

Furthermore, the uniformity that Foucault criticizes here is a synchronic uniformity. The "juridico-discursive" view asserts that all kinds of power at a given time operate according to one model. It is important that we distinguish this synchronic uniformity from a diachronic consistency. I have argued above that part of what qualifies Foucault's analyses as a proper "theory" of power is diachronic consistency or generalizability: it gives us resources to understand the manifestation and operation of power not only in our contemporary epoch but also in earlier periods. (This can be seen in *Discipline and Punish*, as Foucault traces the transformations of penal power from one paradigm or epoch to another. We will return to this point later.) In short, a theory that recognizes multiple models has more resources with which to describe diverse historical periods.

Finally, we should note that the "juridico-discursive" view of power entails a concomitant view of the subject:

> Confronted by a power that is law, the subject who is constituted as subject—who is "subjected"—is he who obeys. To the formal homogeneity of power in these various instances corresponds the general form of submission in the one who is constrained by it—whether the individual in question is the subject opposite the monarch, the citizen opposite the state, the child opposite the parent, or the disciple opposite the master. A legislative power on one side, and an obedient subject on the other. (1976ET, 85)

Note that Foucault here explicitly relates the "obedient subject" who is "subjected" to law as the image of the subject correlated with the juridico-discursive account of power. Many understand Foucault to posit just such an "obedient subject" as the subject of power properly understood; this misunderstanding is at the root of many criticisms of his work. Yet that he defines it as a function of the juridico-discursive view strongly suggests that we should not be so hasty. The implication is that this understanding of the subject is itself mistaken or inadequate, part of the "mask" of this account of power.

It may in fact be the case that Foucault's analyses in this period are somewhat confused and that this understanding of the subject is still at work in his own analyses—that he occasionally lapses into this view and does not entirely peel away the "mask" that this view provides for power. Indeed, his discussions of disciplinary power (in the first moment) do bear a certain resemblance to this juridico-discursive view. One of the motivations behind Foucault's continuous revisions of his analysis of power, as I hope to show, as well as his turn to ethics, is the need to account adequately for agency on the part of individuals and institutions. So we need to remember that part of his ongoing project is to overcome this reductive view of the subject as merely an "obedient subject." As he notes in the introduction to *The Use of Pleasure* (volume 2 of *The History of Sexuality*, which was published months before his death in 1984):

> It appeared that I now had to undertake a third shift, in order to analyze what is termed "the subject." It seemed appropriate to look for the forms and modalities of the relation to self by which the individual constitutes and recognizes himself *qua* subject. (1984aET, 6)

Foucault will come to this new shift on the basis of his new analysis of power. And we can now turn to Foucault's own analysis, having completed our survey of those views of power from which Foucault wishes to free his own analysis.

> It is this image that we must break free of, that is, of the theoretical privilege of law and sovereignty, if we wish to analyze power within the concrete and historical framework of its operation. We must construct an analytics of power that no longer takes law as a model and a code. (1976ET, 90)[4]

A FOUCAULDIAN VIEW OF POWER

It is time now for us to turn to this constructive task and to begin to articulate Foucault's own positive understanding of power. Foucault describes his task as:

a question of forming a different grid of historical decipherment by
starting from a different theory of power; and, at the same time, of
advancing little by little toward a different conception of power through
a closer examination of an entire historical material. (1976ET, 90–91)

The first chapter of Part 4 was devoted to characterizing the view of power
that must be overcome—one of his principal objectives in this work. The
next chapter, "Method," will begin the positive task by outlining Foucault's
new theory of power, which will guide his empirical investigations by providing the hypotheses to be tested.[5] (In this section, I shall offer what is
essentially a commentary upon this chapter, quoting it extensively as Foucault's most condensed presentation of his theory of power in these years.)
He begins:

> It seems to me that power must be understood in the first instance as
> [1] the multiplicity of force relations immanent in the sphere in which
> they operate and which constitute their own organization; as [2] the
> process which, through ceaseless struggles and confrontations, trans-
> forms, strengthens, or reverses them; as [3] the support which these force
> relations find in one another, thus forming a chain or a system, or on
> the contrary, the disjunctions and contradictions which isolate them
> from one another; and lastly, as [4] the strategies in which they take
> effect, whose general design or institutional crystallization is embodied
> in the state apparatus, in the formulation of the law, in the various social
> hegemonies. (1976ET, 92–93; my numeration in brackets)

There is much to unpack in this sentence. The bracketed numbers indicate
four principal aspects of Foucault's initial definition. We have a set of "force
relations," processes by which these relations are transformed, systems or
disjunctions that are constituted by the interplay of these force relations,
and larger strategies (or "terminal forms") with general and institutional
characteristics that emerge from these relations, processes, and systems. He
begins at the micro level, looking at local relations of force rather than at the
macro level of hegemonies and states, which can only be fully understood
as functions of the local relations. (As we'll see later, however, macro forms
of power are not entirely built of these micro forms. Or rather, macro forms
can create a sort of feedback loop that impacts the micro forms, not to men-
tion that there are a number of micro forms that interact with one another
in a variety of ways.)

First of all, then, power must be understood at the micro level as relations of force. Foucault is unambiguous on this point: "It is in this sphere of force relations that we must try to analyze the mechanisms of power" (1976ET, 97). But what are these "force relations" at the basis of power? Force relations seem to be the basic unit, the undefined or given, in this approach to power. Very broadly, force relations consist of whatever in one's social interactions that pushes, urges, or compels one to do something. With this term, Foucault makes an explicit analogy to physics—he refers on numerous occasions, for example, to the "micro-physics of power" (1975ET, 26; CdF74ET, 16; cf. also CdF78ET, 295–296).

We must be careful not to make too much of the analogy to physics—I do not think, for example, that Foucault means to propose that analysis of social relations should be reduced to equations of force relations.[6] As he notes at the Collège de France, "explaining things from below also means explaining them in terms of what is most confused, most obscure, most disorderly, and most subject to chance" (CdF76ET, 54). So to speak of microrelations and force relations is not necessarily to simplify or clarify but to complicate our analysis of events and actions. Furthermore, an important part of my larger argument is that these force relations, while important, do not constitute the whole of social interactions for Foucault. (Modern physicists also tell us that even for physical phenomena, which can be analyzed in terms of equations of force, there are simply too many variables for a complete or accurate analysis [Caraher 2004].) Given this caution, however, we can note certain implications of the analogy.

We can use the analogy to help us understand this notion of force relations as the basic unit of power. In Newtonian physics, force is defined as mass times acceleration. Force is thus the extent to which a body will be put into motion—larger objects (greater mass) will require a greater force to begin moving; a greater force will also be necessary to make an object move more quickly (greater acceleration). The important point here is that "force" is whatever serves to put an object into motion *regardless* of the origin or source of that force. Force may be introduced by gravity, magnetism, or some other means. Its action thus can be described independently of any particular agent or object as the "creator" of that force. Analogously, Foucault speaks of power relations in terms of force relations without reference to a source or agent. This suggests that Foucault does *not* mean to imply that individuals cannot act as agents within power relations but rather to draw our attention, especially for methodological reasons, to the force relations *as such* rather than to agents or actors. Closer examination of the characteristics of these force relations should help make this clearer.

To recall, Foucault began with the claim that "power must be understood in the first instance as the multiplicity of force relations immanent in the sphere in which they operate and which constitute their own organization" (1976ET, 92). Three features of these force relations are thus delineated: there is a multiplicity of force relations, force relations are immanent in social interactions, and these force relations are organized internally.

First, that there is a multiplicity means that we will find many different relations of force intersecting and overlapping in our social interactions. What is more, this suggests that these force relations will not all be of the same quality or kind: there will be multiple sorts of force relations, which may have different particular characteristics or impacts. To draw on the analogy to physics again, we could say that different forces will be present in the same field, as are gravity and magnetism, and that some of these forces will be stronger than others, and some stronger in certain contexts but not in others.

What sort of presence do these relations have, then? The second feature delineated in this description is that force relations are "immanent in the sphere in which they operate." That these relations are "immanent" means that they exist only within a certain domain or discourse. In other words, they are not concrete, like bodies, but incorporeal, like the laws of physics. They are nevertheless genuinely present—and, like laws, their presence can be felt in very concrete ways. The analogy to physics is again useful here. As physical bodies interact, they exert relations of gravity, magnetism, etc. upon each other. Similarly, social interactions are constantly permeated by these relations of force, power relations. Foucault thus describes force relations as a substrate: "it is the moving substrate of force relations which, by virtue of their inequality, constantly engender states of power, but the latter are always local and unstable" (1976ET, 93). He notes in the 1976 Collège de France course that "power is never anything more than a relationship that can, and must, be studied only by looking at the interplay of the terms of the relationship" (CdF76ET, 168).[7] This means that "relations of power are not in a position of exteriority with respect to other types of relationships (economic processes, knowledge relationships, sexual relations), but are immanent in the latter" (1976ET, 94). So "power is not an institution, and not a structure; neither is it a certain strength we are endowed with; it is the name that one attributes to a complex strategical situation in a particular society" (1976ET, 93). This has an important corollary: power is omnipresent (as discussed above) "because it is produced from one moment to the next, at every point, or rather in every relation from one point to another. Power is everywhere; not because it embraces everything, but because it comes from everywhere" (1976ET, 93). (Recall our earlier discussion of power's omnipresence.)

So there is a multiplicity of force relations, which are immanent in social interactions. The third feature in this initial characterization is that these force relations "constitute their own organization." On the one hand, these force relations "are the immediate effects of the divisions, inequalities, and disequilibriums which occur in [other types of relationships]" (1976ET, 94). But on the other hand: "If in fact [these force relations] are intelligible, this is not because they are the effect of another instance that 'explains' them, but rather because they are imbued, through and through, with calculation: there is no power that is exercised without a series of aims and objectives" (1976ET, 94–95). These calculations, these aims and objectives, which Foucault will refer to as "tactics" and "strategies," constitute the internal organization of these power relations. We will come back to explain this more carefully later.

Several other propositions also emerge from this core understanding of power. Foucault delineates five. First, since power emerges in relationships and interactions, power is not possessed but exercised. "It is not the 'privilege,' acquired or preserved, of the dominant class, but the overall effect of its strategic positions" (1975ET, 26). At stake here are two competing models of power—one based on a contract (possession), the other based on perpetual battle (strategies or war). Foucault traces the struggle between these two models in extensive detail in both *Discipline and Punish* and *"Society Must Be Defended."* As he notes in *Discipline and Punish*, his study "presupposes that the power exercised on the body is conceived not as a property, but as a strategy . . . ; that one should take as its model a perpetual battle rather than a contract regulating a transaction or the conquest of a territory" (1975ET, 26).

Second, power relations are not exterior to other relations. This reiterates the point above about immanence.

Third, "power comes from below; that is, there is no binary and all-encompassing opposition between rulers and ruled at the root of power relations and serving as a general matrix" (1976ET, 94). This elaborates upon the observation above that there are a multiplicity of power relations, and

Foucault makes two important points with this observation. First, power is not reducible to a binary relationship; second, power comes from below. That power is not binary means that we cannot reduce all sorts of power to one model. Furthermore, we cannot understand power as a simple relation between ruler and ruled, oppressor and oppressed, master and slave. Rather, power emerges from a variety of overlapping and intertwined relationships.

In part, Foucault insists that power is not binary in order to extricate his view from certain misunderstandings or criticisms (as we saw earlier)— to underscore that this is not a structuralist or deconstructive account of power, nor will it reduce all power to repression or class oppression, as psychoanalytic or Marxist approaches would.

But Foucault also stresses here that power comes from below. We cannot begin to understand power in the first instance by looking at monarchies or states, by looking at the top of any chain of command. Rather, we must look at the complex webs of interwoven relationships—what Foucault calls the "microphysics" of power (1975ET, 26). Power develops in the first instance in specific, local, individual choices, behaviors, and interactions. These combine in myriad ways to constitute larger social patterns, eventually yielding macroforms, which one typically thinks of when one thinks about "power," such as societies, states, and kings—just as everyday objects are constituted by atoms and molecules.

In fact, Foucault's own analysis of power will stress interactions at both the micro level of individuals (which he will describe as disciplinary techniques of the body) and the macro level of populations (which he will term biopolitics). But his work in 1975–1976 is focused almost exclusively on the micro level. He begins to approach an analysis of the macro level only late in this period, at the end of *"Society Must Be Defended"* and the last part of *La volonté de savoir*. A more careful articulation of the macro level, the biopolitics of populations will be developed in the Collège de France courses of 1978 and 1979.

Fourth of the five propositions that emerge from Foucault's conception of power is that "power relations are both intentional and nonsubjective" (1976ET, 94) This juxtaposition is, frankly, puzzling and has led to quite a bit of misunderstanding about Foucault's analysis. First, power is intentional: power relations are "imbued, through and through, with calculation: there is no power that is exercised without a series of aims and objectives" (1976ET, 95). Foucault refers to these aims and objectives as "tactics" and "strategies" and notes that these are what constitute its "rationality." But power, he insists here, is also nonsubjective: "But this does not mean that it results from the choice or decision of an individual subject" (1976ET, 95). Nor, he continues, can it be located in groups such as economic decision makers, governing castes, or the state apparatus.

The problem here, the apparent paradox, is that according to Foucault's description, power has to be exercised by someone or something, but if it is nonsubjective, there can't be a "someone" exercising that power. Given what he says in *Discipline and Punish* about how the subject is constructed by power relations (which we'll discuss in the next chapter), Foucault seems to be erasing agency or locating agency in a noncorporeal "power" rather than individuals and institutions. I think the problem can be resolved with two observations. First, part of his point here is that the effects of the exercise of power reach beyond any individual's (or group's) intentions or control. As we've already seen, Foucault is arguing against the view that "the state" acts as a monolith, and he is arguing for the importance of microevents, with their ripples and interactions, in order to understand macrophenomena. This means that local actions often have unintended macroconsequences and that one's control of macroprocesses will always be limited and incomplete. Macrophenomena result from the concatenation of many microevents, but they are not the direct result of any *particular* individual action or choice. This is, then, an argument for a system-level, rather than individual-level, understanding of power relations. Foucault's distinction between tactics and strategy parallels this micro/macro distinction. Tactics are local, micro; strategies are macro, systemic. But as I've suggested above, Foucault has not yet come to a mature understanding of power at the macro level—that will not emerge clearly until 1978–1979. (This may account for some of the confusion in his language here.)

The second observation to be made here is a logical one. To understand subjectivity as constituted (in part) through power relations is not to deny that subjects can act intentionally. Nevertheless, the status of subjectivity will become a focal point of Foucault's investigations in later years. We will return to this theme in later chapters.[8] It is an important one, because one of the fundamental questions for ethical action has to do with the individual's ability to make decisions that are not "merely" determined by the relations of power in which they emerge—in other words, a question of freedom.

This question may in fact lie at the heart of readers' varied reactions to Foucault's analyses. Those who understand the claim that individuals are constituted by power relations to constitute a denial of freedom find his vision bleak. Those of us who find in his analyses the tools with which to increase our self-awareness, and hence our own freedom, hear wellsprings of hope in his discussion of the continuous transformations of power through history. At a minimum, on the latter view, if power relations are in fact best understood as a necessarily ongoing battle, then the battle is never utterly lost. (We'll return to this question of hope, too, in later chapters.)

Indeed, Foucault seems to anticipate this objection, this worry about freedom, in the fifth of the five propositions that he discusses here. Power is always accompanied by resistance; resistance is in fact a fundamental structural feature of power: "Where there is power, there is resistance, and yet, or rather consequently, this resistance is never in a position of exteriority in relation to power" (1976ET, 95). Without resistance, without two bodies (or minds) pushing or pulling against each other, there is no power relation.

This fifth point encapsulates each of the preceding four. Power is exercised (first proposition) in the very interplay of force and resistance, this interplay is present in all social interactions (second proposition), force and resistance are manifest even in microinteractions between individuals as well as states (third proposition), and while each person may choose to apply force or resist, the ultimate outcome of the relation cannot be controlled by one party (power is intentional and nonsubjective—fourth proposition).

On the role of resistance in constituting power, Foucault's position will not change. In a 1984 interview, for example, Foucault reiterates that "in the relations of power, there is necessarily the possibility of resistance, for if there were no possibility of resistance—of violent resistance, of escape, of ruse, of strategies that reverse the situation—there would be no relations of power" (DE356.2, 12). He adds that "there cannot be relations of power unless the subjects are free. . . . If there are relations of power throughout every social field it is because there is freedom everywhere" (DE356.2, 12).

Let's stop for a moment and recall where we are in the discussion. We began this section with a long quotation, repeated again here, in which Foucault identified four principal aspects of power:

It seems to me that power must be understood in the first instance as [1] the multiplicity of force relations immanent in the sphere in which they operate and which constitute their own organization; as [2] the process which, through ceaseless struggles and confrontations, transforms, strengthens, or reverses them; as [3] the support which these force relations find in one another, thus forming a chain or a system, or on the contrary, the disjunctions and contradictions which isolate them from one another; and lastly, as [4] the strategies in which they take effect, whose general design or institutional crystallization is embodied in the state apparatus, in the formulation of the law, in the various social hegemonies. (1976ET, 92–93; my numeration in brackets)

Our discussion so far has focused on explicating only the first of these, that power consists of multiple force relations. (We've covered a lot of ground along the way.) We can now quickly address the remaining three aspects that Foucault identified here.

The second point that Foucault makes here is that these force relations are processes, not static, and are constantly being transformed. These transformations take the form of ceaseless struggles and confrontations between the original force and its accompanying resistance, and these sometimes strengthen the power relations but other times weaken or reverse it. These processes also produce a number of interrelationships and systems, as various power relations reinforce or undermine one another (third point). Here Foucault introduces a distinction between tactics and strategy: tactics are the local rationalities of power in particular cases; strategies, on the other hand, are the larger systemic or global patterns of power. And (fourth point) these strategies are built out of combinations and concatenations of those local tactics.

> The rationality of power is characterized by tactics that are often quite explicit at the restricted level where they are inscribed (the local cynicism of power), tactics which, becoming connected to one another, attracting and propagating one another, but finding their base of support and their condition elsewhere, end by forming comprehensive systems. (1976ET, 95)

These comprehensive systems, or strategies, constitute "institutional crystallizations" out of the interaction and combination of locally fluid power relations and become recognizable terminal forms like the state and the other types he enumerated.

Foucault elaborates further on strategies and tactics in *Discipline and Punish*:

> If there is a politics-war series that passes through strategy, there is an army-politics series that passes through tactics. It is strategy that makes it possible to understand warfare as a way of conducting politics between

states; it is tactics that makes it possible to understand the army as a principle for maintaining the absence of warfare in civil society. (1975ET, 168)

His use of the army as a symbol for tactics here is part of a broader use of
military metaphors. Just as Foucault has drawn an extended analogy to physics to explain his understanding of power, he also uses an analogy to war—
inverting Clausewitz's saying that war is politics by other means[9]—to underscore the hypothesis that power relations lie at the molecular level of all social
interactions. (Indeed, in his 1973–1974 Collège de France course, he even
acknowledged that his is a "pseudo-military vocabulary" [CdF74ET, 16].)

In this military analogy we can see the "Hobbesian hypothesis" about
power as the organizing principle of society quite clearly articulated in Foucault. Or rather, as I suggested in the Introduction, we can see Foucault's
exploration and testing of the hypothesis—in order to determine its limits,
to show that it is not sufficient, even if necessary, for a complete understanding of social relations.

Foucault makes an interesting and important addition at this point in *La
volonté de savoir*:

> Power's condition of possibility, or in any case the viewpoint which per-
> mits one to understand its exercise, even in its more "peripheral" effects,
> and which also makes it possible to use its mechanisms as a grid of intel-
> ligibility of the social order, must not be sought in the primary existence
> of a central point, in a unique source of sovereignty from which second-
> ary and descendent forms would emanate; it is the moving substrate of
> force relations which, by virtue of their inequality, constantly engender
> states of power, but the latter are always local and unstable. (1976ET, 93)

A number of points can be seen when we consider this long single sentence (portions of which we've already discussed) as a whole. First, Foucault
emphasizes power's peripheral effects—an examination of these peripheral
effects will allow us to observe the actual operation of power, which is obscured and masked if we only look at larger, central forms like the state.
Following from that, this shift in perspective provides a new viewpoint from
which to begin a study of power—and will thus entail a new methodological approach. Third (a point that Foucault has been making throughout this
discussion), this allows us to grasp the actual local basis of power's larger effects. So this approach will make possible a fully realized test of the Hobbes-

ian hypothesis—by using mechanisms of power as our grid of intelligibility for the social order.

Finally, and perhaps most intriguingly, Foucault uses explicitly Kantian language when he speaks of power's "condition of possibility" here—even if he immediately shies away from its implications (his "or in any case the viewpoint . . . " seems to be a rhetoric of retreat). Kant has loomed in the background of Foucault's work throughout his career, from his translation and commentary on Kant's *Anthropology* (1798) for his secondary thesis (OT-61-02), to his analysis of Kant's "What Is Enlightenment?" (1784) in his last years. There Kant's thought will play an important role in the articulation of Foucault's ethical vision, and we will take it up in our final chapter. It is enough for us to note here that he is already using Kantian language in his thinking about power.[10]

The movement of Foucault's analysis here is from the micro level to the macro, from the molecular to the everyday—from (1) specific, individual force relations through (2) their processes of transformation and (3) the networks or systems that their interplay produces, to (4) their larger, strategic manifestations in the state, the law, and other hegemonies, such as ownership of the means of production. In the end-forms that Foucault identifies here, we should recognize the three traditions of analysis that Foucault earlier criticized as partial and inadequate (liberalism, psychoanalysis, Marxism). Even though each of these strategies may be unidimensional, the networks of power taken in sum are multidimensional and cannot be reduced to only one strategic mode, be it juridico-discursive or something else. Foucault's point is that while they may have adequately described some particular strategy (or terminal form) of power, each approach fails to grasp the fundamental form or operation of power at the molecular level. So if, following Hobbes in order to challenge him, we are to understand social relations in terms of power, Foucault's approach will be more effective.

> In short, it is a question of orienting ourselves to a conception of power which replaces the privilege of the law with the viewpoint of the objective, the privilege of prohibition with the viewpoint of tactical efficiency, the privilege of sovereignty with the analysis of a multiple and mobile field of force relations, wherein far-reaching, but never completely stable, effects of domination are produced. . . . And this, not out of speculative choice or theoretical preference, but because in fact it is one of the essential traits of Western societies that the force relationships which for a long

time had found expression in war, in every form of warfare, gradually became invested in the order of political power. (1976ET, 102)

What we have discussed so far provides only a *basic framework*—a set of theoretical presuppositions that constitutes the heart of Foucault's theory of power. There are significant elements of this theory that we have not yet discussed, such as the relationship between power and knowledge and between power and "the subject." (We'll take these up in the next chapter.) And many important aspects of Foucault's analysis of power will evolve over the next decade—for instance, as we will see, he begins by characterizing modern power solely as disciplinary power but then supplements this with an analysis of other forms, like biopower. This basic framework, however, is consistent throughout the theory's subsequent development and elaboration.[11]

METHODOLOGICAL GUIDELINES FOR STUDYING POWER

To review, we have unpacked a dozen or so dense pages at the heart of *La volonté de savoir*. What we've seen so far of Foucault's theory of power, however, is general and formal—it is of little value for engaged social analysis. David Halperin even criticizes Foucault's presentation here as dogmatic:

> Volume One [of Foucault's *History of Sexuality*], for all its admittedly bright ideas, is dogmatic, tediously repetitious, full of hollow assertions, disdainful of historical documentation, and careless in its generalizations . . . (Halperin 1995, 5, quoting Halperin 1986, 277; his brackets).

Halperin's criticism, while not entirely inaccurate, is unfair and fails to consider the book in the context of Foucault's broader investigations.[12] Foucault's analysis of power as presented here is not a series of "hollow assertions" but a "grid of intelligibility" (1976ET, 93) that entails several methodological principles—methodological precautions—that guide his historical investigations. Second, it is based upon an extensive empirical foundation—and much of the "historical documentation" for Foucault's claims here is given in other published works; additional support was intended to be published in subsequent, unrealized volumes.

In his 1976 Collège de France course (given in the months before *La volonté de savoir* was published), Foucault delineates five methodological precautions for his study of power, sovereignty, and domination. First, Foucault notes that "our object is . . . to understand power by looking at its extremities, at its outer limits at the point where it becomes capillary" (CdF76ET, 27), in other words, to study power by observing the infinitesimal, local, micropowers that are its most molecular manifestations rather than by looking at global terminal forms. Second, do not "ask the question (which leads us, I think into a labyrinth from which there is no way out): So who has power?" (CdF76ET, 28). This question is a trap, because power is not possessed but exercised. "The goal was, on the contrary, to study power by looking . . . at the point where it relates directly and immediately to what we might, very provisionally, call its object, its target, its field of application . . . " (CdF76, 28). Again, avoid mistakes based on erroneous theories of power and look to local interactions to see its initial effects.

The third and fourth of Foucault's rules reflect his theory's conception of how the infinitesimal nodes combine and interact in a matrix to create larger effects of domination or sovereignty. Third:

> Do not regard power as a phenomenon of mass and homogeneous domination. . . . Power must, I think, be analyzed as something that circulates, or rather as something that functions only when it is part of a chain. . . . Power is exercised through networks, and individuals do not simply circulate in those networks; they are in a position to both submit to and exercise this power. (CdF76ET, 29)

The circulation of power, exercised by and on individuals, will serve, at least in part, to constitute these individuals as subjects. But it will constitute larger social patterns, strategies, and institutions. Thus the fourth rule:

> We should make an ascending analysis of power, or in other words begin with its infinitesimal mechanisms, which have their own history, their own trajectory, their own techniques and tactics, and then look at how these mechanisms of power, which have their solidity and, in a sense, their own technology, have been and are invested, colonized, used, inflected, transformed, displaced, extended, and so on by increasingly general mechanisms and forms of overall domination. (CdF76ET, 30)

The fifth methodological guideline that Foucault delineates here has to do with the relation between power and knowledge—a relation that we will articulate in more detail shortly: "the delicate mechanisms of power cannot function unless knowledge, or rather knowledge apparatuses, are formed, organized, and put into circulation" (CdF76ET, 33–34).

The common denominator in these five precautions is that one must not misinterpret power by taking one terminal form (sovereignty, prohibition, etc.) as its general form.

> To sum up these five methodological precautions, let me say that rather than orienting our research into power toward the juridical edifice of sovereignty, State apparatuses, and the ideologies that accompany them, I think we should orient our analysis of power toward material operations, forms of subjugation, and the connections among and the uses made of the local systems of subjugation on the one hand, and apparatuses of knowledge on the other. (CdF76ET, 34)

These guidelines thus serve to allow one to interpret historical and sociological data with a new unfiltered lens. And these rules can be adapted to particular contexts—Foucault explicitly does so in his studies of prisons and sexuality.

Discipline and Punish follows four such general rules:

1. Do not concentrate the study of the punitive mechanisms on their "repressive" effects alone. . . . As a consequence, regard punishment as a complex social function.

2. Analyze punitive methods . . . as techniques possessing their own specificity in the more general field of other ways of exercising power. Regard punishment as a political tactic. . . .

3. See whether there is not some common matrix [between the history of penal law and the history of the human sciences] or whether they do not both derive from a single process of "epistemologico-juridical" formation; in short, make the technology of power the very principle both of the humanization of the penal system and of the knowledge of man.

4. Try to discover whether . . . the insertion in legal practice of a whole corpus of "scientific" knowledge, is not the effect of a transformation of the way in which the body itself is invested by power relations. (1975ET, 23–24)

The first two of these rules reiterate what we have seen above: power does not have the general form of "repression"—as the "juridico-discursive" theory would have it—but is exercised in a myriad of specific ways. The various techniques of punishment, and imprisonment in particular, are but a few of the specific micropractices of power in its capillary action. The last two of the rules address the mutually productive relationship between power and knowledge. And this method makes certain new insights possible: as Foucault suggests here, the very humanization of punishment (a movement away from violence inflicted upon the body) may itself be an effect of new technologies of power.

Foucault enumerates four similar rules for his study of sexuality in *La volonté de savoir*. Here again we see that the investigation is grounded in Foucault's new theory of power. The first is what he terms a "rule of immanence": Do not assume that a "sphere of sexuality" exists independently of relations of power.

> If sexuality was constituted as an area of investigation, this was only because relations of power had established it as a possible object; and conversely, if power was able to take it as a target, this was because techniques of knowledge and procedures of discourse were capable of investing it. . . . We will start, therefore, from what might be called "local centers" of power-knowledge. (1976ET, 98)

Beginning from these "local centers," the second and third rules jointly articulate how larger and more complex relations develop. The "rules of continual variations" remind us that "the 'distributions of power' and the 'appropriations of knowledge' never represent only instantaneous slices taken from processes. . . . Relations of power-knowledge are not static forms of distribution, they are 'matrices of transformations'" (1976ET, 99). And the third rule, the "rule of double conditioning," emphasizes that these fluid matrices combine and interact to produce larger patterns and strategies.

> No "local center," no "pattern of transformation" could function if, through a series of sequences, it did not eventually enter into an over-all strategy. And inversely, no strategy could achieve comprehensive effects if it did not gain support from precise and tenuous relations serving, not as its point of application or final outcome, but as its prop and anchor point. (1976ET, 99)

So local interactions and global patterns are mutually interwoven. If Foucault initially emphasizes how the larger strategies are grounded in local power relations (here, for example—local centers are anchoring points, not final outcomes, of these strategies—and more generally in his analysis of disciplinary power), his later analysis of "biopower" will bring out how the global strategies can shape and mold local relations.

The fourth rule, which Foucault terms the "rule of the tactical polyvalence of discourses," underscores the role of resistance as a constituent of relations of power while highlighting the complexities of power's strategies.

> We must make allowance for the complex and unstable process whereby discourse can be both an instrument and an effect of power, but also a hindrance, a stumbling-block, a point of resistance and a starting point for an opposing strategy. Discourse transmits and produces power; it reinforces it, but also undermines and exposes it, renders it fragile and makes it possible to thwart it. In like manner, silence and secrecy are a shelter for power, anchoring its prohibitions; but they also loosen its holds and provide for relatively obscure areas of tolerance. . . . Discourses are tactical elements or blocs operating in the field of force relations; there can exist different and even contradictory discourses within the same strategy; they can, on the contrary, circulate without changing their form from one strategy to another, opposing strategy. (1976ET, 101–102)

Foucault's treatment of discourses here—as part of the tactics and strategies of power, reversible, not monolithic—contrasts explicitly with the "juridico-discursive" view that he had earlier critiqued.

In *La volonté de savoir*, as in the 1976 Collège de France course, Foucault notes that "these are not intended as methodological imperatives; at most they are cautionary prescriptions" (1976ET, 98). This caveat is important. It reminds us that these rules are intended, in the first instance, as "prescriptions" to prevent us from falling into familiar but mistaken habits of thinking—interpreting power according to the discounted approaches. On the other hand, neither Foucault's own approach nor the methodological guidelines that follow from it are "imperatives"; rather, they are tentative proposals, subject to critique and revision in light of the ongoing investigations.

Indeed, these methodological propositions, as well as this theory of power itself, emerged from Foucault's ongoing self-critique. In the opening lecture of his 1974 Collège de France course, *Psychiatric Power*, Foucault began to articulate this new conceptualization of power in response to what he then perceived as shortcomings in the analyses of his first work, *History of Madness*. On the fourth page of that course, he initially observes that

> in the asylum, as everywhere else, power is never something that someone possesses, any more than it is something that emanates from some-

one. Power does not belong to anyone or even to a group; there is only power because there is dispersion, relays, networks, reciprocal supports, differences of potential, discrepancies, etcetera. It is in this system of differences, which have to be analyzed, that power can start to function. (CdF74ET, 4)

Later in the initial lecture, Foucault explicitly identifies this new theoretical approach to power—and to psychiatry in terms of power relations—as a correction to presuppositions in *History of Madness*. "I accorded a privileged role to what could be called the perception of madness. Here . . . I would like to see if it is possible to make a radically different analysis and if . . . we could start from an apparatus of power" (CdF74ET, 13). Arnold Davidson in his introduction notes that

> without having yet developed all of the tools of his own analysis, *Psychiatric Power* already exhibits Foucault's awareness of the shortcomings of available conceptions of power. . . .
>
> *Psychiatric Power* can be read as a kind of experiment in method, one that responds in historical detail to a set of questions that permeated the genealogical period of Foucault's work. (Davidson 2006, xiv, xviii)

Indeed, we might say that this "experiment in method" led to significant results.

We began this discussion of methodology as the first part of a response to Halperin's suggestion that Foucault's analysis of power in *La volonté de savoir* was dogmatic. The second part of this response is to highlight how Foucault's condensed and formal presentation in those pages was grounded in and developed through very careful empirical work. This work, throughout his career, included careful analyses of the development of asylums, hospitals, and prisons, as well as of sexuality. *La volonté de savoir* itself was intended only as the first of six volumes—a schematic overview and a framework for understanding the empirical work of the subsequent volumes. (Of course, that work was not published as such, since Foucault's project had radically changed by the time the two final volumes actually appeared.) To trace this empirical development in detail, and to elaborate further Foucault's conception of disciplinary power, we shall turn next to *Discipline and Punish*.

2

Disciplinary Power:
Testing the Hobbesian Hypothesis

We have traced the core of Foucault's theory of power, as presented in dense form in the fourth part of *La volonté de savoir*. Our next tasks are to develop and refine this analysis by presenting it in more detail, to show how power evolves over time (and how Foucault's own analysis becomes more nuanced and complex), and to document the empirical evidence that supports this theory. We will be able to accomplish these three tasks through a careful discussion of *Discipline and Punish*. It is the last of Foucault's books that can be characterized as a "work of art"—a densely argued, richly layered collection of empirical observations that integrate numerous archival documents into a larger, compelling analysis, one that seduces readers but leaves them vaguely unsatisfied by something that can't quite be nailed down.[1] Before we turn to this text, however, a few observations about Foucault's theory of power are in order.

First, a caution: Foucault's analysis of power is complicated because it is articulated at different levels that are simultaneously at play; it can be imagined as a multidimensional and dynamic puzzle whose pieces must be properly positioned. A few distinctions can help keep these levels clear. First, we must maintain a distinction between "power in general" and specific forms or modalities of power. Much of Foucault's detailed empirical work, the basis for his articulation of power, is devoted to the elaboration of different specific mechanisms through which power is exercised—such as disciplinary power and biopower. Despite their differences, these mechanisms all share certain features in common, which make them mechanisms or forms of power. (Our discussion in the first chapter, highlighting these common characteristics of power, was devoted to "power in general.") To understand Foucault's analyses fully, we must be able to recognize both aspects in his empirical descriptions: what specifies a particular technique as *this* kind of power, and what a particular technique shares with all power, which characterizes power in general or power as such. As we discuss the operation of disciplinary power, we will be simultaneously describing that specific modality and illustrating certain characteristics of any form of power.

Let's briefly recap the general account of power that Foucault presented in *La volonté de savoir*.[2] Power relations are microprocesses, which must be distinguished from the macro forms in which they often manifest themselves. Such macro forms, which include state sovereignty and domination of one group over another, are constituted out of many particular instances of the microrelations. "It seems to me that power must be understood in the first instance as the multiplicity of force relations immanent in the sphere in which they operate and which constitute their own organization" (1976ET, 92).

These microprocesses, these force relations, are strategic relationships. More precisely, "power" is the effect of interactions between unequal positions in the social landscape. "Power's condition of possibility . . . is the moving substrate of force relations which, by virtue of their inequality, constantly engender states of power . . . the latter are always local and unstable" (1976ET, 93). Power circulates through the network of social relations (CdF1976ET, 29). Thus, power is always and "strictly" relational: power relations' "existence depends on a multiplicity of points of resistance: these play the role of adversary, target, support or handle in power relations" (1976ET, 95). Local and unstable, dependent upon many points in relations of inequality and hence resistance, power relations spring from, or are immanent in, the dispersal of positions in a social space, field, or network.

But power relations are not only produced in the dispersion of the social field; power relations are also productive of the dispersions. "They are not univocal; they define innumerable points of confrontation, focuses of instability, each of which has its own risks of conflict, of struggles, and of an at least temporary inversion of the power relations" (1975ET, 27). The power relations immanent and operative in the social field determine the possibilities of transformation, delimiting the possibilities at each point of confrontation.[3]

These possibilities are delimited by the dynamics of the power relations—by the interaction of a struggle between one possible movement and a resistance to that movement. Resistance is part of the logic of power relations, internal to power relations. "Where there is power, there is resistance, and yet, or rather consequently, this resistance is never in a position of exteriority in relation to power" (1976ET, 95), or, as Foucault puts it elsewhere, "there are no relations of power without resistances; . . . [resistances] are formed right at the point where relations of power are exercised" (DE218.1, 142). The exercise of power inevitably creates—is not possible without—resistance, for it is in this opposition between movement in one direction in a social field and resistance to that movement that power relations become clear. The fact that the social field is altered in one or the other direction illustrates that a relation of power has been in operation. It is in this struggle that the "risks" and "inversions" of power relations are realized. As Foucault put it in 1982, "if there was no resistance, there would be no power relations" (DE358.1, 29).[4]

In the opening chapter of *Discipline and Punish*, Foucault presents his general analysis in similar terms. One paragraph in particular, at the heart of the chapter, articulates the core of his theory:

> Now, the study of this micro-physics presupposes that the power exercised on the body is conceived not as a property, but as a strategy, that its effects of domination are attributed not to "appropriation," but to dispositions, manoeuvres, tactics, techniques, functionings; that one should decipher in it a network of relations, constantly in tension, in activity, rather than a privilege that one might possess; that one should take as its model a perpetual battle rather than a contract regulating a transaction or the conquest of a territory. (1975ET, 26)

This single sentence succinctly condenses almost all of the elements of Foucault's theory of power. Power manifests as strategies and tactics within constantly evolving networks of relations, on the model of a perpetual battle—it is not a contract, privilege, or possession held by one but not another. (That he characterizes it here as a *perpetual* battle is significant: that the battle is ongoing means that it cannot be won, once and for all, but by the same token, it is never utterly lost. As long as one is living, then, one will be immersed in, subject to, and participating in power relations, and there is always reason for hope.) Hence, he continues, while the distribution of power may occasionally result in temporary states of domination, it "is not exercised as an obligation or a prohibition on those who 'do not have it'; it invests them, is transmitted by them and through them" (1975ET, 27). This investment (which we will explore more fully later, when we look at disciplinary power in particular) is the site and basis for resistance to that very exercise of power, for relations of power "are not univocal" and can even be reversed (1975ET, 27). Foucault then underscores both the generality and the micro character of these relations of power while also distinguishing his analysis from inadequate approaches (like the Marxist and liberal analyses discussed in *La volonté de savoir*):

> This means that these relations go right down into the depths of society, that they are not localized in the relations between the state and its citizens or on the frontier between classes and that they do not merely reproduce, at the level of individuals, bodies, gestures and behaviour, the general form of the law or government; that, although there is continuity (they are indeed articulated on this form through a whole series of complex mechanisms), there is neither analogy nor homology, but a specificity of mechanism and modality. (1975ET, 27)

The preceding paragraphs constitute a summary of what I just described as "power in general"—an account of power that transcends historical periods. This discussion is even more densely articulated than in the dozen or so pages of *La volonté de savoir* that we discussed in the first chapter, and one other important difference separates these two accounts. While in the latter work Foucault was already beginning to rearticulate his analysis of power in terms of biopower (though still thinking primarily in terms of disciplinary power), here his analysis is exclusively oriented toward disciplinary power. (This is evidenced in part by the way that he speaks here of power's effects on bodies.) We shall begin our detailed exploration of *Discipline and Punish* by tracing how that "specific mode of power," disciplinary power, emerges out of earlier forms.

A "REDISTRIBUTION" OF POWER

The opening pages of *Discipline and Punish* juxtapose two striking—and paradigmatic—images of punishment. The first is a graphic, and often disturbing, eyewitness report of the 1757 execution of the regicide Damiens, who was publicly burned, mutilated, and drawn and quartered. This physically grotesque account is contrasted with an 1838 prisoners' timetable. Just eighty years after Damiens, prisoners are no longer subject to violent torture; instead, the details of their daily routines are carefully regulated and monitored: rise at six a.m., work for nine hours, a schedule for meals and education, etc. Foucault seems to be making two important points with this juxtaposition.

First, there is a shift in the style of punishment: this juxtaposition marks a redistribution of punitive techniques that corresponds to a shift in the dominant modes of power relations in society. Documenting this shift— from what Foucault terms "monarchical" (or sovereign) modes through a transitional phase ("semio-juridical") to a new stabilization in which the prison is the paradigmatic form of punishment, a shift that occurred in the century roughly framed by these two opening images—is the principal task of the first two parts of the book. The prison, Foucault argues, is the paradigmatic example of a new mode of power relations: disciplinary power.

These two opening images suggest that Foucault wants to make a further observation, however. This second, disciplinary mode (punishment through imprisonment, through careful regulation and documentation of a prisoner's each and every activity) perhaps ought to disturb us as much as the first (graphically violent torture). This challenges a certain rhetoric about the reform and "humanization" of punitive practices. "Perhaps it has been attributed too readily and too emphatically to a process of 'humanization,' thus dispensing with the need for further analysis" (1975ET, 7). Foucault's argumentative technique here is similar to that of *La volonté de savoir*: he identifies an understanding that is "taken for granted" or "received wisdom" and shows that it is a *mis*understanding (or at least an only partial and conditional, not essential, understanding)—that beneath it something else is going on, something that is better understood through the lens of power relations—and Foucault thereby recasts our conception of the entire problem. In *La volonté de savoir*, he called into question the accepted view that sexuality was repressed in the Victorian and post-Victorian ages, arguing on the contrary that there has in fact been an explosion of discourses about sexuality in the West. In *Discipline and Punish*, the "false" or "misleading" story with which he begins is one of the gradual humanization of punishment:

> The reduction in penal severity . . . has been regarded in an overall way
> as a quantitative phenomenon: less cruelty, less pain, more kindness,
> more respect, more "humanity." In fact the changes are accompanied by
> a displacement in the very object of the punitive operation. (1975ET, 16)

Indeed, with this displacement, punishment seems to penetrate ever more deeply into prisoners' "souls" by means of their bodies, subtly shaping and molding their habits, actions, and behavior—and this is paralleled by similar transformations in other social institutions, notably schools, factories, and the military.

This recasting or revisioning of fundamental social problems is one of Foucault's most compelling philosophical contributions—and it is part of why his new theory of power is so important. His reframing of the power relations at work in social relations, in the prison or sexuality, not only effects a new understanding of the particular truism challenged in a given volume; it also suggests that this lens of power relations is indispensable for a complete, or even adequate, social analysis. It also creates a new conceptual space in which to confront and articulate an ethics. And Foucault's own ethical orientations and principles will evolve and be recast in response to the evolution of this understanding of how power works.

That the story of the humanization of punishment is a mask for other, perhaps more sinister, transformations of punitive techniques in particular and social relations in general becomes clear as Foucault analyzes and explains the process of transformation from one established, coherent modality of power, which Foucault terms "sovereign," through transitional, hybrid forms ("semio-techniques"), to a new modality, "modern" or "disciplinary" power. Indeed, Nancy Fraser, one of Foucault's most incisive critics (we'll look at her criticisms in Chapter 4), maintains that "Foucault's most valuable accomplishment consists of a rich empirical account of the early stages in the emergence of some distinctively modern modalities of power" (Fraser 1981, 17). (The term "modality" here means a predominant or general form of power relations. If Foucault's theory asserts that certain microrelations are constitutive of *all* relationships of power, ancient and modern, then what is distinct in a particular modality is that certain of those microrelations and techniques are more explicitly or predominantly exercised in the macrorelations between individuals, societies, and states.) Our aim is to trace Foucault's analysis of this "redistribution" of power relations from one regime or modality to another, thereby demonstrating two claims about Foucault's theory: first, that the general analysis given above is not unique to the contemporary, modern regime, and second, that there is a solid empirical basis for his theory.

Before immersing ourselves in *Discipline and Punish*, however, we can see the broad outlines of the argument initially sketched in his 1973–1974 Collège de France course, *Psychiatric Power* (CdF74). There, Foucault began to trace the redistribution from "sovereign" to "disciplinary" power by looking at a very particular example—the emergence of psychiatry as a discipline and a branch of medical science at the beginning of the nineteenth century. This work anticipates his argument about the redistribution of power in *Discipline and Punish*; it also highlights certain limitations of his early hypotheses and the development of his thought. It behooves us therefore to note briefly how he presented the problem in these lectures. Indeed, here too Foucault is debunking myths of "humanization" in favor of analysis in terms of power relations. Liberating the mad from their chains (as the early psychiatrist Philippe Pinel, one of Foucault's principal examples in this course, famously did for the prisoners at Bicêtre),[5] Foucault tells us, "is not exactly a scene of humanism" (Foucault even adds here, "and of course everyone knows this") but rather "the transformation of a certain relationship of power that was one of violence . . . into a relationship of subjection that is a relationship of discipline" (CdF74ET, 29).

Foucault's task in this course is to reassess the emergence of psychiatric practice, and his argument is that this specific historical transition is best understood in terms of, and as based upon, power relations: "The mechanism of psychiatry should be understood starting from the way in which disciplinary power works" (CdF74ET, 41). "So what is organized in the asylum," he notes, "is actually a battlefield" (CdF74ET, 7). A few pages later, he defines "battle": "What is established, therefore, is a battle, a relationship of force" (CdF74ET, 10). (These "relations of force," we should recall, constitute the fundamental elements of Foucault's understanding of power.) There are two important things to note in this characterization of psychiatric practice as a battle. First, Foucault here uses this insight to critique his own earlier analyses of madness and asylums in *History of Madness* (1961)—his emerging emphasis upon power relations grows out of a process of autocritique. (He also uses the occasion to criticize several mistaken frameworks for understanding the birth of psychiatry, frameworks that emphasize representations, institutions, and the family as organizing concepts. This parallels the way that he begins his theory of power in *La volonté de savoir* by first identifying mistaken, or partial, accounts of power.) Second, in this initial, tentative study, Foucault is only looking at a very specific case (psychiatric practice), and he speaks of the relations between doctor and patient as "battles," that is, as specific engagements. Later, as this analytical approach demonstrates its incisiveness, he will generalize the model from specific cases to power relations and social relations as a whole. (This is, in large part, the work of *Discipline and Punish* and *La volonté de savoir*.) He will then speak of power not in terms of battles but rather of "war"—the larger, strategic field within which specific "battles," institutions, individuals, and fields of experience are given significance. For example, in the Collège de France course of 1976, he notes that "if power is indeed the implementation and deployment of a relationship of force . . . shouldn't we be analyzing it first and foremost in terms of conflict, confrontation, and war?" (CdF76ET, 15). This is the background for his famous suggestion that Clausewitz's aphorism should be inverted, that politics be understood as the continuation of war.[6]

Foucault's explicit analysis of these modalities of power is presented in the first four lectures of the 1973–1974 course. Power, he proposes, should be considered as the basis upon which discursive practices are formed. One of his guiding questions is: "How can this deployment of power [in psychiatric practice], these tactics and strategies of power give rise . . . to a game of truth?" (CdF74ET, 13). He goes further to suggest some general hypotheses: "what is essential in all power is that ultimately its point of application is always the body. All power is physical, and there is a direct connection between the body and political power" (CdF74ET, 14).

In the second lecture, Foucault identifies one incident in particular as a critical illustration of the transition from sovereign to disciplinary power: the madness of King George III, who was treated by Sir Francis Willis in 1788–1789. To treat the king, Willis had him held in an isolated palace, away from family and courtesans. All the trappings of royalty were removed. The king was told that "he is no longer sovereign, but that he must henceforth be obedient and submissive" (CdF74ET, 20). Two pages, both physically much stronger than the king, attended to his needs but also kept watch and reminded him of his subservience, restraining him when necessary. On occasion, the pages even had to clean the king forcibly, first stripping him and throwing him on the bed. The doctor, who directed the treatment, received detailed reports from the pages but was rarely present himself. Eventually, the doctor declared, this method "produced a sound cure without relapse" (CdF74ET, 20).[7]

Here in microcosm, Foucault notes, we see the shift from sovereign to disciplinary modes of power clearly enacted.

> I think the confrontation between George III and his servants—which is more or less contemporaneous with the *Panopticon*—this confrontation of the king's madness and medical discipline is one of the historical and symbolic points of the emergence and definitive installation of disciplinary power in society. (CdF74ET, 41)

Indeed, the techniques that Willis used in the treatment (isolation, subservience, constant observation, etc.) will be reproduced in asylum practice in the nineteenth century. (Bentham's *Panopticon Writings*, which Foucault describes here as "the most general political and technical formula of disciplinary power" [CdF74ET, 41], were published in 1791.) The scene of George III's treatment is a particularly striking image precisely because it is the sovereign himself who is brought under disciplinary control by the treatment. This image might also remind us of the opening scenes of *Discipline and Punish*, contrasting the execution of Damiens and the prison timetable. Foucault notes that the image of the pages' forcible cleaning of the king, for example, represents an inversion of a scene of sovereign power, "the scaffold, the scene of public torture" (CdF74ET, 25).

We can quickly review Foucault's analysis of the power of sovereignty, his initial characterization of disciplinary power, and his overview of the transition from the first modality to the second. Sovereign power has, on Foucault's account here, three principal characteristics. First, the sovereign and subject are linked by two asymmetrical relationships. On the one hand the sovereign exacts a levy (tax, tribute, etc.) from subjects; on the other, the sovereign also makes certain expenditures for the subjects (gifts for marriages or births, expenditures for festivals or war, etc.). These are asymmetrical because, first, they are not equal or reciprocal acts (the levies usually exceed the expenditures), and second, they are all determined and executed by the sovereign's agency. Also, these relationships achieve only a temporary, discontinuous control over the subjects: taxes must be paid each year, for example, but the vassal is otherwise largely free to do what he will.

Second, sovereign power takes its justification from a "founding prece-dence," a past event (victory at war, birth or marriage, divine right, etc.) that grounds its authority. So, its authority "is given once and for all but, at the same time, is fragile and always liable to disuse or breakdown" (CdF74ET, 43). Sovereign authority is therefore maintained by occasional reenactment in ceremonies (bowing before the king, public execution of criminals, etc.), but these ceremonies often carry a threat of violence, "which is there behind the relationship of sovereignty, and which sustains it and ensures that it holds" (CdF74ET, 43).

The third characteristic that Foucault identifies about relations of sover-eign power is that "they are not isotopic" (CdF74ET, 43). This means that "they do not constitute a unitary hierarchical table with subordinate and superordinate elements . . . they are heterogeneous and have no common measure" (CdF74ET, 43). The multiple relationships within a sovereign modality (fiefholder/serf, priest/parishioner, king/vassal, etc.), while analo-gously structured, cannot be reduced or assimilated to each other. Sover-eignty can also be exercised with respect to lands or roads as on humans. An important consequence of this heterotopy is that sovereign power tends not to individualize its subjects. On the other hand, sovereign power does individualize the sovereign himself: "there must be a single, individual point which is the summit of this set of heterotopic relationships" (CdF74ET, 45). One consequence of this acute individualization of the king is that "king-ship" must survive the death of the king, thus producing a curious multipli-cation of the king's body.[8]

Sovereign power does not entirely disappear once disciplinary power be-comes the dominant modality of power. On the contrary, "forms of the power of sovereignty can still be found in contemporary society," in the fam-ily (CdF74ET, 79). Describing the family as a "cell" of sovereignty within discipline, Foucault notes how it shares these characteristics of sovereign power: "maximum individualization on the side of the person who exercises power" (the father), establishment of the bond in a past event (marriage or birth), and heterotopic relationships (CdF74ET, 80).

This is, by Foucault's own admission, only a very schematic character-ization of sovereign power. Nevertheless, it is one of his most explicit and extended discussions of the power of sovereignty.

Discipline, Foucault notes, has a history—it is a specific modality of a gen-eral micropower that emerges within and then supersedes sovereign power. Foucault begins his analysis by contrasting it point by point to his description of sovereign power. Discipline does not employ an asymmetrical levy and expenditure but rather aims at "an exhaustive capture of the individual's body, actions, time, and behavior" (CdF74ET, 46). Second, and hence, discipline does not function through occasional rituals and ceremonies; on the contrary it aims for "continuous control": "one is perpetually under someone's gaze, or, at any rate, in the situation of being observed" (CdF74ET, 47). Similarly, discipline does not look to a prior founding event for its justification but rather to the future, "to a final or optimum state" (CdF74ET, 47). Thus discipline is aimed at a constant increase in the forces available to be controlled and used. Third and finally, disciplinary power "is isotopic, or at least tends towards isotopy" (CdF74ET, 52). Foucault delineates what this "isotopy" means: every element has a defined place within the system, with sub- and superordinate elements; movement within the system (up or down) is carefully regulated; different sub-systems are ultimately compatible, able to be linked to each other in a larger, global system; and finally, "the principle of distribution and classification of all the elements necessarily entails something like a residue. That is to say, there is always something like 'the unclassifiable'" (CdF74ET, 53). This last feature is very important: "This will be the stumbling block in the physics of disciplinary power. That is to say, all disciplinary power has its margins" (CdF74ET, 53).

A distinction is in order here. In a 1977 interview, Foucault will famously note that "power *is* 'always already there,' that one is never 'outside' it, that there are no 'margins' for those who break with the system to gambol in" (DE218.1, 141), apparently contradicting this 1973 claim. The point of the 1977 claim is that we can never find ourselves in a situation that is totally free from or immune to power relations—we are never "outside" power. (We could quite legitimately read this as a critique of certain utopian visions or of something like Jürgen Habermas's "ideal speech situation.") But, and this is the point of Foucault's 1973 remark, while we can never be free of power *as such*, we can resist, escape, or be freed from any particular form or instantiation of power, including particular modes of disciplinary power. Thus, there is no contradiction. As Foucault immediately clarifies in the 1977 interview:

> But this does not entail the necessity of accepting an inescapable form
> of domination or an absolute privilege on the side of the law. To say that
> one can never be "outside" power does not mean that one is trapped and
> condemned to defeat no matter what. (DE218.1, 141–142)

Thus, disciplinary power's "margins"—as Foucault refers to them here in 1973—are an important locus of resistance to disciplinary power—and we saw in Chapter 1 that this resistance is a fundamental, even constitutive, feature of all kinds of power. And in the dialectic of hope and despair that motivates Foucault's ethical vision, these margins are clearly an important source for hope, even as the all-encompassing ambition of a disciplinary system (a consequence of its isotopy) could seem to be a cause for despair.

In the fourth lecture, Foucault briefly summarizes the rise of discipline to become the dominant modality of social power. It began, too, in the margins of sovereign power—as islands or pockets within the general sovereign modality—forming principally within religious communities; these islands "functioned positively" and supported the general regime of sovereignty, but "they also played a critical role of opposition and innovation" (CdF74ET, 64). Beginning in the sixteenth and seventeenth centuries, disciplinary power began to extend beyond religious communities and to "colonize" other areas of social life. They did this first within the context of religious orders— Foucault's examples here are schools, overseas colonies, and the confinement of vagrants, prostitutes, and others. In the seventeenth and eighteenth centuries, then, disciplinary techniques become independent of religion and stand alone, as it were—disciplinary practices in armies, factories, mines, and workshops illustrate this transition. Finally, in the nineteenth century, disciplinary power makes its first appearance as a general form, in the practice of psychiatric power: "what appeared openly, as it were, in the naked state, in psychiatric practice at the start of the nineteenth century, was a power with the general form of what I have called discipline" (CdF74ET, 73).

Foucault illustrates this disciplinary modality of power with a discussion of Jeremy Bentham's Panopticon (which Foucault will take up in further detail in *Discipline and Punish*). He notes here that:

> It seems to me that the panoptic mechanism provides the common
> thread to what could be called the power exercised on man as a force
> of work and knowledge of man as an individual. So that panopticism
> could, I think, appear and function within our society as a general form;
> we could speak equally of a disciplinary society or of a panoptic society.
> (CdF74ET, 79)

A number of important themes and examples for the next decade of Foucault's thought are already present in this course. Consider one particularly interesting observation about the early disciplinization of schools:

We find the mould, the first model of the pedagogical colonization of youth, in *this practice of the individual's exercise on himself,* this attempt to transform the individual, this search for a progressive development of the individual up to the point of salvation, in this ascetic work of the individual on himself for his own salvation. (CdF74ET, 67; my italics)

The phrase I have highlighted here—"this practice of the individual's exercise on himself"—marks an example and a line of inquiry that Foucault will continue to pursue long after his theory of power has been more fully elaborated. In fact, this exercise upon oneself will become a case study, the history of which will take Foucault to ancient Greek and Roman practices (as well as the early Christian practices that he alludes to here) and will provide the historical background for the development of his ethics. Just as in this course he began with a reconsideration of—in fact, a *gestalt* shift in relation to—his earlier perspectives on the institution of the asylum, Foucault will bring a new perspective to bear on this phenomenon, too.

Other key insights can be seen in utero in this course, as well. He recognizes in psychiatric power a structure that he will soon apply more broadly: relationships of power are the basis for "the construction of institutional structures, the emergence of discourses of truth, and also the grafting or importation of a number of models" (CdF74ET, 26). Still, there remains a tension, an incomplete formation, in his analysis at this point. He claims that "what is essential in all power is that ultimately its point of application is always the body" (CdF74ET, 14). Notice the strong, absolutist tone: "essential," "all power," "ultimately," "always." This characterization is overdrawn, too crude. In the next years, Foucault will be able to articulate his understanding of power with much greater refinement. His understanding of the contrast between sovereign and disciplinary power, too, is not yet fully articulated:

> There are two absolutely distinct types of power corresponding to two systems, two different ways of functioning: the macrophysics of sovereignty, the power that could be put to work in a post-feudal, pre-industrial government, and then the microphysics of disciplinary power . . . (CdF74ET, 27)

Foucault does not yet see that sovereign power, too, is constituted by micropowers; likewise, he doesn't yet see that discipline has macropowers. (This latter insight will not come for several more years and will be the focus of

Chapter 3.) Foucault's survey at this point provides the general outline and structure for his developing argument about the historical redistribution of power, but in 1973–1974, it is clearly only rudimentarily articulated.

THE EMERGENCE OF A NEW MODALITY:
FROM "SOVEREIGN" TO "DISCIPLINARY" POWER

Our brief review of Foucault's 1973–1974 characterization of the transition from "sovereign" to "disciplinary" modalities of power nicely prepares us to see how he refines, expands, and develops that account in *Discipline and Punish*. To begin, let's briefly look at how the book is organized as a whole. *Discipline and Punish* consists of four parts, each subdivided into chapters. The first part, "Torture," consists of two chapters: the first provides a condensed overview of the argument of the book as a whole, as well as a theorization of power relations; the second chapter presents in more detail certain key features of the sovereign modality. Part 2, "Punishment," looks at the emergence of unstable, transitional modes of power: the first of two chapters here emphasizes how these transitional forms emerge out of the sovereign form; the second emphasizes how the modern modality itself emerges from these transitional forms. Parts 1 and 2 together tell the story of redistribution that we will focus upon now. The third part, "Discipline," constitutes an analysis of the central mechanisms or techniques of disciplinary power. We'll look at Part 3 in more detail later in this chapter, when we more fully articulate Foucault's analysis of disciplinary power. The fourth and final part of the book, "Prison," examines this paradigmatic example of disciplinary power and suggests the extent to which this new modality has shaped the landscape of society, painting a bleak portrait that seems to resemble Weber's "iron cage." Part 4 is quite interesting, first because it shows the limitations of Foucault's theorization at this point (it works from the *incorrect* hypothesis that disciplinary power by itself constitutes the full range of power relations in society), but also because, given this incorrect hypothesis, it raises important issues for what I have termed Foucault's larger Hobbesian hypothesis and for questions of hope and despair at the heart of his work. We will return to these themes later, as well.

Foucault begins in Chapter 2 of Part 1 with an articulation of the "logic," or mechanisms, of sovereign power. A number of shifts—in perspective as well as in presuppositions—are recognizable in these new analyses. Whereas he had focused on psychiatric practice in his earlier analyses, here he focuses on penal practices as paradigmatic of the functioning of power. While he continues to recognize the importance of the body in the exercise of power relations, he no longer speaks in the reductive, universalizing language we noted earlier ("essentially," "always," etc.); this allows him to articulate a broader, theoretically more inclusive and useful analysis of power. And finally, Foucault begins to integrate micro- and macroanalyses as he describes the sovereign mode of power—sovereign power is no longer presented as merely a macro form, and Foucault turns to the microlevel in order to articulate its techniques. In the 1974 Collège de France course, Foucault had described the transition from sovereign to disciplinary power as "the transformation of a certain relationship of power that was one of violence . . . into a relationship of subjection that is a relationship of discipline" (CdF74ET, 29). In *Discipline and Punish*, that sovereign relationship of violence is made concrete and specific—Foucault refers to the importance of torture within the legal and penal manifestations of sovereign power. He will thus analyze the micropolitics of torture at multiple levels: as the form of punishment itself but also as a vehicle for the legal establishment of truth (thus as a mechanism on both sides of the legal operation, the establishment of guilt and the punishment of it), and, finally, as the linchpin that binds these legal practices to political practices that maintain and reinforce the authority of the sovereign.

At the beginning of his discussion of torture, Foucault acknowledges that it was not the only means of punishment in the seventeenth century. Nevertheless, it was a central technique, symbolically significant, and, as he notes, "every penalty of a certain seriousness had to involve an element of torture, of *supplice*" (1975ET, 33). And at its basis, "torture is a technique" (1975ET, 33). This technique is characterized by three criteria: torture produces pain, the production and the pain are regulated, and "torture forms part of a ritual" (1975ET, 34). The ritual thus constituted through torture is itself bifocal: on the one side, this ritual targets the criminal—"it must mark the victim," the traces of the pain record the infamy of the crime upon the criminal's body; on the other side, this ritual speaks to the entire community or kingdom of the sovereign's power—"public torture and execution must be spectacular, it must be seen by all almost as its triumph" (1975ET, 34). Thus, "in the 'excesses' of torture, a whole economy of power [that is, sovereign power] is invested" (1975ET, 35). That economy of power is made evident in both foci, in other words, at both the micro- and the macro levels.

At the micro level, the level of the individual, torture is at the heart of both the punishment and the investigation. It applies itself directly to an individual's body, one person at a time. That torture constitutes a significant part of punishment is amply illustrated by the case of Damiens, with which Foucault opened the book. Its role in investigation merits further elaboration. Confession constituted one of the strongest proofs of guilt, so "judicial torture," the use of torture in order to produce a confession, played an important, if dangerous, part of an investigation. It bears certain elements of the *épreuve*, a test or trial to determine guilt, and constitutes a kind of duel between the examiner and the accused. Here we see the possibility of resistance even in such an extremely lopsided power relation: "the examining magistrate . . . had a stake in the game . . . ; for the rule was that if the accused 'held out' and did not confess, the magistrate was forced to drop the charges. The tortured man had won" (1975ET, 40–41). If an accused could bear the pain, the accusation would be reversed.

At the macro level, torture is the conduit that ties these penal practices of investigation and punishment to larger social and political forces and publicly illustrates the extent of the monarch's power. First, Foucault notes, "the right to punish . . . is an aspect of the sovereign's right to make war on his enemies: to punish belongs to 'that absolute power of life and death . . .'" (1975ET, 48, quoting Muyart de Vouglans). This phrase is significant for the development of Foucault's understanding of power relations: it is also the starting point for his introduction of the term "biopower," in Part 5 of *La volonté de savoir* and in his 1976 Collège de France course. (We shall examine how he introduces and revises this term in Chapter 3.)

Second, punishment—and in particular, public execution—also performs a symbolic function, restoring and reenacting the monarch's authority: It "has a juridico-political function. It is a ceremonial by which a momentarily injured sovereignty is reconstituted. . . . [It] belongs to a whole series of great rituals in which power is eclipsed and restored" (1975ET, 48). The public display of a king's power—in the case of Damiens, for example, to rend his body limb from limb, to inflict intense pain—serves to remind the populace that the monarch is "in control" and to undo any damage to his reputation that a crime may have caused. It served "to make everyone aware, through the body of the criminal, of the unrestrained presence of the sovereign. The public execution did not re-establish justice, it reactivated power" (1975ET, 49). In making "everyone" aware, this serves as a social restraint, an exercise of the king's authority not only on the criminal, but on all those subject to his power who may witness or hear of the punishment. It thus constitutes a "political operation" (1975ET:53). In short, it was a vehicle for the maintenance of sovereignty. This political operation that reinscribes the sovereign's power for all to see is a macro-level manifestation of sovereign power, realized through the very same mechanisms (torture and punishment) that inhabited its micro-level phenomena. Foucault summarizes the macro-level aspects of sovereign power in the final paragraph of this discussion:

> It was the effect, in the rites of punishment, of a certain mechanism of power: of a power that not only did not hesitate to exert itself directly on bodies, but was exalted and strengthened by its visible manifestations . . . of a power which, in the absence of continual supervision, sought a renewal of its effect in the spectacle of its individual manifestations; of a power that was recharged in the ritual display of its reality as "super-power." (1975ET, 57)

The "continual supervision" that Foucault mentions here is the form that disciplinary power will take. He is thus contrasting these two different modalities of power: in sovereign power, the masses are controlled not by being themselves under surveillance but rather by witnessing the exercise and effects of the monarch's power. There is also an important similarity in these two modalities: in both cases, the macroeffects emerge from practices that are fundamentally micropractices. The monarch's power is renewed for all his subjects through the visible application of it upon only one, the criminal. So we can perhaps understand why, at this point in his analysis, Foucault mistakenly understood all macro-level relations of power to be grounded in micro-level power relations.

Though it certainly was not the only, or even the most common, form of punishment, torture thus functioned as paradigmatic for the exercise of sovereign power. It thus functions for Foucault's analyses as the microtechnique that undergirds the larger sovereign modality, and it is a key for our understanding of the operation of sovereign power. "If torture was so strongly embedded in legal practice, it was because it revealed truth and showed the operation of power" (1975ET, 55). It revealed the truth and showed the operation of power in particular investigations when an accused's guilt or innocence hung in the balance, and it also revealed the truth and showed the operation of the king's sovereignty itself. It thus allows us to see not only how sovereign power is distinct from disciplinary power but also (and just as importantly) how they share a common fundamental relational structure. One important example of this commonality is in the relationship between knowledge and power at the heart of any sort of power relations. Torture, whether as a means for determination of guilt or as the vehicle for punishment (and thus for a reinscription of the "truth" of the sovereign's authority), is a technique in which relations of truth or knowledge and relations of power are intimately, indeed, essentially, interwoven and mutually productive. Foucault adds here: "We shall see later [in his discussion of disciplinary power in Part 3] that the truth-power relation remains at the heart of *all* mechanisms of punishment and that it is still to be found in contemporary penal practice—but in a quite different form and with very different effects" (1975ET, 55; my italics). This sentence is, in many ways, a key for our understanding of the entire book: A basic characteristic of all power relations—essential for our understanding of, but not unique to, the contemporary disciplinary modality—is this truth-power relation. So Foucault is underlining the claim that his analysis of power relations is a general analysis while noting that this does not elide the important differences in modalities' forms and effects (and hence in the form that our ethical responses to these modalities ought to take).

The practice of torture at the heart of sovereign power also constituted an important site of resistance to that power, a point of resistance in both phases or aspects of the manifestation of power. We already saw how an accused man, by refusing to confess under torture, could overturn any other evidence that had been gathered and thereby escape conviction. At the macro level, too, resistance was possible in the exercise of sovereign power. Crowds did not always respond to these public manifestations of power with the appropriate awe and submission—sometimes the rituals would backfire: "In these executions, which ought to show only the terrorizing power of the prince, there was a whole aspect of the carnival, in which rules were inverted, authority mocked and criminals transformed into heroes . . . executions could easily lead to the beginnings of social disturbances" (1975ET, 61). The public would sometimes respond with sympathy or solidarity for the criminal, rejecting the authority that the execution was meant to demonstrate, and so the very mechanism for asserting monarchical authority could become "a political danger" (1975ET, 63). Indeed, "out of the ceremony of the public execution, out of that uncertain festival in which violence was instantaneously reversible, it was this solidarity *much more than sovereign power* that was likely to emerge with redoubled strength" (1975ET, 63; my italics). This mechanism at the heart of sovereign power, then, proved to be dangerous, unstable, and ultimately driven to a fundamental transformation—a transformation, in fact, of the very modalities by which power was exercised and a movement away from this sovereign form.

Recall that Foucault began this book by questioning the "received wisdom" that punishment was becoming more humane. Here we see a "political" explanation for the transformation of punitive techniques, an explanation in terms of the power relations at play: sovereign power was ultimately unstable and self-defeating. As Marx would put it, a new social order emerges out of the contradictions of the old order (cf., for example, Marx 1859, 4–5).[9] Here Foucault gives us an alternative explanation for the transformation of penal practice away from torture and toward imprisonment—an explanation grounded in an analysis of power relations at the core of social interactions.

How, then, is sovereign power as the principal modality of the exercise of power transformed into—or, rather, displaced and superseded by—disciplinary power? Foucault traces this development in Part 2 of *Discipline and Punish*. What Foucault describes is a two-part transformation. The first is a movement from the modalities of monarchical or sovereign power to a transitional phase, in which they are displaced by what Foucault called "semio-techniques." Then these "semio-techniques" are superseded by "a new politics of the body" (1975ET, 103), namely, disciplinary power. In the two chapters of Part 2, Foucault examines these processes through two lenses. Chapter 1, "Generalized Punishment," articulates the perspective of the theorists and reformers; Chapter 2, "The Gentle Way in Punishment," looks at the practice of punishment, tracing the rise of the prison as the principal instrument. Finally, he closes by merging these two lenses and showing how the practice and the theory were interdependent.

These historical transformations date from either side of the turn from the eighteenth to the nineteenth century. These events are framed by the two opening images of the book, the 1757 execution of Damiens and the 1838 prison timetable. Foucault has little to say in this book about the origins of sovereign power. At times, he seems to imply that "it was ever so"; at others, he seems to recognize that it, too, emerged from earlier modalities. He will have little of significance to say about the origins of sovereign power until later—first in the 1976 Collège de France course, where he will look at the development of monarchical forms, in particular in light of Henri de Boulainvilliers' theories, then more extensively in his surveys of early Christian monastic practices in the first centuries C.E. But his dating of the transformation from sovereign to disciplinary power in his study of the prison correlates with his earlier analyses in the 1974 Collège de France course on psychiatric power. Indeed, his analysis of penal techniques gives us an even clearer picture of the practices and techniques of discipline, and of the process by which it came to be predominant, than did his earlier studies of psychiatry. *Discipline and Punish* argues that disciplinary power became the new dominant modality in the heart of the nineteenth century and continues as such in the present day.

Indeed, this is why understanding disciplinary power is a necessary prolegomena for a Foucauldian ethics. An ethics must address its actual circumstances, and the techniques of disciplinary power constitute a very important, if not the only, part of our contemporary social situation. Or as Foucault put it in the first chapter of the book, this history of the prison "as an instrument and vector of power . . . this whole technology of power over the body that the technology of the 'soul' . . . fails either to conceal or to compensate" is intended as "the history of the present" (1975ET, 30, 31). This "history of the present" is a project that takes its structure from the Kantian project of interrogating Enlightenment and its motivation from an implicitly ethical attitude.[10]

I noted a few moments ago that this transformation of power is framed by a public execution and a prison timetable—the opening images of the book. Foucault observed in tracing this shift in power's modes that "it is understandable that the criticism of the public execution should have assumed such importance in penal reform: for it was the form in which, in the most visible way, the unlimited power of the sovereign and the ever-active illegality of the people came together" (1975ET, 88–89). An important feature of the transformation is a reversal of these two poles—the sovereign and the common people—as the focus of the apparatuses of power shifts from the former to the latter. The opening pages (73–82) of Part 2 give us a schematic of the underlying transformations.

The transformations in penal practice reflected, Foucault notes, "an effort to adjust the mechanisms of power that frame the everyday lives of individuals" (1975ET, 77) and manifested "as a tendency towards a more finely tuned justice, towards a closer penal mapping of the social body" (1975ET, 78). These efforts and tendencies were motivated not through a concern for humanitarian treatment but rather for efficiency and effectiveness. "The criticism of the reformers was directed not so much at the weakness or cruelty of those in authority, as at a bad economy of power" (1975ET, 79). Thus "the paralysis of justice was due not so much to a weakening as to a badly regulated distribution of power, to its concentration at a certain number of points and to the conflicts and discontinuities that resulted" (1975ET, 79–80). Therefore, "penal reform was born at the point of junction between the struggle against the super-power of the sovereign and that against the infra-power of acquired and tolerated illegalities" (1975ET, 87). The manifestation of the sovereign's power in displays such as a public execution often prompted, as we discussed earlier, resentments or rebellion, sympathies with the convict; it also left many others free to do as they pleased far from the authorities' eyes. "This dysfunction of power was related to a central excess: what might be called the monarchical 'super-power'" (1975ET, 80). The very characteristics that enabled a sovereign form of power to be exercised also served to undermine its authority, to lead to arbitrariness in the administration of punishment, as some crimes would go unpunished. "By placing on the side of the sovereign the additional burden of a spectacular, unlimited, personal, irregular and discontinuous power, the form of monarchical sovereignty left the subjects free to practice a constant illegality; this illegality was like the correlative of this type of power" (1975ET, 88). Many common people would find that their rights—especially property rights among a growing mercantile class—were left unprotected by the sovereign power, thus prompting a movement of reform:

> The reform of criminal law must be read as a strategy for the rearrangement of the power to punish, according to modalities that render it more regular, more effective, more constant and more detailed in its effects; in short, which increase its effects while diminishing its economic costs . . . and its political cost (by dissociating it from the arbitrariness of monarchical power). The new juridical theory of penality corresponds in fact to a new "political economy" of the power to punish. (1975ET, 80–81)

This rearrangement, expressed in eighteenth-century theories of reform, created a new network of relations and marked "a new strategy for the exercise of the power to punish" (and note how Foucault has articulated this in terms of his own general analysis or theory of power—in terms of strategies and exercise of power), a strategy that aims "to make of the punishment and repression of illegalities a regular function, coextensive with society; not to punish less, but to punish better; to punish with an attenuated severity perhaps, but in order to punish with more universality and necessity; to insert the power to punish more deeply into the social body" (1975ET, 82). The task of the penal theorists, reformers, and critics was "in short, to constitute a new economy and a new technology of the power to punish: these are no doubt the essential *raisons d'être* of penal reform in the eighteenth century" (1975ET, 89). Indeed, as Foucault tries to show us in this history, they were remarkably successful in this project.

To make punishment more effective, the reformers argued, it must be capable of touching every criminal act, so that everyone and every crime is assured of its "just deserts." The techniques that were proposed to achieve such a correspondence between crime and punishment Foucault called "semio-techniques," since they constituted a "technique of punitive signs" in which any crime would be accompanied, like a word with its meaning, by its punishment (1975ET, 94). Foucault spells out a number of the key principles underlying these reforms: "the rule of minimum quantity," "the rule of sufficient ideality," "the rule of lateral effects," "the rule of perfect certainty," "the rule of common truth," and "the rule of optimal specification" (1975ET, 94–98). We needn't dwell on the details of these rules but should note that they contribute to an increasing supervision of the general population, so that each and every crime could be appropriately punished—we are thus clearly on the road toward disciplinary power.

> This discourse provided, in effect . . . a sort of general recipe for the exercise of power over men: the "mind" as a surface of inscription of power, with semiology as its tool; the submission of bodies through the control of ideas; the analysis of representations as a principle in a politics of bodies that was much more effective than the ritual anatomy of torture and execution. (1975ET, 102)

One important consequence of these techniques is an increase in individualization: "the codification of the offences-punishments system and the modulation of the criminal-punishment dyad go side by side, each requiring the other. Individualization appears as the ultimate aim of a precisely adapted code" (1975ET, 99).

These reforms, these "semio-techniques," however, remained very theoretical—they still needed to be conjoined in penal practice with techniques that might actually achieve these targets. Prisons were not the reformers' preferred method; nevertheless, detention quickly became the principal means of punishment. A number of penitentiary models emerged—in Belgium, in England, and in Philadelphia in the United States—that would facilitate the realization of these theoretical goals. In these models, over a period of roughly twenty years, the prison emerged as a central and, ultimately, virtually the only institution for punishment, in part because it allowed for a closer supervision of convicts but also because it would allow a very precise metering of punishment to crime: some acts would require days of detention, others months or years. Prisons serve to hide the power to punish behind walls (in contrast to the very public display in executions); it also served to reorient punishment upon convicts' bodies—the very bodies whose liberties were restricted, who were trapped behind bars.

> The scaffold, where the body of the tortured criminal had been exposed to the ritually manifested force of the sovereign, the punitive theatre in which the representation of punishment was permanently available to the social body, was replaced by a great enclosed, complex and hierarchized structure that was integrated into the very body of the state apparatus. A quite different materiality, *a quite different physics of power*, a quite different way of investing men's bodies, had emerged. (1975ET, 115–116; my italics)

Note that in this evolution, the sovereign has been supplanted by the "state"—this will be important for Foucault's later analyses; note also Foucault's use of the guiding metaphor of physics for his analyses of different modes of power. This new "physics of power" also led ("both as a condition and as a consequence") to the development of new kinds of knowledge about individuals (1975ET, 125). "A whole new corpus of individualizing knowledge was being organized that took as its field of reference . . . the potentiality of danger that lies hidden in an individual and which is manifested in his observed everyday conduct. The prison functions in this as an apparatus of knowledge" (1975ET, 126).

Foucault had sketched this analysis in the 1974 Collège de France course:

> We could say, if you like, that there is a kind of juridico-disciplinary pincers of individualism. There is the juridical individual as he appears in these philosophical or juridical theories [which Foucault traced from Hobbes in the preceding paragraph]: the individual as abstract subject, defined by individual rights that no power can limit unless agreed by contract. And then, beneath this, alongside it, there was the development of a whole disciplinary technology that produced the individual as an historical reality, as an element of the productive forces, and as an element also of political forces. This individual is a subjected body held

in a system of supervision and subjected to procedures of normalization. (CdF74ET, 57)

Here we see the two sides of this individualization—the juridical theory and the penal practice—explicitly paired. That pairing, as the more detailed analysis in this part of *Discipline and Punish* shows, is only in the process of being worked out at the turn of the eighteenth and nineteenth centuries. It is the product of two connected but ultimately independent historical developments.

In Part 2 of *Discipline and Punish*, Foucault has outlined three different "ways of organizing the power to punish": monarchical law (or sovereign power), the reforming jurists' vision, and "the project for a prison institution" (1975ET, 130, 131). The latter two, the reformers' semiological project and the prison project, although they both challenged the sovereign modality, were far from identical—and a struggle between them marks the transitional period as sovereign power waned. Eventually, Foucault argues, the prison model would win out. Despite important divergences between the practice of prisons as penal institutions and the reformers' initial visions (in particular, the prisons' emphasis on bodies rather than ideas), their semiotechniques were to be taken up into a penitentiary model that became the dominant form for punishment in the nineteenth century. The integration of these two alternative mechanisms of punishment provided the key elements of disciplinary power and marked its emergence as the new paradigmatic form of social power (1975ET, 256).

DISCIPLINARY POWER

"Discipline is a political anatomy of detail" (1975ET, 139). Discipline is, in other words, power at the microscopic level, power at the level of discrete individuals. In a 1976 lecture that Foucault gave in Brazil, he defined discipline as "basically the mechanism of power through which we come to control the social body in its finest elements, through which we arrive at the very atoms of society, which is to say individuals" (DE297.1, 159). This inverts the monarchical model and focuses its attention, its apparatuses of knowledge and power, not on the majesty of the sovereign but on each one of the individuals that constitute "the masses." "How to oversee someone, how to control their conduct, their behaviour, their aptitudes, how to intensify their performance, multiply their capacities, how to put them in the place where they will be most useful: this is what discipline is, in my sense" (DE297.1, 159). This shift in focus was the end toward which the reformers' efforts were ultimately oriented. He elaborates in *Discipline and Punish* that the techniques of disciplinary power

> were always meticulous, often minute, techniques, but they had their importance: because they defined a certain mode of detailed political investment of the body, a "new micro-physics" of power; and because, since the seventeenth century, they had constantly reached out to ever broader domains, as if they tended to cover the entire social body.
> (1975ET, 139)

This orientation to detail, to individuals' corporal and mental habits, constitutes, Foucault notes, an application of power at the tactical level. It also marks a significant shift in focus away from the sovereign as the locus of power's manifestation and to the individuals who constitute "the masses," to each and every one of those who are trained in schools, who work in factories, who serve in the army, or who commit crimes and are punished in prisons. Thus, "disciplines mark the moment when the reversal of the political axis of individualization—as one might call it—takes place" (1975ET, 192).

"'Discipline' may be identified neither with an institution nor with an apparatus; it is a type of power, a modality for its exercise, comprising a whole set of instruments, techniques, procedures, levels of application, targets; it is a 'physics' or an 'anatomy' of power, a technology" (1975ET, 215). Discipline is a micropower: it focuses on the infinitesimal. This does not mean that it focuses on individuals; rather, it focuses on specific behaviors, postures, attitudes, outlooks—the elements that constitute one's individuality. (We've already discussed the analogy to physics; here we can see why Foucault also suggests the analogy to anatomy: like the subatomic particles that constitute a molecule, but also like organs and cells that constitute the body, these are the elements that make an individual a social being. Thus, "discipline 'makes' individuals; it is the specific technique of a power that regards individuals both as objects and as instruments of its exercise" [1975ET, 170].) An individual's character is—at least in part but perhaps in its entirety—thus constituted by these various and interwoven techniques and relations of power. In Part 3 of *Discipline and Punish* Foucault analyzes how these techniques work together to constitute individuals as "docile bodies." We shall look at a few paradigmatic examples and then see how these tactical techniques of disciplinary micropower operate.

The soldier, the student, and the prisoner are each paradigmatic examples of disciplined individuals. They serve not only to illustrate how disciplinary practices condition individuals but also to underscore Foucault's claim that prisons are not exceptional but typical of larger social norms and practices. These three examples thus support the claim that the Foucauldian analysis of power encompasses social practices in general, not just penal practices.

Indeed, Foucault opens his discussion of discipline in Part 2 with an analysis of the soldier. Whereas in the seventeenth century, the soldier was considered a natural type (one whose body and disposition, which communicated strength and courage, were well-suited for fighting), "by the late eighteenth century, the soldier has come to be something that can be made" (1975ET, 135). These two contrasting images of the soldier, corresponding to two different historical periods, parallels and maps onto the two juxtaposed images of Damiens and the prison timetable. The "making" of a soldier—turning anyone, of any body type or character, into a fighting machine—was effected through a series of training and conditioning: "posture is gradually corrected; a calculated constraint runs slowly through each part of the body, mastering it, making it pliable, ready at all times, turning slowly into the automatism of habit" (1975ET, 135). This image of the soldier is especially important because Foucault will explore and test the hypothesis, implicit in a vision of a disciplinary society as well as Foucault's own emphasis on power relations at the heart of social interactions, that politics be considered as a species of war. (We'll take this up in more detail later.) Furthermore, the soldier is a paradigmatic example of discipline because the soldier is housed, indeed, formed, in military camps, which served as a kind of "ideal model" for a disciplinary milieu (1975ET, 171). Finally, the image of the soldier also illustrates the importance of the body as a locus of disciplinary techniques: rather than merely destroying it (as in the case of Damiens), it can be shaped, molded, and conditioned, thereby shaping and molding the "soul," too.

The second paradigmatic figure, the student, illustrates how this "soul" or "mind" comes to be conditioned. Like the soldier, a student can be trained and conditioned to certain behaviors, through techniques of observation and pressure to conform. Schools—from elementary through higher levels—are reorganized in the nineteenth century to facilitate this kind of surveillance, and examinations constitute the culmination of many disciplinary techniques. Students' desks are arranged in the classroom so that students can be ordered—alphabetically by name, by class rank, or by some other standard—and regular examinations measure each student's progress in learning prescribed material. "The examination in the school was a constant exchanger of knowledge; it guaranteed the movement of knowledge from the teacher to the pupil, but it extracted from the pupil a knowledge destined and reserved for the teacher . . . the age of the 'examining' school marked the beginnings of a pedagogy that functions as a science" (1975ET, 187). The student thus embodies what Foucault here calls "the power of normalization" (though, as we shall see in Chapter 3, he will significantly revise his understanding of normalization in 1978): "the power of normalization imposes homogeneity; but it individualizes by making it possible to measure gaps, to determine levels, to fix specialities and to render the differences useful" (1975ET, 184).

The third paradigmatic image of discipline is the prisoner—which should come as no surprise, given that *Discipline and Punish* is a history of, as its subtitle indicates, "the birth of the prison." Many of the various techniques and mechanisms of disciplinary power developed or were perfected in penal practice, and the prison and the prisoner represent a focal point where multiple trajectories and techniques would intersect. Indeed, as Foucault suggested at the end of Part 2, penal mechanisms and reforms were instrumental in the transition from sovereign to disciplinary modalities. Jeremy Bentham's Panopticon, which Foucault presents as an almost perfect architectural expression of disciplinary power, was most widely employed in the design of prisons (though Bentham had in fact intended the panopticon for much wider social application). As Foucault notes, "at the heart of all disciplinary systems functions a small penal mechanism" (1975ET, 177).

Given these three paradigmatic examples of disciplined individuals, what do they share in common? What are the characteristics of disciplinary power? In each of the three cases, a personage is shaped, certain behaviors are encouraged or suppressed, in part by placing the individual in a carefully regimented situation—the military camp, the school classroom, or the prison cell—and in part by conditioning the individual's behavior so that certain responses become habitual or automatic. For this conditioning to be successful, a detailed knowledge of the individual becomes necessary, so that progress can be measured and the desired results obtained.

Foucault details three principal characteristics of disciplinary power: hierarchized observation, normalizing judgment, and the integration of these two elements in examinations. These three aspects of disciplinary power produce what Foucault calls "docile bodies," habituated to act or think in certain ways. Power and knowledge are thus interwoven into a tight fabric and become mutually productive, and individuals' own subjectivity is, at least in part, a product of the kinds of power relations that have shaped them. Thus has emerged, Foucault suggests in *Discipline and Punish*, a new "micro-physics" of power that has supplanted sovereign power as the dominant mode of social power, a modality whose dominance continues to the present day. This microphysics is composed of "a multiplicity of minor procedures," "humble modalities," and "simple instruments" (1975ET, 138, 170). The three techniques—observation, normalization, and examination—are just such simple instruments, whose combination nevertheless can produce a network of profound scope and power.

The first element is hierarchical observation: "the exercise of discipline presupposes a mechanism that coerces by means of observation" (1975ET, 170). Through "multiple and intersecting observations" (1975ET, 171), individuals' behaviors can be carefully monitored and thus controlled. To be most effective, these observations must be both complete and discrete. Both of these goals, completeness and discreteness, can be advanced through architecture, designing spaces to facilitate complete observation while masking the observers, and through social practices and hierarchies; ultimately, architecture, practices, and hierarchies can be integrated into a unified institution. Supervision and surveillance are key elements of this observation—in, for example, factories, workshops, and classrooms—and can be linked to other "productive" tasks, such as the training of students or soldiers and the exploitation of workers' labor. In the classroom, for example, "surveillance . . . is inscribed at the heart of the practice of teaching, not as an additional or adjacent part, but as a mechanism that is inherent to it and which increases its efficiency" (1975ET, 176). These techniques, simultaneously increasing discipline and productivity, function throughout the economy and every other aspect of society as a whole. And these observational techniques conform to Foucault's general analysis of power relations and how power is exercised: "The power in the hierarchized surveillance of the disciplines is not possessed as a thing, or transferred as a property; it functions like a piece of machinery" (1975ET, 177).

But observation in and of itself is insufficient; it provides a grid and a set of data about those who are observed, but it does not specify how the behaviors of the observed are to be altered. A second element of disciplinary power is required—normative judgment.

The workshop, the school, the army were subject to a whole micro-penality of time (latenesses, absences, interruptions of task), of activity (inattention, negligence, lack of zeal), of behavior (impoliteness, disobedience), of speech (idle chatter, insolence), of the body ("incorrect" attitudes, irregular gestures, lack of cleanliness), of sexuality (impurity, indecency). (1975ET, 178)

These normative judgments, these "micro-penalities," function through "a double system: gratification-punishment" and thus make possible

> a number of operations characteristic of disciplinary penality. First, the definition of behaviour and performance on the basis of the two opposed values of good and evil . . . we have a distribution between a positive pole and a negative pole; all behavior falls in the field between good and bad marks, good and bad points. Moreover, it is possible to quantify this field and work out an arithmetical economy based on it. (1975ET, 180)

We can first note that this normative judgment is thereby linked to and builds upon the hierarchical observation, which provides the data to determine what sort of behavior the student, worker, or soldier has demonstrated. Furthermore, Foucault notes here, it links these micropractices with larger macropatterns, "an arithmetical economy." (This unidirectional linkage is important because it contributes to the "bleak" outlook of Part 4 and is the central "problem" that Foucault will correct in his later analyses of biopower—all of which will be discussed below.) When normative judgment and hierarchical observation are thus united,

> the disciplinary apparatuses hierarchized the "good" and the "bad" subjects in relation to one another. Through this micro-economy of a perpetual penality operates a differentiation that is not one of acts, but of individuals themselves, of their nature, their potentialities, their level or their value. (1975ET, 181)

Hierarchical observation conjoined with a set of normative judgments serves to distribute and differentiate the "individuals themselves." "The perpetual penality that traverses all points and supervises every instant in the disciplinary institutions compares, differentiates, hierarchizes, homogenizes, excludes. In short, it *normalizes*" (1975ET, 183). This normalization functions in two directions: it pressures each individual to be just like everyone else—to be more like the norm—and it brings greater specificity and attention to each individual, by locating that individual within the grids of observation and evaluation. "The power of normalization imposes homogeneity; but it individualizes by making it possible to measure gaps, to determine levels, to fix specialities and to render the differences useful by fitting them one to another" (1975ET, 184).

These two disciplinary techniques—observation and normalizing judgment—are united in the third paradigmatic technique: the examination, which "will have the triple function of [a] showing whether the subject has reached the level required, [b] of guaranteeing that each subject undergoes the same apprenticeship and [c] of differentiating the abilities of each individual" (1975ET, 158; my brackets). Thus,

> the examination opened up two correlative possibilities: firstly, the constitution of the individual as a describable, analyzable object . . . in order to maintain him in his individual features, in his particular evolution, in his own aptitudes or abilities, under the gaze of a permanent corpus of knowledge; and secondly, the constitution of a comparative system that made possible the measurement of overall phenomena, the description of groups, the characterization of collective facts, the calculation of the gaps between individuals, their distribution in a given "population." (1975ET, 190)[11]

Foucault's point is that disciplinary power works to create and constitute "individuals": "The individual is no doubt the fictitious atom of an 'ideological' representation of society; but he is also a reality fabricated by this specific technology of power that I have called 'discipline'" (1975ET, 194).

An important point to observe here is the all-encompassing character of disciplinary power, methods, and institutions. Foucault has consistently described discipline as constituting a "perpetual penality"—one that is constant and uninterrupted. This consistency and completeness suggest two corollary observations. First, it suggests an inescapability, a network closed in both space and time in which we all are trapped, defined by the techniques and methods of disciplinary power. A second corollary is that "all resistance is futile." Indeed, in Part 4 of *Discipline and Punish*, Foucault is effectively developing and testing both of these corollary hypotheses—within the enclosed space of a prison (and, by implication within the other institutions of society),[12] can discipline constitute a "complete and austere" "carceral society"? However, these corollary implications are in fact mistaken, as should be clear if we recall the characteristics that Foucault has identified of power in general. First, power is not merely repressive but profoundly productive. To be sure, disciplinary power as described here "produces" normalized individuals. But the system is not (and could not be) perfect—it also produces other, nonconforming, abnormal individuals. Resistance is a constituent element without which power relations cannot obtain. And so, as Foucault puts it in "Power and Strategies," a 1977 interview,

> It seems to me that power *is* "always already there," that one is never "outside" it, that there are no "margins" for those who break with the system to gambol in. But this does not entail the necessity of accepting an inescapable form of domination or an absolute privilege on the side of the law. To say that one can never be "outside" power does not mean that one is trapped and condemned to defeat no matter what. (DE218.1, 141–142)

Though we cannot step "outside" of power, though disciplinary techniques may impose a "perpetual penality," there is still (and of necessity) space for resistance. Not every individual will be successfully normalized. Resistance to any particular application of power—in various forms and guises—will continue to emerge, all along the continuum.[13]

We must also ask another very important question, however: where do these norms come from? How do the values by which individuals are to be classified and evaluated come to be adopted and justified? These questions will ultimately push Foucault toward a fuller articulation of what constitutes ethics and will challenge the apparent completeness of this disciplinary analysis. His answer at this point seems to be reductive, explaining these norms in terms of the power relations that obtain in and frame a given situation. So the schoolmasters, factory owners, or military leaders will determine what norms, what ideals, those who are observed and judged will be conditioned to adopt. Indeed, Foucault will recognize the importance of these questions about the origins of norms in his 1978 Collège de France course (as he also realizes that all macro forms of power may not be reducible to the disciplinary micro forms):

> Disciplinary normalization consists first of all in positing a model, an optimal model that is constructed in terms of a certain result, and the operation of disciplinary normalization consists in trying to get people,

movements, and actions to conform to this model, the normal being precisely that which can conform to this norm, and the abnormal that which is incapable of conforming to the norm. In other words, it is not the normal and the abnormal that is fundamental and primary in disciplinary normalization, it is the norm. That is, there is an originally prescriptive character of the norm and the determination and the identification of the normal and the abnormal becomes possible in relation to this posited norm. Due to the primacy of the norm in relation to the normal, to the fact that disciplinary normalization goes from the norm to the final division between the normal and the abnormal, I would rather say that what is involved in disciplinary techniques is a normation rather than normalization. Forgive the barbaric word, I use it to underline the primary and fundamental character of the norm. (CdF78ET, 57)

Disciplinary power, as a technique, presupposes a given norm, in terms of which its subjects are sorted into normal and abnormal categories. The giving and specification of those norms is prior to the exercise of discipline in the cultivating of those norms—in effect, the norms are determined by the contexts, the institutions and their aims, in which they are applied. Thus, in a school, the "normal" student is one who obeys teachers' directives and learns the assigned material; in a factory, "normal" workers are docile and perform their tasks efficiently. But we can (and should) still ask, how did *these* norms come to be adopted? Indeed, this question is an absolutely essential element of Foucault's conception of the *"critical attitude,"* itself a central aspect of Foucault's ethics: "'How not to be governed *like that*, by that, in the name of these principles, in view of such objectives, and by the means of such methods, not like that, not for that, not by them?'" (OT-78-01.1, 384).

A DISCIPLINARY INSTITUTION

Discipline and Punish closes with a striking image, what Foucault terms—in a clear allusion to Aleksandr Solzhenitsyn's contemporaneous work on Soviet labor camps and prisons, or gulags[14]—the "carceral archipelago" (1975ET, 286). This carceral archipelago constitutes a paradigmatic symbol of what Foucault calls "the disciplinary society," "the gradual extension of the mechanisms of discipline throughout the seventeenth and eighteenth centuries, their spread throughout the whole social body" (1975ET, 209). A different example of disciplinary power at work in the construction of a nineteenth-century carceral society would perhaps be useful here. Kenneth M. Stampp, in his 1956 study of American slavery, *The Peculiar Institution: Slavery in the Ante-Bellum South*, shows how disciplinary techniques were deployed in the management of slaves.[15] The institution and practice of slavery in the thirty years prior to the American Civil War illustrate how these disciplinary techniques could underpin an entire society and economy. "Let us say that discipline is the unitary technique by which the body is reduced as a 'political' force at the least cost and maximized as a useful force" (1975ET, 221). Slavery was the system in which people of African descent were deprived of political and civil rights while their useful labor force was simultaneously exploited to the fullest extent possible: slavery marked slaves' bodies, "their social status, their legal status, and their private lives—but they felt it most acutely in their lack of control over their own time and labor" (Stampp 1956, 86).

Just as discipline marked a new vision of the soldier, no longer someone "born" with natural endowments but "something that can be made" (Part 3 of *Discipline and Punish* opens with this image [1975ET, 135]), so too

> A wise master did not take seriously the belief that Negroes were natural-born slaves.[16] He knew better. He knew that Negroes freshly imported from Africa had to be broken into bondage; that each succeeding generation had to be carefully trained. . . . In most cases there was no end to the need for control. (Stampp 1956, 144)

This disciplinary control was effected through slave codes enacted into state laws, which "rigidly controlled the slave's movements and his communications with others," often specifying the forms of observation and surveillance to be employed ("under the supervision of white men, and not left to the sole direction of slave foremen") and what sorts of behaviors were to be banned—reading and writing, preaching, traveling off the plantation without a pass, and various behaviors that could constitute "insolence"—including "'a look, the point of a finger, a refusal or neglect to step out of the way when a white person is seen to approach . . . [which] if tolerated would destroy that subordination, upon which our social system rests'" (208).

Stampp identifies five steps in the process of disciplining slaves. First of all "was to establish and maintain strict discipline" (144). This was effected through what Foucault has called the "disciplinary techniques," through careful observation and individualization of all the slaves on a plantation, with incentives and punishments tailored to each individual's situation. Second, a sense of personal inferiority, particularly with respect to whites, had to be implanted in slaves' self-consciousnesses to discourage impudence or indocility (145). Thus, slaves are simultaneously situated on a hierarchy, and their behaviors and aspirations—their subjectivities—are normalized. "The third step in the training of slaves was to awe them with a sense of their master's enormous power" (146). This third step more closely resembles the sovereign forms of power, illustrating how these different modalities can be adapted and integrated within a predominantly disciplinary framework. Fourth "was to persuade the bondsmen to take an interest in the master's enterprise and to accept his standards of good conduct" (147). Slaves must, in other words, internalize the enslavers' norms of behavior and values, just like prisoners in a panoptic institution. Finally, slaves must be given to understand "their helplessness, to create in them 'a habit of perfect dependence' upon their masters" (147).

> To achieve the "perfect" submission of his slaves, to utilize their labor profitably, each master devised a set of rules by which he governed. These were the laws of his private domain—and the techniques which enabled him to minimize the bondsmen's resistance to servitude. The techniques of control were many and varied, some subtle, some ingenious, some brutal. (143)

Frederick Douglass, in his first autobiography, recounts an incident in which these disciplinary techniques effectively turned him into a docile subject:

> I was somewhat unmanageable when I first went there [to a new farm with a slave-breaking overseer], but a few months of this discipline tamed me. Mr. Covey succeeded in breaking me. I was broken in body, soul, and spirit. My natural elasticity was crushed, my intellect languished, the disposition to read departed, the cheerful spark that lingered about my eye died; the dark night of slavery closed in upon me; and behold a man transformed into a brute! (Douglass 1845, 49)

As Stampp documents and Douglass recounts, the disciplinary techniques of slavery often employed physically brutal, even cruel methods. "Physical cruelty . . . was always a possible consequence of the master's power to punish. . . . [But t]he great majority preferred to use as little violence as possible" (Stampp 1956, 178). The use of cruelty as one of the enslavers' tactics thus constituted part of a "political technology of the body" (1975ET, 26). Indeed, this reflects the *disciplinary* character of the power exercised over slaves—the point of this kind of power is to find just the right amount or just the right kind of force to compel or induce a particular behavior. This is reflected in what Foucault terms the "military dream of society" embodied in discipline:

> Its fundamental reference was not to the state of nature, but to the meticulously subordinated cogs of a machine, not to the primal social contract, but to permanent coercions, not to fundamental rights, but to indefinitely progressive forms of training, not to the general will but to automatic docility. (1975ET, 169)

Discipline's ultimate goal would be the elimination—or rather, the taming, harnessing—of any resistance: "It must master all the forces that are formed from the very constitution of an organized multiplicity; it must neutralize the effects of counter-power that spring from them and which form a resistance to the power that wishes to dominate it" (1975ET, 219). Of course, discipline is not always successful; it is never entirely free from resistance. Anyone familiar with Frederick Douglass's story knows that the moment recounted above was the nadir of his experience: his love of freedom and his will to resist were later rekindled; he successfully escaped from slavery to a free state and became one of the most powerful voices of the abolitionist movement.[17] Indeed, as Stampp documents, slaves employed a number of techniques—individual and collective, subtle and overt—to resist enslavers' power. Escape—whether a genuine attempt to leave the South entirely, or to rejoin family from whom one was removed, or simply for a respite from the disciplinary regime of the enslaver and overseers—was an important and often (at least somewhat) successful resistance technique: "Sometimes these escapes resembled strikes, and master or overseer had to negotiate terms upon which the slaves would agree to return" (Stampp 1956, 113). At other times, enslavers would choose to reunite a slave with his or her family rather than be troubled by repeated attempts to escape or return to family. A perpetual problem in the antebellum South was the ongoing, continuous threat of slaves' resistance, which the enslavers were never able to eliminate: "The masses of slaves, for whom freedom could have been little more than an idle dream, found countless ways to exasperate their masters—and thus saw to it that bondage as a labor system had its limitations as well as its advantages" (97).

In its most extreme form, slaves' resistance manifested in armed insurrections and rebellions. But, as Stampp observed, "in truth, no slave uprising ever had a chance of ultimate success, even though it might have cost the master class heavy casualties" (140).

This impulse to resist and to seek freedom will be an important touchstone for Foucault's ethics. But as Stampp noted, slaves "longed for liberty and resisted bondage as much as any people could have done in their circumstances, but their longing and their resistance were not enough even to render the institution unprofitable to most masters. The masters had power and . . . they developed an elaborate technique of slave control" (140). American slaves' experience in the antebellum South thus raises a question that Foucault's "Hobbesian hypothesis" must confront: is it possible for all resistance—some spontaneous, subversive, undisciplined, or unnormalized behavior—to be eliminated or controlled in a complete and carceral institution or society? This is the question behind Part 4 of *Discipline and Punish*.

"ALL HOPE ABANDON YE WHO ENTER HERE"

Foucault concludes Part 3 (his presentation of the emergence of disciplinary power) with this summation:

> On the whole, therefore, one can speak of the formation of a disciplinary society in this movement that stretches from the enclosed disciplines, a sort of social "quarantine," to an indefinitely generalizable mechanism of "panopticism." Not because the disciplinary modality of power has replaced all the others; but because it has infiltrated the others, sometimes undermining them, but serving as an intermediary between them, linking them together, extending them and above all making it possible to bring the effects of power to the most minute and distant elements. It assures an infinitesimal distribution of the power relations. (1975ET, 216)

This suggests that disciplinary power has in fact "infiltrated" the whole of society, creating a closed web of interwoven micropowers. It may seem that Foucault's analysis of disciplinary power serves principally to demonstrate, as Tocqueville phrased it a little over a century earlier, that "formerly, tyranny used the clumsy weapons of chains and hangmen; nowadays even despotism, though it seemed to have nothing more to learn, has been perfected by civilization" (Tocqueville 1835, 255). The bleak implication—the "Hobbesian hypothesis," as I characterized it in the Introduction—is that the exercise and flow of power in and of itself is sufficient to explain the functioning of modern society writ large and the individuals that constitute it. Indeed, Part 4 develops this implication further, examining how the prison has become a "complete and austere" carceral institution—mirroring, perhaps, and indisputably connected with the larger society—that is reinforced and perpetuated even by the criticisms meant to undermine it.

Prisons, which emerge as the virtually exclusive form of criminal punishment, Foucault argues, attempt to constitute "complete and austere" institutions that would regulate every aspect of prisoners' lives within a web of disciplinary observation. In the process of creating this space of punishment, the "object" of criminal justice shifts, from an act, "the crime," to an actor, a personage, "the delinquent." Thus the criminal is constituted as a knowable individual whose history and past are linked to one's current behavior and outlook. In this way, the scope of prisons' impact goes beyond their walls to infiltrate society as a whole. This disciplinary personage, the "delinquent," organizes the whole of criminal justice, from trial courts to police investigation, to parole and reform institutions. "What [the penitentiary apparatus] must apply itself to is not, of course the offence, nor even exactly the offender, but a rather different object . . . the *delinquent*. . . . It is not so much his act as his life that is relevant in characterizing him" (1975ET, 251). "Now the 'delinquent' makes it possible to join the two lines and to constitute . . . an individual in whom the offender of the law and the object of a scientific discourse are superimposed—or almost—one upon the other" (1975ET, 256).[18]

The delinquent is but one example of a larger phenomenon—the constitution of individuals through these power relations' effects upon their bodies and habits. As Foucault will later define it, this "is a form of power that makes individuals subjects" in two senses, subject to others' control and bound to one's own identity, both of which "suggest a form of power that subjugates and makes subject to" (DE306.4, 331). This has implications for the whole of society: "The history of the punitive power would then be a genealogy or an element in a genealogy of the modern 'soul' . . . the present correlative of a certain technology of power over the body" (1975ET, 29). Indeed, "on this reality-reference, various concepts have been constructed and domains of analysis carved out: psyche, subjectivity, personality, consciousness, etc.; on it have been built scientific techniques and discourses, and the moral claims of humanism" (1975ET, 29–30).

The disciplinary society as realized in the architecture and operation of prisons constitutes a "meticulous observation of detail . . . for the control and use of men . . . [composed of] a whole set of techniques, a whole corpus of methods and knowledge, descriptions, plans, and data. And from such trifles, no doubt, the man of modern humanism was born" (1975ET, 141). (We cannot help but hear echoes of the closing pages of *The Order of Things*, where Foucault imagines this "man" to be "an invention of recent date. And one perhaps nearing its end" [1966ET, 387].)

Nevertheless, prisons—at the center of the disciplinary grid that constructs our individuality—seem consistently to fail at the task they were ostensibly created to accomplish, namely, reducing crime. "For the prison, in its reality and visible effects, was denounced at once as the great failure of penal justice" (1975ET, 264). Imprisonment leads most directly to recidivism, to an increase in crime. But even this "failure" is an element in its overall success. Indeed, Foucault argues—and here we can see the extent to which prisons have infiltrated other institutions—the only apparent response to our "solution" for reformers' critiques of prisons is "more prisons." So he asks,

> Is not the supposed failure part of the functioning of the prison? Is it
> not to be included among those effects of power that discipline and the
> auxiliary technology of imprisonment have induced in the apparatus of
> justice, and in society in general, and which may be grouped together
> under the name of "carceral system"? (1975ET, 271)

And the disciplinary techniques that can be perfected within the prison, too, can be seen more and more widely distributed throughout society—in education, in factories, in the military, in the ways we perceive others in daily life—which parallel the various institutions connected in their functioning to the prison:

> It is this complex ensemble that constitutes the "carceral system," not
> only the institution of the prison, with its walls, its staff, its regula-
> tions and its violence. The carceral system combines in a single fig-
> ure discourses and architectures, coercive regulations and scientific
> propositions, real social effects and invincible utopias, programmes for

correcting delinquents and mechanisms that reinforce delinquency. (1975ET, 271)

Thus, it seems, society is progressively becoming more and more imprisoning—a Weberian "iron cage" within whose inescapably tentacular grasp we have no other choice but to despair. "Discipline makes possible the operation of a relational power that sustains itself by its own mechanism and which, for the spectacle of public events, substitutes the uninterrupted play of calculated gazes" (1975ET, 177). Two elements here suggest this bleak, despairing outlook: First, that this power "sustains itself by its own mechanisms," and second, that it places us within an "*uninterrupted* play" of gazes. A power that is uninterrupted and self-sustaining seems to offer little opening for resistance. Nancy Fraser succinctly articulates this reading:

> Michel Foucault was the great theorist of the fordist mode of social regulation. Writing at the zenith of the postwar Keynesian welfare state, he taught us to see the dark underside of even its most vaunted achievements. Viewed through his eyes, social services became disciplinary apparatuses, humanist reforms became panoptical surveillance regimes, public health measures became deployments of biopower, and therapeutic practices became vehicles of subjection. From his perspective, the components of the postwar social state constituted a carceral archipelago of disciplinary domination, all the more insidious because self-imposed. (Fraser 2003, 160)

If Fraser's view is correct, then Foucault's analysis of power seems to leave us little alternative but despair. Remember, however, that we should interpret this hypothesis as a *thought experiment*: this conclusion is precisely what is being tested—whether disciplinary power *can* entirely explain social organization. Foucault here is testing the limits of this hypothesis by trying to explain the individual entirely as a correlate of power relations, as not only socially constituted but constructed exclusively through the effects of power, and thus entirely predictable. If such an explanation were to succeed, if it provided a complete and total—an uninterrupted and self-sustaining—analysis, then it would offer a very bleak portrait, one echoing that of, for example, Adorno and Horkheimer's *Dialectic of Enlightenment*. But this thought experiment leads us to the contrary conclusion. For even if individuals (and, he will later add, states)[19] are "correlates" of power relations, it does not follow that they are entirely and exclusively the product of power relations. For correlates can be productive as well as derivative; correlatives can have other sources from which they are constituted besides power relations. Foucault's thought experiment functions as a sort of modus tollens (if P then Q, and not Q, therefore, not P, where P is a social analysis exclusively in terms of power relations and Q is a closed, inescapable carceral society and a subject constituted entirely through power relations). Foucault's discussion of the prison in the concluding chapters of *Discipline and Punish* is testing the hypothesis that all power reduces to discipline and that it encompasses all social interactions. But such a reductive analysis is too tight, and it fails—the closed system won't hold. Discipline—or, more generally, power—*cannot* be the sole analytical framework for an understanding of social relations. This insight is similar, to draw another analogy to physics, to Gödel's incompleteness theorem, which states that no mathematical system can be fully expressed in a closed set of axioms. As Foucault explained in a 1984 interview, "I had to reject a priori theories of the subject in order to analyze the relationships that may exist between the constitution of the subject or different forms of the subject and games of truth, practices of power, and so on" (DE356.4, 290). This experimental Hobbesian reduction was methodologically necessary in order to discover how the theoretical landscape could be opened up without naïvely presupposing some other, more attractive view of the subject and society. That the social system cannot be reduced to a "disciplinary society" thus leaves open at least a thread of hope—a path for investigation—to counter its apparently bleak portrait.

This experiment indicates new directions for Foucault's analysis—directions that he will take in the Collège de France courses immediately following a sabbatical year: First, Foucault realized that discipline is inadequate and incomplete as a description of power—not all modern power is disciplinary—and so he will articulate a new focus on macropowers as irreducible to, independent of, micropowers. Second, building upon the first new direction, this reframing of power will make possible a more definitive escape from the Hobbesian hypothesis—a way to posit ethical precepts without a naïve or false sense of foundations, because an analysis exclusively in terms of power is inadequate. As Foucault will (revisionistically) assert in a 1978 interview with Duccio Trombadori, "I've never argued that a power mechanism suffices to characterize a society" (DE281.2, 293).

Though many have understood Foucault's message in *Discipline and Punish* to echo Dante's inscription over the gates of Hell, "All hope abandon ye who enter here" (where "here" would mean our modern society), the real message of *Discipline and Punish* is closer in spirit to Alexis de Tocqueville's observation in *Democracy in America*: "I do think that . . . if we despair of imparting to all citizens those ideas and sentiments which first prepare them for freedom and then allow them to enjoy it, there will be no independence left for anybody . . . but only an equal tyranny for all" (Tocqueville 1835, 315). In other words, Foucault's analysis of power relations is an important one of "the ideas and sentiments which first prepare [citizens] for freedom." And as Sandra Bartky observes about the coming to be of a feminist consciousness,

> This picture is not as bleak as it appears; indeed, its "bleakness" would
> be seen in proper perspective had I described what things were like
> *before.* Coming to have a feminist consciousness is the experience of
> coming to see things about oneself and one's society that were heretofore
> hidden. This experience, the acquiring of a "raised" consciousness, in
> spite of its disturbing aspects, is an immeasurable advance over that false
> consciousness which it replaces. (Bartky 1990, 21)

Discipline and Punish's analysis of the micropowers at work in the new punitive regime of discipline is better than the preceding misunderstanding of these power dynamics. Indeed, a reduction of all power to discipline is not possible, but the recognition of discipline as one of the modes of power marks an important contribution:

> I would like to suggest another way to go further toward a new economy
> of power relations, a way that is more empirical, more directly related
> to our present situation, and one that implies more relations between
> theory and practice. It consists in taking the forms of resistance against
> different forms of power as a starting point. (DE306.4, 329)

Foucault's articulation of disciplinary power in *Discipline and Punish* does demonstrate the central importance—even ontological necessity—of resistance within and for power relations. And it is on the basis of that understanding of power relations (as, for Bartky, on the basis of a feminist consciousness) that a new agenda for action—an ethics—can be articulated.

But first, we must follow Foucault's intellectual trajectory and see how this Foucauldian analysis of power will be opened up and supplemented. Foucault closes *Discipline and Punish* with the note that it "must serve as a historical background to various studies of the power of normalization and the formation of knowledge in society" (1975ET, 308). Indeed, Foucault will use this work as the background, the frame, for his subsequent work on "the power of normalization," which he terms biopower (CdF78ET, 9)—and which will in turn contextualize, reassess, and qualify or "soften" the understanding of power presented here. Nancy Fraser, after painting her bleak portrait of the Foucauldian outlook, asserts that we need "to creatively transform Foucauldian categories to account for new modes of 'governmentality' in the era of neo-liberal globalization" (Fraser 2003, 161). (Her own sketched proposal of a form this might take is what she calls "flexibilization," "a process of self-constitution that correlates with, arises from, and resembles a mode of social organization" [169].) Foucault accomplished just such a "creative transformation" of his account of power in the years immediately following *Discipline and Punish*—and this transformation was largely completed in his 1978 course at the Collège de France. He will recognize a new facet or aspect of power relations, biopower, which marks a critical new element and rearticulation of his own theory of power and will thus complete the overall analysis of power within which Foucault's ethics emerges.

Reframing the Theory:
Biopower and Governmentality

Much of Foucault's initial analysis of power has now been presented—we've got the general theory or framework, and we've seen Foucault's analysis of disciplinary power, a form of power found at the molecular level of modern society. But Foucault came to realize that disciplinary power alone is not adequate to explain the entirety of modern power. He thus introduces a new element, which he initially termed "biopower," to encompass important macrophenomena that cannot be characterized as "sovereign power" or in terms of the "juridico-discursive model." This in turn forced him to revise his initial hypothesis that all macro forms of power could be derived entirely from micro forms. Instead, Foucault's analysis of power is reframed—most explicitly in the 1978 course at the Collège de France—so that macro and micro forms of power can be understood as interrelated but not necessarily reducible the one to the other. To effect this reframing Foucault introduces two new central concepts into his analysis of power: biopower and governmentality.

Biopower denotes certain macro forms of power, especially those made possible through statistical analysis, power that is exercised at the level not of individuals (as was the case in disciplinary power) but populations. Norms (a point of difficulty or tension for Foucault's earlier analyses, which failed to appreciate the independence of the macro level), then, can be more adequately understood as one of the important conduits or interfaces between macropowers of populations and micropowers of individuals.

Governmentality emerges in Foucault's discussions as a sort of umbrella term—encompassing both macro and micro forms of power, both the institutions of the state and more local institutions like schools, hospitals, and barracks—that also includes within its penumbra "the government of oneself," an orientation that will loom increasingly important in Foucault's later work. (One could even use a phrase such as "the logic of government" as a rough synonym for "governmentality." But the term "governmentality," in both English and French, contains the term "mentality," thus perhaps suggesting that the mechanisms described are not just a logic but a mentality—something more pervasive than a mere logic, something like what William James terms a "temperament" [James 1907, 8ff.]. Admittedly, this observation is a bit "cutesy," but its suggestiveness is helpful for seeing how a Foucauldian ethics will orient itself and, in particular, how such an ethics is rooted in an attitude of critique.)

My agenda in this chapter is to "complete" our survey of Foucault's analysis of power, so that we can see how it constitutes the "background" or framework for his ethical thinking and how it provides certain resources for an ethical project. We shall see how tensions in the account so far—centered on the emergence of disciplinary techniques and their diffusion throughout society—lead Foucault to supplement and reconfigure this analysis with an entirely different "macro" level of power relations, ones not reducible to the microrelations of discipline. This new, more general understanding of how power works serves to reframe its problems in terms of "governmentality," thus providing an opening for ethical possibilities that would seem to have been eliminated at the end of *Discipline and Punish*.

Foucault's move away from the bleak portrait of his Hobbesian hypotheses would be clarified by 1978 in his Collège de France course that year, *Security, Territory, Population*. But tensions in the closed account that he attempted to articulate in *Discipline and Punish* would begin to emerge almost immediately. The clearest indication of these tensions—and the new directions that his analysis of the "power of normalization" will take—emerge in two texts from 1976: his Collège de France course that year, *"Society Must Be Defended,"* and the fifth (and final) part of *La volonté de savoir* (*The History of Sexuality*, volume 1, whose fourth part, as we saw in Chapter 1, produced a critical articulation of his general theory of power), in both of which he explicitly explores the extent to which politics can be understood as "the continuation of war."

POLITICS AS THE CONTINUATION OF WAR

We can hear this theme in *Discipline and Punish*: "it must not be forgotten that 'politics' has been conceived as a continuation, if not exactly and directly of war, at least of the military model as a fundamental means of preventing civil disorder" (1975ET, 168). Indeed, Foucault had been thinking along these lines since at least 1973: in the November 7, 1973, opening lecture of his Collège de France course, for example, he described the dynamics of power and knowledge in the asylum as "actually a battlefield" (CdF74ET, 7). But the theme of politics (and society) as a kind of war becomes his explicit focus in the 1976 Collège de France course: the final lecture summarizes that "I have been trying to raise the problem of war, seen as a grid for understanding historical processes" (CdF76ET, 239). Arnold Davidson, in his introduction to this course, agrees that this course "is Foucault's most concentrated and detailed historical examination of the model of war as a grid for analyzing politics" (Davidson 2003, xviii).

Foucault opens this lecture course with the question, "What is power?" (CdF76ET, 13), to which he answers (following the argument I've presented in the first two chapters) that "it is primarily, in itself, a relationship of force" (CdF76ET, 15). Which leads to a new question—"shouldn't we be analyzing it first and foremost in terms of conflict, confrontation, and war?"—and a new hypothesis to be tested: "Power is war, the continuation of war by other means. At this point, we can invert Clausewitz's proposition and say that politics is the continuation of war by other means" (CdF76ET, 15). Giving us the theme for the year's lectures, Foucault makes this hypothesis quite explicit:

> I would like to try to see the extent to which the binary schema of war
> and struggle, of the clash between forces, can really be identified as the

basis of civil society, as both the principle and motor of the exercise of political power. (CdF76ET, 18)

Is something analogous to war really "the basis of civil society," its "principle and motor," as would be suggested by Foucault's Hobbesian hypothesis and the reduction of all power to a disciplinary "relationship of forces"? This is the hypothesis *to be tested* in these courses. And while we might anticipate that his examination would *confirm* this hypothesis, on the contrary, in fact, it will lead us to reexamine and reassess it.

Foucault opens the second lecture by reiterating that this course constitutes "a series of investigations into whether or not war can possibly provide a principle for the analysis of power relations: can we find in bellicose relations, in the model of war, in the schema of struggle or struggles, a principle that can help us understand and analyze political power" (CdF76ET, 23). He then notes several "methodological cautions" that should guide these investigations—cautions that reiterate the elements of his general theory of power. Two of these are particularly important.

First, although "the system of right and the judiciary field are permanent vehicles for relations of domination, and for polymorphous techniques of subjugation" (CdF76ET, 27), we must "not regard power as a phenomenon of mass and homogenous domination" (CdF76ET, 29). Thus, while our institutions can serve to dominate us, power is not exclusively or essentially something that dominates.

Second,

we should make an ascending analysis of power, or in other words begin with its infinitesimal mechanisms, which have their own history, their own trajectory, their own techniques and tactics, and then look at how these mechanisms of power . . . have been and are invested, colonized, used, inflected, transformed, displaced extended, and so on by increasingly general mechanisms and forms of overall domination. (CdF76ET, 30)

Begin, in other words, with the local microrelations of power, and then look to see how they combine to constitute macrorelations such as a general domination.

These cautions remind us of the contrast with other, inadequate and in-complete, analyses of power, which distinguishes Foucault's analysis as a "theory" of power. More particularly, they fit with—and bring into relief—

the implications that *Discipline and Punish* left us with: that power operates at an infinitesimal or micro level upon individuals in ways that lead to larger macroeffects of domination. However, what Foucault proposes here is that our method should *begin with* infinitesimal microrelations; this methodological caution does not necessarily entail that macro power relations are entirely analyzable *in terms of* microrelations. This is the insight toward which Foucault is beginning to work. It will open up both a way out of the apparent "iron cage" and an intriguing ethico-strategic possibility, with which the lecture closes:

> Truth to tell, if we are to struggle against disciplines, or rather against
> disciplinary power, in our search for a nondisciplinary power, we should
> not be turning to the old right of sovereignty; we should be looking
> for a new right that is both nondisciplinary and emancipated from the
> principle of sovereignty. (CdF76ET, 39–40)

The first two lectures had been published independently of the rest of the course as "Two Lectures" (DE193, DE194). They offer a nice summary of the stakes and scope of Foucault's analysis of power, but in themselves they do not allow us to see how Foucault will ultimately assess this Hobbesian hypothesis. The fifth lecture, however, almost halfway through the course, explicitly addresses Hobbes on war. "Hobbes . . . does, at first glance, appear to be the man who said that war is both the basis of power relations and the principle that explains them" (CdF76ET, 89). For Hobbes, war is what characterizes the "state of nature" out of which sovereignty is born. We create sovereignty out of fear, to protect us from others; thus, "the will to prefer life to death: that is what founds sovereignty" (CdF76ET, 95) and constitutes the right of the sovereign to take life or let one live. Thus, "for sovereignty to exist there must be—and this is all there must be—a certain radical will that makes us want to live" (CdF76ET, 96). This effects a sort of reversal in how we should read Hobbes, Foucault argues: "far from being the theorist of the relationship between war and political power, Hobbes wanted to eliminate the historical reality of war, as though he wanted to eliminate the genesis of sovereignty" (CdF76ET, 97). By making war the "state of nature" left behind in the establishment of sovereignty, by making sovereignty a kind of perpetual given, war becomes in a certain sense "off the table" for contemporary struggles.

What would such an elimination accomplish? "The enemy—or rather, the enemy discourse Hobbes is addressing—is the discourse that could be heard in the civil struggles that were tearing the State apart in England at this time" (CdF76ET, 99). And so "What Hobbes is trying, then, not to refute, but to eliminate and render impossible . . . is a certain way of making historical knowledge work within the political struggle" (CdF76ET, 98). But Foucault's entire project is devoted first of all to showing that and how historical knowledge and historical particularities *do* work within political struggles, and second and just as importantly, to harnessing and *using* historical knowledge within ongoing struggles. His analysis of Hobbes—and of what Hobbes was arguing against (indeed, Foucault is more interested in Hobbes's discursive opponents' insights)—shows, Foucault thinks, that "the logical and historical need for rebellion is therefore inscribed within a whole historical analysis that reveals war to be a permanent feature of social relations" (CdF76ET, 110). So taking war to be a "permanent feature of social relations" has a particular value: it entails a "need for rebellion," that is, it implies that the status quo cannot become entirely closed in domination, that historical knowledge and circumstances can be exploited in resistance.

Foucault's insight contra Hobbes here—that understanding social relations on the model of war makes it possible to cognize and strategize resistance to those social relations—echoes a point Simone de Beauvoir had made in *The Ethics of Ambiguity*:

> To the idea of present war there is opposed that of a future peace when man will again find, along with a stable situation, the possibility of a morality. But the truth is that if division and violence define war, the world has always been at war and always will be; if man is waiting for universal peace in order to establish his existence validly, he will wait indefinitely: there will never be any *other* future. (de Beauvoir 1948, 119)

Beauvoir's point (oriented not toward a mythical past, as in Hobbes's account, but a mythical future) is that we will never be "free" from the struggle and division that make society seem to be a sort of ongoing war. She rejects the view that "the possibility of morality" would obtain only in some "future peace" because such a peace will never come to be. But Beauvoir also insists that we can "establish [our] existence validly" in our current (and inevitable) circumstances of ongoing struggle—indeed, these are the conditions upon which, for her, morality must be created. I note this parallel here because Foucault will make a very similar move (and we can already see the first step in his discussion here): ethics becomes possible within the circumstances of struggle, within the network of power relations in which we are situated.

Indeed (this is the first step), that those power relations can be understood in terms of struggle opens up certain possibilities for what kinds of ethics might emerge.

However, Foucault will recognize that this analogy of political power, and social relations more generally, to war is, while useful, incomplete and limited—especially if those power relations are understood only in terms of discipline. He acknowledged or suspected these limitations even at the beginning of the course: "I think that the twin notions of 'repression' and 'war' have to be considerably modified, and ultimately, perhaps, abandoned" (CdF76ET, 17). We saw in Chapter 1 that "repression" as an exhaustive model of power clearly must be abandoned. But the model of "war," too, must be modified. He had attempted to understand power in the light of this analogy as "strategic relations" best exemplified in disciplinary techniques. But by the course's conclusion, in fact, Foucault is already articulating a major addition and alteration to his understanding of disciplinary power:

> And I think that one of the greatest transformations political right
> underwent in the nineteenth century was precisely that . . . sovereignty's
> old right—to take life or let live— . . . came to be complemented by
> a new right which does not erase the old right but which does pen-
> etrate it, permeate it. . . . It is the power to "make" live and "let" die.
> (CdF76ET, 241)

This new, inverted, "opposite" "right" reveals the "inner logic," one might say, of what he will call "bio-politics." This is especially intriguing, given that Foucault had closed the second lecture by noting that we needed just such a "new right" to "struggle against disciplinary power" (CdF76ET, 39–40). A new right, corresponding to a kind of power that cannot be reduced to discipline, will (even if it poses new dangers of domination) at the very least add new dimensions for any struggles of resistance and new openings through which to escape a seemingly "complete and austere" prison.

Though we will return shortly to this final lecture of his 1976 course, we can get a clearer picture of this new biopolitical right "to 'make' live and 'let' die" in the final part (entitled "Right of Death and Power Over Life") of *La volonté de savoir*: "one would have to speak of *bio-power* to designate what brought life and its mechanisms into the realm of explicit calculations and made knowledge-power an agent of transformation of human life" (1976ET, 143). As Foucault presents it, "this power over life evolved in two basic forms"—the micro form of discipline and the macro form of biopower—"these forms were not antithetical, however; they constituted rather two poles of development linked together by a whole intermediary cluster of relations" (1976ET, 139). Foucault is here reorganizing the landscape of his analysis of power relations: having just completed an analysis premised upon the assumption that end-forms like the state can and must be analyzed in terms of more general micro forms in Part 4, he is now altering that analysis to allow for a macro form that is also "basic"—one that is not antithetical to but linked together with disciplinary micropower.

Foucault explicitly identifies disciplinary power as the first of these two forms:

> One of these poles—the first to be formed, it seems [an interesting caveat, given how Foucault's analysis has developed]—centered on the body as a machine: its disciplining, the optimization of its capabilities, the extortion of its forces, the parallel increase of its usefulness and its docility, its integration into systems of efficient and economic controls, all this was ensured by the procedures of power that characterized the *disciplines*: an *anatomo-politics of the human body*. (1976ET, 139)

He thus recharacterizes disciplinary power as an "anatomo-politics" to highlight the parallelism between it and the second form, "bio-power" or "bio-politics," which is addressed not to the individual anatomy but to the *bios*, life in general:

> The second, formed somewhat later, focused on the species body, the body imbued with the mechanics of life and serving as the basis of the biological processes: propagation, births and mortality, the level of health, life expectancy and longevity, with all the conditions that can cause these to vary. Their supervision was effected through an entire series of interventions and *regulatory controls: a bio-politics of the population*. (1976ET, 139)

Thus, Foucault has begun to recognize a macropower, aimed at the species and populations through regulatory mechanisms, distinct from disciplinary micropower. As he describes it in the final lecture of *"Society Must Be Defended,"* "This new technique does not simply do away with the disciplinary technique, because it exists at a different level, on a different scale, and because it has a different bearing area, and makes use of different instruments" (CdF76ET, 242). A "different level," a "different scale," and a "different bearing area" are all ways of saying that this power functions between and upon macrophenomena. And so this macropower "does not exclude disciplinary technology, but it does dovetail into it, integrate it, modify it to some extent, and above all, use it by sort of infiltrating it, embedding itself in existing disciplinary techniques" (CdF76ET, 242). The two modes of power are distinct and irreducible to the other; they are also—even if he is not yet sure exactly how—interwoven and integrated: "the two sets of mechanisms—one disciplinary and the other regulatory—do not exist at the same level. Which means of course that they are not mutually exclusive and can be articulated with each other" (CdF76ET, 250).

Together, in their mutual articulation, "this great bipolar technology—anatomical and biological . . . —characterized a power whose highest function was perhaps no longer to kill, but to invest life through and through" (1976ET, 139). Power at all levels is, in other words, fundamentally productive. And the two technologies, the micro- and the macro-, are conjoined and integrated not "at the level of a speculative discourse, but in the form of concrete arrangements that would go to make up the great technology of power in the nineteenth century: the deployment of sexuality would be one of them, and one of the most important" (1976ET, 140).

> This is the background that enables us to understand the importance assumed by sex as a political issue. It was at the pivot of the two axes along which developed the entire political technology of life. On the one hand it was tied to the disciplines of the body. . . . On the other hand, it was applied to the regulation of populations through all the far-reaching effects of its activity. (1976ET, 145)

Foucault defines "sex" not as a drive but as "the most internal element in a deployment of sexuality" (1976ET, 155), which is itself "an especially dense transfer point for relations of power: between men and women, young people and old people, parents and offspring, teachers and students, priests and laity, an administration and a population" (1976ET, 103). Note the pairings that Foucault has included here—these indicate the scope of power relations to penetrate something as seemingly intimate as sexuality and the different ways that sexuality can become a vehicle for both micro- and macrorelations. "Sexuality exists at the point where body and population meet" (CdF76ET, 251–252). Foucault continues that "sexuality is not the most intractable element in power relations, but rather one of those endowed with the greatest instrumentality: useful for the greatest number of maneuvers and capable of serving as a point of support, as a linchpin, for the most varied strategies"

(1976ET, 103). Indeed, "it is through sex—in fact, an imaginary point determined by the deployment of sexuality—that each individual has to pass in order to have access to his own intelligibility . . . to the whole of his body . . . to his identity" (1976ET, 155–156).

In Part 4, Foucault sketched four especially significant such points of support: "it seems that we can distinguish four great strategic unities which, beginning in the eighteenth century, formed specific mechanisms of knowledge and power centering on sex" (1976ET, 103). Foucault identified these four strategies or "deployments" as "hysterization of women's bodies," "pedegogization of children's sex," "socialization of procreative behavior," and "psychiatrization of perverse pleasure" (1976ET, 104–105). All four of these strategies are composed of both disciplinary techniques and larger macro-level power relations such as the regulation of populations and the construction of racial identities. We can thus situate the planned trajectory of Foucault's subsequent volumes in the *History of Sexuality* series—studies that this first volume was meant to inaugurate but which were never published; each was to focus on one of these "deployments of sexuality."

In these two 1976 texts, Foucault does begin to articulate *how* the connection between disciplinary micropowers and biopolitical macropowers is effected—through the vehicle of norms:

> There is one element that will circulate between the disciplinary and the regulatory, which will be applied to body and population alike, which will make it possible to control both the disciplinary order of the body and the aleatory events that occur in the biological multiplicity. The element that circulates between the two is the norm. . . . The normalizing society is a society in which the norm of discipline and the norm of regulation intersect along an orthogonal articulation. (CdF76ET, 252–253)

And so, for example, sexuality will be one of the points or lines of orthogonal articulation. He adds that biopower "needs continuous regulatory and corrective mechanisms. . . . Such a power . . . effects distributions around the norm" (1976ET, 144). Thus, to pull this together, "a normalizing society is the historical outcome of a technology of power centered on life" (1976ET, 144). Foucault will have more to say about the details of how norms work in his 1978 course, which we'll turn to shortly. But he makes another important connection here, linking these norms with the function of racism.

Racism "is primarily a way of introducing a break into the domain of life that is under power's control . . . . It is a way of separating out the groups that exist within a population" (CdF76, 245–255). Kenneth Stampp's discussion of slavery, which I earlier used to illustrate disciplinary power, supports this analysis as well: "Slavery was, above all, a method of regulating race relations, an instrument of social control" (Stampp 1956, 387). Stampp goes on to connect his analysis with the framework that had driven Foucault's investigations here (bringing our discussion full circle): to the hypothesis of understanding power relations (and society in general) in terms of war. He notes that slaves' basic attitude toward whites (and especially enslavers) was "an attitude of deep suspicion." He continues: "When this was the Negro's basic attitude, the resulting relationship was an amoral one which resembled an unending civil war; the slave then seemed to think that he was entitled to use every tactic of deception and chicanery he could devise" (380). The most basic relationship structuring the social life of the South could be construed as a sort of "war," which authorized slaves to employ whatever tactics that were available for their resistance.

I suspect that Foucault's continuing analysis of these examples—the deployments of sexuality and racism—may have been what helped Foucault understand a key error in his analysis up to this point, namely that many of these macrorelations cannot be entirely analyzed in terms of micropractices. This realization will drive the next great theoretical shift in Foucault's understanding of power and in Foucault's understanding of the contexts for ethics. For as he notes here:

> It is the agency of sex that we must break away from, if we aim—
> through a tactical reversal of the various mechanisms of sexuality—to
> counter the grips of power with the claims of bodies, pleasures, and
> knowledges, in their multiplicity and their possibility of resistance.
> (1976ET, 157)

We will return to these remarks—which herald one launching point for Foucauldian ethics—in Chapter 4.

However, elements remain in both of these texts from 1976 that could be construed to support the bleak view of power as an all-encompassing iron cage. Consider two passages from *The History of Sexuality*. First, a longer passage that ends on a bad note:

> If the development of the great instruments of the state, as *institutions*
> of power, ensured the maintenance of production relations, the rudi-

ments of anatomo- and bio-politics, created in the eighteenth century as *techniques* of power present at every level of the social body and utilized by very diverse institutions (the family and the army, schools and the police, individual medicine and the administration of collective bodies) . . . acted as factors of segregation and social hierarchization . . . guaranteeing relations of domination and effects of hegemony. (1976ET, 141)

This list of institutions includes those that he had studied in *Discipline and Punish* (the army, schools, and police), in *The History of Sexuality* (the family), and in another text that I will discuss in the next section, "The Politics of Health in the Eighteenth Century" (individual and collective medicine). Thus, it would not be unreasonable to hear, when Foucault says these techniques "guarantee" domination and hegemony, a continuation of the bleak analyses of the end of *Discipline and Punish*. He continues (in the second passage I want to highlight in this regard) that "power would no longer be dealing simply with legal subjects over whom the ultimate domination was death, but with living beings, and the mastery it would be able to exercise over them would have to be applied at the level of life itself" (1976ET, 142–143). So, it seems, hegemony and domination are guaranteed through mastery of living being. These passages seem to cohere with one from the final lecture of the Collège de France course:

> Beneath that great absolute power, beneath the dramatic and somber absolute power that was the power of sovereignty, and which consisted in the power to take life, we now have the emergence, with this technology of biopower, of this technology of power over "the" population as such, over men insofar as they are living beings. . . . Sovereignty took life and let live. And now we have the emergence of a power that I would call the power of regularization, and it, in contrast, consists in making live and letting die. (CdF76ET, 247)

These three passages *could* be read, as I've suggested, in a negative way. In saying that that power guarantees domination and hegemony and that its mastery now extends over all life, by making it live and letting it die, Foucault could be understood to connote that "war" organizes all of our relationships, that our options have been foreclosed by the emergence of these new technologies of power. But this interpretation is not the only one available. And Foucault gives us a clear indication that, while he may have seriously explored that possibility, it is a mistaken reading:

The normalizing society is therefore not, under these conditions, a sort of generalized disciplinary society whose disciplinary institutions have swarmed and finally taken over everything—that, I think, is no more than a first and inadequate interpretation of a normalizing society. (CdF76ET, 253)

THE IMPORTANCE OF POPULATION

In both the 1976 Collège de France course and *La volonté de savoir* Foucault has clearly begun a process of autocritique, revising and complicating the understanding of power whose articulation he had just completed. The tension that emerges in both of these texts, but is not yet fully controlled, inheres in the claim that all power could be analyzed in terms of disciplinary relations. Indeed, Foucault was already beginning to recognize that this reduction cannot be maintained and that there are certain macrophenomena (and macro power relations) that must be explained in other terms. The notion of "population" is central for this clarification.

We can see how Foucault's conception of population evolved by contrasting his discussions of it between 1974 and 1979. In a lecture given in October 1974 in Rio de Janeiro, Brazil (lectures that reflect Foucault's then-current view of power as principally disciplinary),[1] Foucault discusses "populations" as essentially reducible to individuals embedded in microrelations:

The individual thus emerges as an object of medical knowledge and practice.

At the same time, through the same system of disciplined hospital space, one can observe a great number of individuals . . .

Thanks to hospital technology, the individual and the population simultaneously present themselves as objects of knowledge and medical intervention. (DE229.1, 151, trans. mod.)

For Foucault in 1974, populations are essentially "a great number of individuals," an epiphenomenon or byproduct, as it were, of disciplinary power's effects upon discrete individuals, that emerges simultaneously with them. He still holds this view in 1975's *Discipline and Punish*, defining a population as simply constituted by a "multiplicity of bodies and forces" (1975ET, 77–78). In 1976, as we saw in the preceding section, Foucault's understanding has begun to evolve, and "populations" point to larger phenomena that are not simply or strictly reducible to "groups of individuals." Finally, in the 1979 essay, "The Politics of Health in the Eighteenth Century," he is describing populations as discrete entities requiring their own level of analysis (and rebutting his 1974 remark that populations were merely "great numbers" or a "sum" of individuals):

> In appearance, it [population] is a question of nothing but the sum
> of individual phenomena; nevertheless, one observes there constants
> and variables which are proper to the population; and if one wishes to
> modify them, specific interventions are necessary. (DE257, III-730-731;
> DE257.1, 117)

As the tensions we saw in his Collège de France course and *La volonté de savoir* illustrate, 1976 was a critical year in Foucault's evolving understanding of populations. A key moment in this transformation is indicated in his review of a biological text by Jacques Ruffié, *De la biologie à la culture* [*From Biology to Culture*]. Foucault takes a number of insights from Ruffié, most importantly his understanding of populations not simply as collections of individuals but rather statistical entities, "ensembles of variations" that "are unceasingly formed and dissolved" and that can function independently of the individuals they encompass (DE179, III-97; DE179.1, 129). Importantly, especially given his remarks about racism in the final lecture of his Collège de France course, he also draws from Ruffié's work for his understanding of "race" as a concept to be challenged and rejected—especially as it is employed by states as a mechanism of control:

> Hemato-typology now authorizes the dissolution of the idea of human
> race. With a whole series of supporting evidence from prehistory and
> paleontology, it can be established that there never were "races" in the
> human species; but at the very most a process of "raciation," tied to
> the existence of certain isolated groups. This process, far from having
> succeeded, reversed itself beginning with the Neolithic era and, through
> the effect of migrations, displacements, exchanges, and diverse intermin-
> glings, it was succeeded by a constant "deraciation." We must conceive
> of a humanity not as juxtaposed races, but as "clouds" of populations
> that are interwoven together and combine a genetic inheritance that
> is all the more valuable the more its polymorphism is accentuated.
> (DE179, III-96; DE179.1, 129)

"Race" is a kind of fiction that may come to seem permanent, perhaps even a priori, but in fact "race" and "races" are contingent historical constructs that can be dissolved through other historical shifts. Foucault finds Ruffié's text valuable because, as he closes his review,

> one sees very clearly formulated here the questions of a "bio-history" that would no longer be the unitary and mythological history of the human species across time, and a "bio-politics" which would not be one of divisions, self-preservation, and hierarchies but of communication and polymorphism. (DE179, III-97; DE179.1, 129)[2]

For Foucault, "bio-politics" and biopower are addressed not to particular individuals but to larger shifts in human populations—and, in contrast to the disciplinary techniques of division and hierarchy, they open a space for "communication and polymorphism" (important notions for a Foucauldian ethics).

Perhaps the best illustration of how Foucault's rethinking of the concept of population allows his larger analysis to advance can be seen in the changes he made in two versions of an essay published in 1976 and 1979—initially as he is just discovering the inadequacies of his current analysis, and later, after he has reconstructed his theory. The essay is "The Politics of Health in the Eighteenth Century."

The bibliographical history of this text is tricky. Both versions were published in a monograph, which itself has the same title in both editions—*Les machines à guérir* [*Curing Machines*]. The 1976 edition (DE168) was published in Paris by the Institut de l'Environnement, however, whereas the 1979 edition (DE257) was published in Brussels by Pierre Mardaga. (An English translation of the 1976 version was published in the early collection *Power/Knowledge* [DE168.1]; the 1979 version did not appear in English until 2014 [DE257.1].) Despite superficial similarities, the second version has been substantially rewritten. Though they are approximately the same length, and the second halves of the two essays are virtually identical (one paragraph from the 1976 version is omitted in 1979), the essays' first halves, however, differ in significant ways.[3] Foucault has rewritten the first half of this essay in light of his insights in the intervening years about populations as macro-phenomena to which correspond nondisciplinary forms of power—and the essay is, as a result, frankly much clearer.

His aim in this essay is to articulate the emerging interconnections be-

GARY PUBLIC LIBRARY

tween "private" medicine (clinical practice between doctors and patients) and state-supported "assistance" (public health and welfare programs). Already in 1976, Foucault recognizes that these are distinct but related: that version of the essay begins by noting that "what the eighteenth century shows, in any case, is a double-sided process. The development of a medical market in the form of private clienteles . . . cannot be divorced from the concurrent organization of a politics of health" (DE168.1, 166). But his attempts to articulate the framework in which both obtain are strained. His "solution"—inelegant and unclear—is to speak of what he calls "noso-politics," literally medical- or hospital-politics. "The most striking trait of this noso-politics . . . no doubt consists in the displacement of health problems relative to problems of assistance" (DE168.1, 168). This neologism does little to help us understand how these two trends are interwoven; nevertheless, it is the organizing theme of the 1976 version. He does speak of "populations" in this version but still reads them as the cumulative effects of multiple applications of power upon individual bodies rather than as autonomous (DE168.1, 171–172).

Whereas Foucault was struggling (unsatisfactorily) to use "noso-politics" as a kind of framing concept in 1976, this term has entirely disappeared from the 1979 version. As I noted above, Foucault now recognizes populations as discrete entities (not merely Benthamite "sums of individuals") upon which discrete forms of power may operate. As this concept allows him to analyze different *kinds* of power relations at different levels, Foucault's problem of articulating the interrelationships between these levels (the clinical and the public) becomes much more straightforward—as is reflected in his prose and his abandonment of awkward neologisms. Thus, the later version begins by asserting that

> what is important is rather the specific manner in which, at a given moment and in a specified society, the individual interaction between the doctor and the sick person is articulated upon the collective intervention with respect to illness in general or to this sick person in particular (DE257, III-726; DE257.1, 114).

This clarity was facilitated by his realization that populations function at a macro level in a way analogous (but not reducible) to individuals at the micro level:

> But an element appeared at the center of this materiality, an element whose importance unceasingly asserted itself and grew in the seven-

teenth and eighteenth centuries: it was the *population*, understood in the already traditional sense of the number of inhabitants in proportion to the habitable area, but equally in the sense of an ensemble of individuals having between them relations of coexistence and constituting therefore a specific reality. (DE257, III-730; DE257.1, 117)

Populations constitute "a specific reality" "at the center of this materiality," which is to be managed through other, nondisciplinary techniques— "collective interventions" that he terms "the functions of police." And so the "politics of health" in the eighteenth century is characterized by the interweaving of two related but distinct forms of power—disciplinary power over (sick) individuals and a macropower over populations, whose aim was not to treat but prevent illnesses.

As the changes in this essay illustrate, his shift away from an exclusive emphasis upon individualizing microfunctions of power toward the dynamics of populations and power at a larger scale will enable Foucault to analyze better social processes such as normalization and to spell out a new aspect of power: biopower. Indeed, my explication of the latter risks jumping too far ahead, as it presupposes concepts that Foucault had developed in more detail in the intervening years. Articulating the concepts that facilitate this shift in his understanding of power was the primary task in his 1978 Collège de France course, *Security, Territory, Population.*

APPARATUSES OF SECURITY

After a sabbatical year in 1977, Foucault's 1978 course at the Collège de France gave him the opportunity to articulate the major alteration to the theory of power that he had been working out over the past several years. Here he articulates the irreducibility of macrophenomena to microphenomena, even as he begins to show some of the ways in which they are interwoven. This analysis builds upon Foucault's recognition of "populations" as irreducible macrophenomena; it also brings a renewed subtlety to his analysis of the processes of normalization. He articulates what we could characterize as a "structural" analysis of biopower, explicitly contrasting its mechanisms and orientation with those of disciplinary power, describing this macropower as one oriented toward "security," in particular, the security and the preservation of the modern state. But this task constitutes only the first of three central, interconnected foci that emerge in *Security,*

Territory, Population. Further, Foucault is able to trace the emergence of biopower back to much earlier, premodern forms of power that developed in the eastern Judeo-Christian tradition—this constitutes the second focal theme; he calls this premodern form "pastoral power." (This connection also shows how the application and utility of Foucault's theory of power is not restricted to modern Western societies and cultures.) The third theme of the course—to which I will devote less attention—returns to the original concern with states' security, identifying two particular technologies or mechanisms by which states were able to exercise this macropower: what Foucault terms "raison d'état" and "police." (The latter of which, in particular, constitutes an interface between biopolitical and disciplinary modes of power.) With the modifications and reelaboration that Foucault accomplishes here, his theory of power becomes much more complex—and, as a corollary, so do the landscape of and possibilities for resistance, self-articulation, and ethics within these multifaceted relations of power. Reconceived in this way, the problem of "power" becomes instead the "problem of government," or (as he will call it) "governmentality." This problem of governmentality explicitly thematizes certain ethical dimensions—it thus constitutes a background, a stable social analysis, within which a Foucauldian ethics can begin to be articulated.

Indeed, the very first remark Foucault makes to inaugurate the course is that "This year I would like to begin studying something that I have called, somewhat vaguely, bio-power" (CdF78ET, 1). He then defines it in two ways. First, biopower is "the set of mechanisms through which the basic biological features of the human species became the object of a political strategy, of a general strategy of power" (CdF78ET, 1); it can also be understood as "how, starting from the eighteenth century, modern Western societies took on board the fundamental biological fact that human beings are a species" (CdF78ET, 1). These two definitions, while largely overlapping, are not identical. The second includes both a temporal specification—modernity, especially since the eighteenth century (which fits with the temporal focus of his 1976/1979 essay on the politics of health)—and a geographical specification—Western, that is, European, societies—that are not present in the first. Indeed, the origins of biopower, he will argue, come from beyond both of these specifications; nevertheless, modern Western society is of particular importance because it constitutes our situation, the circumstances within which we must act.

Foucault next defines "security," or the "apparatuses of security," which represent a modulation or shift effected upon certain disciplinary techniques, so that they now function in a different way, upon a different object. He illustrates this with two examples: law and medicine, in each of which we can see several modulations. Law, for example, may begin with a simple prohibition such as "Do not steal" and its accompanying punishment. He here calls this the "legal or juridical mechanism" (CdF78ET, 5). It can then be modulated by disciplinary techniques: it is still the same law, "but now everything is framed by . . . a series of supervisions, checks, inspections, and varied controls that, even before the thief has stolen, make it possible to identify whether or not he is going to steal, and so on" (CdF78ET, 4). Finally, there is a biopolitical modulation, "based on the same matrix, with the same penal law, the same punishments, and the same type of framework of surveillance on one side and correction on the other, but now [all this] will be governed by" (CdF78ET, 4) a different organizing principle: "The general question basically will be how to keep a type of criminality, theft for instance, within socially and economically acceptable limits and around an average that will be considered as optimal for a given social functioning" (CdF78ET, 5). Medicine, too, offers an illustration of these different modulations. Biopolitical medicine is oriented not toward particular sick individuals but rather "the statistical effects on the population in general" of medical practices such as inoculation and vaccination (CdF78ET, 10). "In short, it will no longer be the problem of exclusion, as with leprosy, or of quarantine, as with the plague [a disciplinary medicine], but of epidemics and the medical campaigns that try to halt epidemic or endemic phenomena" (CdF78ET, 10). These "modulations," Foucault immediately notes, however, do not displace or eliminate the earlier forms; rather they are overlaid upon each other: "there is not a succession of law, then discipline, then security, but that security is a way of making the old armatures of law and discipline function in addition to the specific mechanisms of security" (CdF78ET, 10).

Having thus illustrated how "security" or biopower functions simultaneously with, alongside, disciplinary power, Foucault devotes the remainder of the first three lectures of this course to articulating four "general features of these apparatuses of security" (CdF78ET, 11), in each case showing how biopower is distinct from disciplinary power. These four characteristics concern the way these different kinds of power deal with space (or geography), their respective treatments of uncertainty, "the form of normalization specific to security which seems to me to be different from the disciplinary type of normalization," and "the correlation between the technique of security and population as both the object and subject of these mechanisms of security" (CdF78ET, 11). Of these four—space, uncertainty, normalization, and population—the latter two are clearly the most important. For Foucault had closed *Discipline and Punish* by noting that it "must serve as a historical background to various studies of the power of normalization" (1976ET, 308), and as I have argued, Foucault's reconceptualization of "population" had compelled and facilitated his analysis of biopower as a distinct type of power. Speaking of the historical transformations that he is tracing in governmental technologies and practices, but in language that is equally applicable to the development of his own understanding of power, Foucault observes that:

> it is thanks to the perception of the specific problems of the population, and thanks to the isolation of the level of reality that we call the economy, that it was possible to think, reflect, and calculate the problem of government outside the juridical framework of sovereignty [or discipline]. (CdF78ET, 104)

We can briefly discuss the first feature (space), and then will turn to a more extended presentation of normalization and populations—the heart of the contrast—before finally returning to the second feature (uncertainty, which is importantly linked to possibilities for freedom). In constructing a panopticon, a prison, a barracks, or any architecture designed to facilitate observation and hierarchy, "discipline works in an empty, artificial space that is to be completely constructed" (CdF78ET, 19). By contrast,

> Security will rely on a number of material givens . . . this given will not be reconstructed to arrive at a point of perfection, as in a disciplinary town. It is simply a matter of maximizing the positive elements, for which one provides the best possible circulation, and of minimizing what is risky and inconvenient, like theft and disease, while knowing that they will never be completely suppressed. [Thus,] one works on probabilities. (CdF78ET, 19)

Thus, biopower does not aim at a complete control but begins with "givens," historical realities that can shift and change independently and thus can only be maximized or minimized, never entirely eliminated or perfected. It cannot control every individual in a population; instead it aims at probabilities rather than totalities. As a result, biopower "works on the future, that is to say, the town will not be conceived or planned according to a static perception that would ensure the perfection of the function there and then, but will open onto a future that is not exactly controllable, not exactly measured or measurable" (CdF78ET, 20). In this contrasting approach to problems of space, we see the emerging importance of both norms—those not completely controllable but probabilistically predictable patterns—and population—the set of human beings taken not as discrete individuals but as a collectivity.

The lecture of 25 January 1978—the third lecture of the course—is devoted to these two topics. First, Foucault corrects and clarifies his own understanding of norms by introducing a distinction between what he terms "normation" and "normalization"—a distinction corresponding to micro- and macro forms, though the micro form, what he now terms "normation," is what he had earlier (in *Discipline and Punish*) called "normalization." The second task is to begin to excavate the significance of "population"—a concept that as we've seen is centrally organizing for his understanding of these macro forms of power. The purpose behind both of these tasks is, he notes at the very beginning of the lecture, "to emphasize the opposition, or at any rate the distinction, between security and discipline" (CdF78ET, 55). (We can hear in this softening, from "opposition" to "distinction," the movement toward complementing rather than replacing the original analysis of disciplinary power.)

So, strictly speaking, what is this distinction between "normation" (Foucault's own neologism, which he himself describes as a "barbaric word" [CdF78ET, 57]) and normalization? Discipline "normalizes" (in the loose sense) in a five-step process. First, it analyzes and isolates discrete "individuals, places, times, movements, actions, and operations" (CdF78ET, 56). Next, these discrete analytical units (individuals, behaviors, etc.) are classified "according to definite objectives" (CdF78ET, 57). Then optimal sequences, links, and coordinations are established between them—in other words, the individuals are sorted and hierarchized in light of their classifications. Fourth, "discipline fixes the processes of progressive training and permanent control" (CdF78ET, 57) in light of the given objectives. Finally, "on the basis of this, it establishes the division between those considered unsuitable or incapable and the others. That is to say, on this basis it divides the normal from the abnormal" (CdF78ET, 57). This analysis is itself very schematic, but Foucault has already done the detail work: recall Part 3 of *Discipline and Punish*, and you will find a rich empirical analysis of this process in armies, in prisons, and in schools. But, as Foucault now observes,

> Disciplinary normalization consists first of all in positing a model, an optimal model that is constructed in terms of a certain result [step 2 of the five he has just delineated], and the operation of disciplinary normalization consists in trying to get people, movements, and actions to conform to this model, the normal being precisely that which can conform to this norm. (CdF78ET, 57)

The force of this insight is that disciplinary power *presupposes* something beyond its own techniques, something that gives content to its distinctions—something that Foucault here refers to as a "model." This model determines the "definite objectives" as well as the optimal sequences and hierarchies. But the disciplinary micropower itself does not and cannot determine what that model is; it merely operates with the values (or variables, if you'd like to think about this mathematically) that are provided by that model. "In other words," Foucault notes, "it is not the normal and the abnormal that is fundamental and primary in disciplinary normalization, it is the norm" (CdF78ET, 57). The norm, then, is the model that is presupposed by disciplinary normalization, and so:

> Due to the primacy of the norm in relation to the normal, to the fact that disciplinary normalization goes from the norm to the final division between the normal and the abnormal, I would rather say that what is involved in disciplinary techniques is a normation rather than normalization. (CdF78ET, 57)

How, then, are these norms—norms that are given externally and prior to the operation of disciplinary apparatuses—determined? The identification and emergence of norms is the product of a macrorelation, and Foucault finds this macrorelation at work in the emerging medical practices of vaccination and inoculation. This macroprocess involves several elements. First, there is the "case,"

> which is not the individual case but a way of individualizing the collective phenomenon of the disease, or of collectivizing the phenomena, integrating individual phenomena within a collective field, but in the form of quantification and of the rational and identifiable. (CdF78ET, 60)

A case can be identified only if individuals are considered not as discrete individuals but as tokens of a type within a larger field. Along with "cases" come the elements of "risk" and "danger": variations in individual circumstances (all children in France, or those in towns compared those in the country, or adults compared to children, etc.) will account for a greater or lesser risk of contracting, for example, smallpox. The quantitative calculation of these risks

> shows straightaway that risks are not the same for all individuals, all ages, or in every condition, place or milieu. There are therefore differential risks that reveal, as it were, zones of higher risk and, on the other hand, zones of less or lower risk. This means that one can thus identify what is dangerous. (CdF78ET, 61)

We are not speaking of discrete individuals but of groups, patterns, and populations when we speak of these zones of higher or lower risk. This macroapparatus "is not the division between those who are sick and those who are not" (CdF78ET, 62), which would be the disciplinary technique. Rather,

> It takes all who are sick and all who are not as a whole, that is to say, in short, the population, and it identifies . . . the normal expectation in the population of being affected by the disease and of death linked to the disease. . . . Thus we get the idea of a "normal" morbidity or mortality. (CdF78ET, 62)

It then subdivides the population as a whole "to disengage different normalities in relation to each other" (CdF78ET, 63). "It is at this level of the interplay of differential normalities [all established in terms of populations, not individuals] . . . that . . . the medicine of prevention will act" (CdF78ET, 63). This analysis at the level of populations gives us

> a plotting of the normal and the abnormal, of different curves of normality, and the operation of normalization consists in establishing an interplay between these different distributions of normality and [in] acting to bring the most unfavorable in line with the more favorable. . . . These distributions will serve as the norm. (CdF78ET, 63)

Norms emerge, then, through macroanalyses, macrorelations of power and knowledge that cannot be explained in disciplinary terms. Foucault is unambiguous on this point: "The government of populations is, I think, com-

pletely different from the exercise of sovereignty over the fine grain of individual behaviors. It seems to me that we have two completely different
systems of power" (CdF78ET, 66).

(Of course, while he was unambiguous in the assertion that these are two
"completely different" systems of power, he did speak here of an "exercise
of sovereignty" when he should have said "of discipline." That he is speaking of discipline is clear not only from the phrasing here of "the fine grain
of individual behaviors" but because he is referring to the Panopticon, "a
power that takes the form of an exhaustive surveillance of individuals" and
is the paradigmatic architecture of disciplinary power.)

Foucault has now grasped that the macro power relations that determine
norms are not reducible to disciplinary microtechniques. This macroprocess
of determining norms is what Foucault now terms "normalization in the
strict sense" (CdF78ET, 63). We should also note, however, that these two
processes (disciplinary normation and macronormalization) are not isolated
phenomena and can reciprocally influence each other. How the macronorms
motivate microdiscipline is, I hope, already clear. But the influence can flow
in the opposite direction, too—constituting a sort of feedback loop. Micropractices can, over time, produce new norms, or at least produce individuals
that, when considered as part of a collective whole, shift the values of the
norm in new directions. (Thus are constituted the "material givens" with
which apparatuses of security must begin.) Norms inform and frame discipline's classification of the normal and abnormal, but the new, altered
individuals produced by these disciplinary practices can also shift the values
of the norms. (This is, in effect, a process of evolution.)

And so, if his earlier analyses showed that an individual is the locus of,
and in part constituted by, disciplinary micro forms of power, then we can
now understand a population as the analogous object of the normalizing
(in the strict sense) macro forms of power. For mechanisms of security, like
preventative medicine, the "pertinent level of government is not the actual
totality of the subjects in every single detail but the population with its
specific phenomena and processes" (CdF78ET, 66). Populations come to be
understood as "natural" and as a "set of processes to be managed" "not from
the standpoint of the juridical-political notion of the subject, but as a sort of
technical-political object of management and government" (CdF78ET, 70).
This "natural phenomenon" is marked by several characteristics: it "is not
the simple sum of individuals inhabiting a territory" (CdF78ET, 70); it "is
not a primary datum; it is dependent upon a series of variables" (CdF78ET,

70) such as climate, commerce, etc.; and thus, "the relation between the population and sovereign cannot simply be one of obedience or the refusal of obedience, or obedience or revolt" (CdF78ET, 71). Nevertheless, a population "is constantly accessible to agents and techniques of transformation, on condition that these agents and techniques are at once enlightened, reflected, analytical, calculated, and calculating" (CdF78ET, 71). A population thus constitutes

> a set of elements that, on one side, are immersed within the general regime of living beings and that, on another side, offer a surface on which authoritarian, but reflected and calculated transformations can get a hold.
>   . . . we have here a whole field of new realities in the sense that they are the pertinent elements for mechanisms of power. (CdF78ET, 75)

We can hear in this evocation of "the general regime of living beings" the perspective that led Foucault to define biopower initially as a power that targets humans as a species (CdF78ET, 1). We can hear, too, in the description of population as an object of management and rational, calculated government the origins of his term "governmentality."

The discovery or recognition of these macro forms of power, and the central importance of this notion of population as the object of these macro forms, is a shift of profound significance in Foucault's understanding of power relations. (Hence, perhaps, the proliferation of terms for this new macro form of power.) However, there are important continuities. Structurally or theoretically, the macro forms of biopower and disciplinary micropower are, as Foucault understands them, quite similar: they are both relational; neither is understood as a property to be possessed; they are both productive, not prohibitive in function; they both constitute and are constituted by knowledges; and both in their very relational logic necessarily presuppose a possibility for resistance—indeed, freedoms. It is in light of these profound commonalities that I think we can best understand biopower as a complement to, an enrichment of, Foucault's analyses of discipline.

Foucault's closing remarks in this third lecture offer some important suggestions about how this reelaborated analysis of power opens new possibilities for Foucault's ethical thinking. He ends by noting that

> Hence the theme of man, and the "human sciences" that analyze him as a living being, working individual, and speaking subject, should be

understood on the basis of the emergence of population as the correlate of power and the object of knowledge. (CdF78ET, 79)

This "theme of man" is, of course, a famous trope that runs throughout Foucault's work: In 1966 he closed *The Order of Things* with the quasi-hopeful/quasi-despairing claim that "one can certainly wager that man would be erased, like a face drawn in sand at the edge of the sea" (1966ET, 387); *Discipline and Punish* opened with the claim that "the man described for us, whom we are invited to free, is already in himself the effect of a subjection much more profound than himself" (1975ET, 30).

Discipline and Punish, which grasped disciplinary power in its details, mistakenly hypothesized that all power relations are reducible to microrelations, thus leading to its seemingly bleak portrayal of a "carceral society." "This process that constitutes delinquency as an object of knowledge is one with the political operation that dissociates illegalities and isolates delinquency from them. The prison is the hinge of these two mechanisms" (1975ET, 277). But as Foucault can now recognize, his earlier analyses conflated disciplinary microprocesses (the former process) with macroprocesses (the latter political operation, which we can now understand in the terms he has introduced in 1978). If there is no escape from the ever-tightening net of discipline, if we are the effects of "a subjection much more profound" than ourselves, then resistance may be ultimately futile. But if these distinct forms of power are not "one with" each other but rather sometimes collaborative and sometimes opposed forces, then for those who find themselves enmeshed in these power relations (in other words, all of us), the possibilities for freedom have been greatly enlarged and multiplied. The power relations in which our subjectivities are constituted are not monolithic. The field has opened up. A framework is opening in which Foucault (and we) will be able to reexamine our subjectivities—not merely as passive products of "subjectivation" but also as active, "self-interpreting animals" (to borrow a phrase from Charles Taylor),[4] engaged in what Foucault in 1984 will call "practices of liberty" (cf. DE356). This insight will guide the trajectory of his Collège de France courses from 1980 until his death.

The notion of freedom raised here also brings us back to the second feature that distinguishes biopower—its treatment of uncertainty. In the second lecture of the course (18 January 1978), Foucault explores this theme through the example of scarcity—food shortages and how governments could attempt to prevent or ameliorate them. A disciplinary approach would attempt to regulate finely all aspects of production—through quotas, import/export regulations, and price controls, for example—to ensure that there is always an adequate supply of grain. But this cannot account for the uncontrollable variability of "material givens" such as climate (drought, flood, or ideal conditions), harvest (a shortage or a surplus—both of which play havoc with the supply mechanisms), etc. But these techniques, frankly, typically failed to prevent shortages; they also often contributed to unrest and revolts. A biopolitical approach, "by contrast . . . 'lets things happen'" (CdF78ET, 45). Rather than imposing infinitesimal and tight regulations, it is oriented toward solving the problem at the level of the collectivity or population and allows "market mechanisms" (CdF78ET, 40) to regulate themselves, solving the problems of excess supply or demand through price variations, increasing or decreasing exports, or planting of larger or smaller crops. Thus, the "problem" of scarcity dissolves itself and becomes a chimera:

> It is a chimera when, in fact, people conduct themselves properly, that is to say when some accept to endure scarcity-dearness, others sell their wheat at the right moment, that is to say very soon, and when exporters send their product when prices begin to rise. This is all very well and we have here, I don't say the good elements of the population, but behavior such that every individual functions well as a member, as an element of the thing we want to manage in the best way possible, namely the population. (CdF78ET, 43)

Note that this mode of power, too, attempts to impose certain conceptions of "conducting oneself properly"—but this proper conduct will be geared toward the ends of the population as a whole, not the discrete individual. Some will do without; others will raise or lower their prices, release more grain or alternatively export grain to reduce domestic supply: the integration of all these behaviors serve to regulate the supply of grain for the population as a whole. The mechanisms of security are not only markedly different from the mechanisms of discipline; in this case they actually work against each other.

The laissez-faire approach of security—accepting the uncertainty of given reality—"this fundamental principle that political technique must never get away from the interplay of reality with itself is profoundly linked to the general principle of what is called liberalism" (CdF78ET, 48).[5] It thus brings to the fore what Foucault calls "this problem of freedom," with which he closes this lecture. First, "it cannot be false . . . that this ideology of freedom really was one of the conditions of development of modern or, if you like, capitalist forms of the economy" (CdF78ET, 48). (Thus, an ideology of freedom is a kind of "condition of possibility" for a capitalist economy.) But second, this leads Foucault to make a significant revision to the portrayal given in *Discipline and Punish*.

> I said somewhere[6] that we could not understand the establishment of liberal ideologies and a liberal politics in the eighteenth century without keeping in mind that the same eighteenth century, which made such a strong demand for freedoms, had all the same ballasted these freedoms with a disciplinary technique that, taking children, soldiers, and workers where they were, considerably restricted freedom and provided, as it were, guarantees for this freedom. Well, I think I was wrong. I was not completely wrong, of course, but, in short, it was not exactly this. (CdF78ET, 48)

Whereas (following his Hobbesian hypothesis) he had earlier read freedom as a "mirage" produced through disciplinary normation of individuals, he now understands freedom in a wider context—it is not merely an epiphenomenon of discipline and control. But it remains fundamentally conjoined with power relations—the macrorelations of biopower as much as if not more than the microrelations of discipline: "this freedom, both ideology and technique of government, should in fact be understood within the mutations and transformations of technologies of power. More precisely and particularly, freedom is nothing else but the correlative of the deployment of apparatuses of security" (CdF78ET, 48). Of course, we should recognize this language of "correlates"—the soul, he had said, is "the present correlative of a certain technology of power over the body" (1975ET, 29)—but two very important shifts are being made here. First, freedom is primarily correlated with the macrotechniques of apparatuses of security, not discipline. But also, and for our purposes more importantly, "an apparatus of security . . . cannot operate well except on condition that it is given freedom . . . the possibility of movement, change of place, and processes of circulation of both people and things" (CdF78ET, 48–49). Freedom is a correlate of power relations, but those very power relations cannot function without that very freedom—freedom is also a condition for the possibility of these very power relations.

Let me close this discussion with an illustration from the eighteenth century—like my discussion of Stampp on slavery, this is an example that Foucault himself does not cite—a long and dense passage from the opening of Immanuel Kant's 1784 "Idea for a Universal History with a Cosmopolitan Intent":

> History—which concerns itself with providing a narrative of these appearances, regardless of how deeply hidden their causes may be—allows us to hope that if we examine *the play of the human will's freedom in the large*, we can discover its course to conform to rules as well as to hope that what strikes us as complicated and unpredictable in the single individual may in the history of the entire species be discovered to be the steady progress and slow development of its original capacities. Since the free wills of men seem to have so great an influence on marriage, the births consequent to it, and death, it appears that they are not subject to any rule by which one can in advance determine their number; and yet the annual charts that large countries make of them show that they occur in conformity with natural laws as invariable as those [governing] the unpredictable weather. . . . Individual men and even entire peoples give little thought to the fact that while each according to his own ways pursues his own end—often at cross purposes with each other—they unconsciously proceed toward an unknown natural end, as if following a guiding thread; and they work to promote an end they would set little store by, even if they were aware of it. (Kant 1784b, 29; Ak. 8:17)

Kant here articulates the interplay between individuals and populations that Foucault has been analyzing; Kant also shows how norms that seem to "obey natural laws" or "follow a guiding thread" emerge even through the interplay of free individuals. But Kant also takes this uniformity amid chaos as a reason for various kinds of hope—for Kant, hope for the progress of the human species and for our ability to discover the moral law within ourselves. Perhaps Foucault would hope for other things. But the emergence of this hope out of the interplay of freedom and norms shows, I think, a genuine alternative to the bleak and despairing outlook that *Discipline and Punish* could (from mistaken premises, as Foucault notes here) foster.

PASTORAL POWER AS THE "ART OF GOVERNING"

Foucault's presentation of "security" or "biopower" in these first three lectures allow him to bring into focus a new problem—the modern problem of justifying the state's claim to sovereignty, after the displacement of "sovereign power"—which emerged in discourses about "the art of government." Indeed, he suggests, "the unblocking of the art of government was linked to the emergence of the problem of population" (CdF78ET, 103–104). "In fact," he notes, "we have a triangle: sovereignty, discipline, and governmental management, which has population as its main target and apparatuses of security as its essential mechanism" (CdF78ET, 107–108). And at the pinnacle of this triangle are the arts of government, so that "from the eighteenth century, these three movements—government, population, political economy—form a solid series that has certainly not been dismantled even today" (CdF78ET, 108).[7] This allows Foucault to specify the "challenge" or the "stakes" of these lectures: "Can we talk of something like a 'governmentality' that would be to the state what techniques of segregation were to psychiatry, what techniques of discipline were to the penal system, and what biopolitics was to medical institutions?" (CdF78ET, 120).

To answer this question—to assess what constitutes an "art of governing"—Foucault first attempts to trace this notion's genealogy. "I will now try to show you how this governmentality was born from the archaic model of the Christian pastorate and, second, by drawing support from a new diplomatic-military model, or rather, technique, and finally, third . . . thanks to a set of very specific instruments . . . which is called . . . police" (CdF78ET, 110). These latter two elements are less important for my discussion; instead I will focus on its origins in the Christian pastoral and on Foucault's understanding and use of the notion of "governmentality."

He begins by examining the meaning of the verb "to govern," looking not at its contemporary "political, rigourous statist meaning" (CdF78ET, 120) but its earlier, variable meanings from the thirteenth through fifteenth centuries. There are a number of material senses: first, a very simple, physical meaning, "to direct, move forward, or even to move forward oneself on a track, a road" (CdF78ET, 121). There is a broader sense of "supporting by providing means of subsistence" (CdF78ET, 121) to one's family or to a city; finally, this second sense can be abstracted even farther, to encompass the sources of one's subsistence, such that a town "is governed by" its principal industry. Beyond these material meanings, however, there are also a number of moral senses to this term. At its core, the moral element of "governing" involves the guidance or direction of someone's conduct—in a spiritual sense of "the government of souls" or in a more secular sense of "imposing a regimen." One could guide another's conduct, as doctors direct their patients, or one can guide oneself, as a patient "who imposes treatment on himself, governs himself" (CdF78ET, 121). "Government" could be a synonym for conduct (a misbehaving daughter would be described as of "bad government"); "governing" could mean a variety of relationships, from command and control to engaging in conversation with someone. It could also refer to having sexual relations with someone. Thus, from its beginning, the notion of governing and government combine material elements encompassing the power to bring about a certain end *and* moral elements encompassing how to exercise this power well or poorly, for the good or not. "One thing clearly emerges through all these meanings, which is that one never governs a state, a territory, or a political structure. Those whom one governs are people, individuals, or groups" (CdF78ET, 122).

This notion of governing *people* does not come from the Western (Greek or Roman) political traditions. Foucault engages in an extended reading of Plato's *Statesman* to show how in this exemplar of the Western tradition such an understanding of governing is mentioned only to be quickly dismissed. Rather, this notion of government came to the West from Christianity in the Mediterranean East—from the practices of the pastorate, which offered the shepherd as the model of good governing:

> The Christian Church coagulated all these themes [which Foucault
> had just listed, and I will discuss next] of pastoral power into precise
> mechanisms and definite institutions, it organized a pastoral power that
> was both specific and autonomous, it implanted its apparatuses within
> the Roman Empire, and at the heart of the Empire it organized a type
> of power that I think was unknown to any other civilization. (CdF78ET,
> 129–130)

This pastoral power is distinguished by four key characteristics. As Foucault enumerates them, it is exercised over a "multiplicity in movement" (CdF78ET, 125); second, it "is fundamentally a beneficent power" (CdF78ET, 126); its form is of "someone who keeps watch" (CdF78ET, 127); and, finally, it "is an individualizing power" (CdF78ET, 128). Each of these is quite significant; however, I will discuss the second trait only after I have discussed the other three.

First, pastoral power is exercised over "the flock in its movement from one place to another" (CdF78ET, 125). In contrast to Greek conceptions, in which gods are tied to a particular place or territory, a shepherd (and the Hebrew God) governs a group that is constantly in motion, constantly in search of new grazing. Thus, this power is not "exercised on the unity of a territory"(CdF78ET, 126) but rather over a group—the multiplicity, the flock as a whole, as it moves from pasture to pasture. This first characteristic anticipates the structure of biopower, which will be concerned with populations, groups of individuals, taken as a whole, populations that can fluctuate and are in constant motion.

Further, "the form it takes is not first of all the striking display of strength and superiority" (CdF78ET, 127), as, for example, would be the case in Greek gods' manifestations or in the exercise of "sovereign power." Rather, the shepherd "will keep watch over the flock and avoid the misfortune that may threaten the least of its members. He will see to it that things are best for each of the animals of his flock" (CdF78ET, 127). Rather than drawing others' attention to the shepherd's majesty and glory, pastoral power is exercised by directing the shepherd's attention to its flock. He is concerned with the flock *as a whole* and with *each individual member* (even "the least") of the flock, keeping watch over them to avoid dangers. Here we can recognize rudimentary elements of *both* biopower (again, in the concern for the entire flock, anticipating dangers to be avoided) *and* discipline (in its watchful attention to each individual sheep).

Thus, pastoral power is individualizing. The shepherd must take note of each individual sheep, not just the flock as a whole. He does so by counting the sheep, morning and night, and may even be compelled to put the rest of the flock at risk to rescue a single stray sheep. In its individualizing function, as well as through its mechanism of keeping watch, we can hear early elements of what will become disciplinary power.

Pastoral power is an ancestral form of what will be bifurcated into micro and macro forms, discipline and biopower. This tension is captured in what Foucault calls "the paradox of the shepherd," which takes two forms. First,

> the shepherd must keep his eye on all and on each, *omnes et singulatim*, which will be the great problem both of the techniques of power in Christian pastorship, and of the, let's say, modern techniques of power deployed in the technologies of population I have spoken about. (CdF78ET, 128)

Further, just as the shepherd must be willing to sacrifice the entire flock to save even the least of the sheep, he must be willing to sacrifice himself to save the entire flock. This constitutes a "moral paradox": "the sacrifice of one for all, and the sacrifice of all for one, which will be at the absolute heart of the

Christian problematic of the pastorate" (CdF78ET, 129). And so the problematic revealed in this paradox—how to exercise pastoral power in the government of Christians' souls—will become for Saint Gregory of Nazianzus in the fourth century C.E. "the 'art of arts,' the 'science of sciences'" (CdF78ET, 151). This early precursor of "the art of governing" thus "was the art by which some people were taught the government of others, and others were taught to let themselves be governed by certain people" (CdF78ET, 151).

This paradox only arises—the question of whom to sacrifice only becomes an issue—because of the final (Foucault's second) feature of pastoral power: "pastoral power is fundamentally beneficent power" (CdF78ET, 126). Foucault puts this simply and unambiguously: "Pastoral power is a power of care" (CdF78ET, 127). And this feature is *fundamental*: "pastoral power is, I think, entirely defined by its beneficence; its only *raison d'être* is doing good, and in order to do good. In fact the essential objective of pastoral power is the salvation of the flock" (CdF78ET, 126). This power exists on ethical grounds—it is exercised precisely and "entirely" for the good, the salvation, of those upon whom it is exercised. It thus constitutes "a duty, a task to be undertaken" for the one who exercises it, the shepherd (CdF78ET, 127). "The shepherd directs all his care towards others and never towards himself. This is precisely the difference between the good and the bad shepherd" (CdF78ET, 127–128). The prominence of this term "care" here is important for at least two reasons. First of all, this form of power, which is a precursor to both discipline and biopower, has an ethical dimension at its core. Second, as we shall see, some of Foucault's own ethical trajectories will explore the possibilities for such caring within a framework marked by the later, more developed forms of power.

Foucault presented this analysis of pastoral power again in his October 1979 Tanner Lectures at Stanford University (DE291; in effect, these two lectures serve as a condensed version of the 1978 Collège de France course). Two key points emerge quite clearly in the Tanner Lectures rearticulation.

First, the theme of care is underscored: "The shepherd's role is to ensure the salvation of his flock. . . . It's a matter of constant, individualized, and final kindness" (DE291.4, 302). And so his "duty," his "shepherdly kindness[,] is much closer to 'devotedness'" (DE291.4, 302), which manifests in a constant concern to keep watch over the flock: "He pays attention to them all and scans each one of them. He's got to know his flock as a whole, and in detail" (DE291.4, 303). In pastoral power, the ethics and the techniques of power are interwoven. And the final phrase here, "as a whole and in detail," again reminds us that pastoral power is at the root of both biopolitical and disciplinary forms of modern power. It can even be seen in contemporary political struggles: "The well-known 'welfare state problem' . . . must be recognized for what it is: one of the extremely numerous reappearances of the tricky adjustment between political power wielded over legal subjects and pastoral power wielded over live individuals" (DE291.4, 307).

The second important point that Foucault brings out in the Tanner Lectures is pastoral power's legacy in the construction of modern subjectivity. For in the history of the Christian Church, the original theme of pastoral power was to be rearticulated and reformulated in various techniques and institutions. Most important among these are the practices of self-examination and confession. The shepherd has a certain responsibility to "render an account—not only of each sheep, but of all their actions" (DE291.4, 308). So each member of the flock must confess its sins to the shepherd, so that he can, in his turn, render an account. Correspondingly, each sheep must be obedient to the shepherd, taking on a "personal submission to him" (DE291.4, 309). Taken together, these relations of responsibility and obedience serve to constitute "a peculiar type of knowledge" (DE291.4, 309) of each sheep's particular needs—but also of each one's sins. We can hear in this description an anticipation of what Foucault will call in *Discipline and Punish* "the modern 'soul.'" Understanding this legacy—the constitution of the modern subject—will also guide Foucault's continuing itinerary. The title of the 1982 Collège de France course, *The Hermeneutics of the Subject*, is explicitly devoted to the genealogy of this subjectivity; in fact, it is a central theme of many of his courses in the 1980s.

A particular example can be seen in another 1982 text, "The Subject and Power" (DE306). Returning to the questions of "the state" that had initially guided his 1978 Collège de France inquiry, Foucault again situates pastoral power at the root of these developments: "we can see the state as a modern matrix of individualization, or a new form of pastoral power" (DE306.4, 334). In enumerating how pastoral power is present in the state and in the forms of modern subjectivity, he concludes by evoking the twin poles of macro biopower and micro disciplinary power:

> Finally, the multiplication of the aims and agents of pastoral power
> focused the development of knowledge of man around two roles: one,
> globalizing and quantitative, concerning the population; the other, ana-
> lytical, concerning the individual. (DE306.4, 335)

Significantly, immediately following this observation, Foucault cites Immanuel Kant's 1784 essay "What Is Enlightenment?" as "an analysis of both us and our present" (DE306.4, 335). Foucault continues that "the task of philosophy as a critical analysis of our world is something that is more and more important" (DE306.4, 336). And he notes that this has important ethical implications:

> The conclusion would be then that the political, ethical, social, philosophical problem of our days is not to try to liberate the individual from the state, and from the state's institutions, but to liberate us both from the state and from the type of individualization linked to the state. We have to promote new forms of subjectivity through the refusal of this kind of individuality that has been imposed on us for several centuries. (DE306.4, 336)

Freedom, liberation, is here identified as the task toward which philosophy ought to work. Indeed, Foucault closed his Tanner Lectures in noting that "Liberation can come only from attacking not just one of these two effects [individualization and totalitarianism] but political rationality's very roots" (DE291.4:325). And as he noted in the 1978 course, "there has never been an anti-pastoral revolution" (CdF78ET, 150).[8] Exploring what possibilities there could be for "new forms of subjectivity" will be one of Foucault's tasks in the years to come—one of the trajectories of a Foucauldian ethics. But just as importantly, we can note that this freedom, the telos of philosophy, is also—as he has shown in the first part of the 1978 course—a condition for the possibility of the power relations from which we seek to be liberated. This is an important insight, to which we shall return.

GOVERNMENTALITY

Pastoral power, then, "is the prelude to this governmentality in two ways" (CdF78ET, 184). It establishes new types of relationships, and it gives rise to, constitutes, a specific sort of subject. And so, Foucault explains, "by this word 'governmentality' I mean three things" (CdF78ET, 108).

First, it encompasses

> the ensemble formed by institutions, procedures, analyses, and reflections, calculations, and tactics that allow the exercise of this very specific, albeit very complex, power that has the population as its target,

political economy as its major form of knowledge, and apparatuses of security as its essential technical instrument. (CdF78ET, 108)

As the last half of this passage makes explicit, Foucault means biopower, the macropower that he has been describing in the first lectures of the course. But if we were to consider only the first half of this passage (ending with "this very specific, albeit very complex, power"), we could rightly infer that Foucault was talking about modern power more generally—not only bio-power but also disciplinary power—for they each are constituted through all of the elements and techniques he has adumbrated.

Second, "governmentality" means

the tendency, the line of force, that for a long time, and throughout the West, has constantly led towards the pre-eminence over all other types of power—sovereignty, discipline, and so on—of the type of power that we can call "government" and which has led to the development of a series of specific governmental apparatuses on the one hand, [and, on the other] to the development of a series of knowledges. (CdF78ET, 108)

We can note the same bivalence in this statement, as well. On the one hand, Foucault is clearly specifying biopower in this description and even suggests that it has become preeminent over other forms, including discipline. There is a sense in which this is correct: biopower as a specific technique emerged somewhat later than discipline and was able to "piggyback" on disciplinary modes in the articulation of its knowledges about populations. However, two points can be noted in response. First, Foucault has been quite clear (and correctly so) that biopower does not "displace" but rather "overlays" disciplinary power—the latter is not superseded; rather, they both simulta-neously function in the same social field. Second, as Foucault's discussion of pastoral power (which we have already seen but would actually be given in the lecture following this one) makes clear, discipline and biopower share a common ancestor in pastoral power. So the "tendency" or "line of force" that leads to the preeminence of a particular form of power might be better understood as referring not to biopower in its specificity but rather to the modern distribution of power, which is only adequately described when both forms are interwoven.

Third and finally, "governmentality" connotes "the result of the process by which the state of justice of the Middle Ages became the administrative state in the fifteenth and sixteenth centuries and was gradually 'governmentalized'" (CdF78ET, 108–109). Again, in the strict sense, Foucault is referring to a state whose administrative apparatus is aimed at the population, that is, biopower. But in a broader sense, the administrative institutions and techniques that constitute the state are also represented by what Foucault calls "police," and "police" techniques are disciplinary through and through. (Indeed, "police" represents the interface where disciplinary and biopolitical techniques are integrated for the management or government of the state.) Discipline is, just as much as biopower, the result of these administrative transformations of the state since the Middle Ages.

So with each of these specifications of "governmentality," Foucault could be speaking exclusively of biopower, or he could be speaking of a framework of modern power that incorporates discipline and biopower into the constitution and management of states. As Michel Senellart notes, "the concept of 'governmentality' progressively shifts from a precise, historically determinate sense, to a more general and abstract meaning" (Senellart 2004, 387–388). While we do need to be aware of that "determinate" sense (the forms of raison d'état and police, which I mentioned earlier, are such historically specific developments), the more general meaning is in fact the more important.

Even by the end of these lectures, though the specific sense has not been entirely abandoned, "governmentality" comes to function as a sort of umbrella term that brings the different kinds of power (sovereign, disciplinary, and biopower) into a coherent frame; it also underscores, in the multiple senses of "governing," the capacities or resources for ethics implicit within his analysis of power—resources that Foucault will continue to excavate for the remainder of his life, most explicitly in his final Collège de France courses. In the very last paragraph of the entire course, Foucault sums up its work:

All I wanted to do this year was a mere experiment of method in order to show how starting from the relatively local and microscopic analysis of those typical forms of power of the pastorate it was possible, without paradox or contradiction, to return to the general problems of the state, on condition precisely that we [do not make] the state [into] a transcendent reality whose history could be undertaken on the basis of itself. It must be possible to do the history of the state on the basis of men's actual practice, on the basis of what they do and how they think . . . there is not a sort of break between the level of micro-power and the level of macro-power, and that talking about one [does not] exclude talking about the other. (CdF78ET, 358)

We must not take the state as a transcendent reality. On the contrary, we must talk about the micropowers and macropowers—disciplines and bio-powers—together. As we move from the local to the global and back, "on the basis of what men do and how they think," "governmentality," and "the arts of governing" serve well as a framework and background for this critical work. Using this concept of "government" as a frame will, in fact, help Foucault clarify his own thinking as he turns from the analysis *of* power to questions of ethics *within* power. We can see such a schema being sketched in Foucault's January 1984 interview, "The Ethics of the Concern for the Self as a Practice of Freedom":

> We must distinguish between power relations understood as strategic games between liberties—in which some try to control the conduct of others, who in turn try to avoid allowing their conduct to be controlled or try to control the conduct of others—and the states of domination that people ordinarily call "power." And between the two, between games of power and states of domination, you have technologies of government—understood, of course, in a very broad sense that includes not only the way institutions are governed but also the way one governs one's wife and children. (DE356.4, 299)

"Governing," guiding the conduct of others, is an integral part of the games of power. "States of domination" are not "nation-states" but rather reified situations in which no resistance would be possible. The "technologies of government," which Foucault notes here should be understood in the broadest sense, encompass both states ("governmentality" in the strict biopolitical sense) and microrelations such as families. (And lest we mistakenly accuse Foucault of antifeminism here, we should note that he drew these examples from his study of ancient Roman society, in which one did speak of governing one's wife.) In 1982's "The Subject and Power," Foucault had spoken of liberation "both from the state and from the type of individualization linked to the state" (DE306.4, 336). Here, in 1984, he will note that

> I believe that this problem [how power is to be used] must be framed in terms of rules of law, rational techniques of government and *ethos*, practices of the self and of freedom.

I believe that this is, in fact, the hinge point of ethical concerns and the political struggle for respect of rights, of critical thought against abusive techniques of government and research in ethics that seeks to ground individual freedom. (DE356.4, 299)

The framework with which we understand power—"governmentality," encompassing government of the state, the economy, and the self—is a hinge point for ethical concerns as well as political struggle. This new frame will be indicated in the titles of several of his later Collège de France courses: from 1980's "The Government of the Living" to "The Government of Self and Others" in 1983 and 1984. The 1980 title reflects a lingering emphasis upon biopolitical themes, concerned with the management of macrogroups through institutions such as the state (which had been his focus in 1979). It nevertheless continues two important and parallel shifts, initially indicated in Foucault's 1978 discussion of pastoral power's roots in early Christianity: first, a shift away from contemporary transformations to earlier, ancient practices—as can be seen in his opening image of the Roman emperor Septimus Severus—and second, a deemphasis of states in favor of individuals. As Foucault stressed at the beginning of the third lecture of the 1980 course, "This is what I'd like to study a little this year . . . the element of the first person, of the 'I,' of the '*autos*,' of the 'myself' in what could be called alethurgy or veridiction of oneself" (CdF80ET, 48; trans. mod. based on the audio recordings; cf. CdF80, 48).

Thus, the structural elaboration of how power works is essentially complete, with the emergence of this notion of "governmentality." We are given a clear and succinct (if dense) statement of Foucault's "mature" view in the 1982 Collège de France course:

In other words, what I mean is this: if we take the question of power, of political power, situating it in the more general question of governmentality understood as a strategic field of power relations in the broadest and not merely political sense of the term, if we understand by governmentality a strategic field of power relations in their mobility, transformability, and reversibility, then I do not think that reflection on this notion of governmentality can avoid passing through, theoretically and practically, the element of a subject defined by the relationship of self to self . . . the analysis of governmentality—that is to say, of power as the ensemble of reversible relations—must refer to an ethics of the subject defined by the relationship of self to self. Quite simply, this means that in the type of analysis I have been trying to advance for some time you can see that power relations, governmentality, the government of the self and others, and the relationship of self to self constitute a chain, a thread, and I think it is around these notions, that we should be able to connect together the question of politics and the question of ethics. (CdF82ET, 252; trans. mod.; cf. CdF82, 241–242)

Inevitably, there will be details to be revised in this analysis of power and governmentality, but the core of the theory of power has been articulated, and (as these passages from 1982 and 1984 nicely encapsulate) this theory marks a key intersection between empirical and ethical concerns. We are now, therefore, in a position to identify the linkages that Foucault points to between his analyses of power and ethics.

ETHICS WITHIN POWER

We have achieved a number of insights. First, the mechanisms of modern (or any) power cannot be analyzed exclusively in terms of disciplinary micropractices. On the contrary, macropowers aimed at populations are coextensive with and irreducible to the disciplinary micropowers. Indeed, both forms of power share a common ancestor in premodern Christian pastoral power. Second, since there are multiple, irreducible forms or modes of power constantly at play with and against one another, the field of power relations has become exponentially more complex. This complexity actually means that there is more "freedom" within the system—multiple kinds of power that are overlaid upon each other create more possibilities for resistance against any particular form. Thus, the "Hobbesian hypothesis," as I've termed it—that since all social relations are inflected by power we are trapped in an inescapable cage—is unsustainable. Consider again one of Kenneth Stampp's observations about slavery:

> In truth, no slave uprising ever had a chance of ultimate success. . . . The bondsmen themselves lacked the power to destroy the web of bondage. They would have to have the aid of free men inside or outside the South. (Stampp 1956, 140)

Even though the slaves themselves could not completely break their state of domination, there were other vectors of power, recourse to which would bring the institution of slavery to an end. (Of course, even the end of slavery was not the final end of all struggle but the inauguration of a new one that continues today in the civil rights movement and Black Lives Matter a century and a half later.) While we should be suspicious of power, we need not despair. On the contrary, the very sources of power and resistance can give us cause for hope in a struggle against domination.

This brings us to two absolutely critical and interwoven Foucauldian insights.

First, this analysis of power provides a framework and basis for ethical concerns. On the one hand, this means that we cannot engage in an ethical analysis without first understanding how power relations have shaped and conditioned our selves. On the other hand, this means that ethics must be articulated *within* a framework of power relations—ethics is not "outside of" or "beyond" power relations but rather emerges explicitly and necessarily within and through those very relations.

This point is intimated in the very opening remarks of Foucault's 1978 Collège de France course—at the end of which he remarks, "Now I would like to begin the lectures" (CdF78ET, 4). In these prefatory remarks, he lays down a series of "indications of choice or statements of intent" (CdF78ET, 1) that delineate how he wants to situate his developing analysis of power. These general indications implicitly give the outline for a new shift that will reorient virtually all of Foucault's subsequent thinking—a new explicit foregrounding of ethical questions that will displace power relations from their central place. These indications also articulate power relations' newly emerging status as the context for, the inescapable frame or condition of possibility within which these ethical questions obtain.

Foucault's five general indications are as follows: First, his ongoing analysis of power is "not in any way a general theory of what power is" (CdF78ET, 1) but rather "could and would only be at most a beginning of a theory" (CdF78ET, 2) of mechanisms of power's functions. Of course, we have heard this claim that Foucault is not doing a "theory of power" before. But in this iteration, he qualifies and specifies the de rigeur disclaimer in interesting ways.

The second "indication of choice" is thus that power relations "are not 'self-generating' or 'self-subsistant'; they are not founded upon themselves" (CdF78ET, 2). Power relations are not sui generis; on the contrary, they are interwoven with a wide variety of and different types of social relations. "Mechanisms of power are an intrinsic part of all these relations and, in a circular way, are both their effect and cause" (CdF78ET, 2).

This leads us to the third indication: because power relations are interwoven with other kinds of relations throughout society, "the analysis of these power relations may, of course, open out onto or initiate something like the overall analysis of a society" (CdF78ET, 2). In other words, this analysis can certainly begin (as it has) with an analysis of power, but it must then go beyond power relations to the other kinds of relations that constitute society. And, Foucault adds, this means that "what I am doing is something that concerns philosophy" (CdF78ET, 3). The analysis of power relations that he has developed can be linked and integrated with "history, sociology, or economics" (CdF78ET, 3), but for Foucault, the important connection that he wants to develop is to philosophy, "that is to say, the politics of truth, for I do not see many other definitions of the word 'philosophy' apart from this" (CdF78ET, 3). When Foucault speaks of "the politics of truth" he means adopting a certain kind of critical attitude—which is, as he will make clear in later years, the heart of an ethical project. Thus the connection to ethics, though only implicit, is nonetheless beginning to be articulated.

It becomes much clearer, if still tentative, in the final two indications. The fourth indication is that all "theoretical or analytical discourses" are "permeated or underpinned in one way or another by something like an imperative discourse" (CdF78ET, 3). This is, quite frankly, strong and surprising language: the analytical work that Foucault has been doing to articulate a theory of power, he tells us, is "permeated or underpinned" by imperative discourses—value claims. In other words, normativity, or some sort of ethical or moral discourse, is unavoidable. He immediately qualifies this statement, however, adding that such an imperative "seems to me, at present at any rate, to be no more than an aesthetic discourse that can only be based on choices of an aesthetic order" (CdF78ET, 3). We can hear in this remark the roots of Foucault's later exploration of the possibilities available within a "merely" aesthetic approach, of "one's self as a work of art," for example. And we can recognize a larger pattern of argument being repeated here: suppose a most-limited-case scenario, and only when it is demonstrated to be inadequate can we safely posit a stronger claim—one that we wanted but were initially reluctant to embrace. (This was, after all, how the Hobbesian hypothesis was refuted.) For "the dimension of what is to be done can only appear within a field of real forces that cannot be created by a speaking subject alone" (CdF78ET, 3)—that is, ethical work can only be done within a field analyzable in terms of power relations.

This has direct implications for how Foucault will conceive his own work.

> So, since there has to be an imperative, I would like the one under-
> pinning the theoretical analysis we are attempting to be quite simply
> a conditional imperative of the kind: If you want to struggle, here are
> some key points, here are some lines of force, here are some constric-
> tions and blockages. In other words, I would like these imperatives to
> be no more than tactical pointers. (CdF78ET, 3)

If Foucault's own imperatives have the status of mere "tactical pointers," then he will be able to resist efforts to make his word a sort of gospel—a role he consistently denied. "You don't have to do (or think) this, but you might want to try X," not "Here is what must be done." There are many reasons for Foucault's reluctance to make such proclamations; among the most important is his profound appreciation for the contingency of any particular situation and the rich and unpredictable results of resistance in "a field of real forces"—what one would recommend now could in fact make things worse, and other strategies might turn out to be more productive toward a given end. And so, as he will put it later, "My point is not that everything is bad, but that everything is dangerous" (DE326.4, 256). Yet even as Foucault marks his ethical norms as mere "conditional imperatives" and "tactical pointers," he will be more willing to make them explicit. And they will thus pull him deeper into what he terms "the circle of struggle and truth, that is to say, precisely, of philosophical practice" (CdF78ET, 3), for as he later notes, "ethics is a practice" (DE341.1, 377).

This brings us to Foucault's fifth and final indication: "this serious and fundamental relation between struggle and truth . . . becomes emaciated, and loses its meaning and effectiveness in polemics. . . . So in all of this I will therefore propose only one imperative, but it will be categorical and un-conditional: Never engage in polemics" (CdF78ET, 3–4). Even as it claims to be "merely methodological," this imperative, too, carries rich ethical im-plications. For as he will note in a 1983 interview, "polemics allows for no possibility of an equal discussion" (DE342.2, 112).

> The polemicist, on the other hand, proceeds encased in privileges that he
> possesses in advance and will never agree to question. . . . For him, then,
> the game consists . . . of abolishing [an interlocutor] from any possible

dialogue; and his final objective will be not to come as close as possible to a difficult truth but to bring about the triumph of the just cause he has been manifestly upholding from the beginning. (DE342.2, 112)

In explicit contrast to "polemics," Foucault will distinguish his own work—indeed his "attitude"—as investigations into the politics of truth, that is, philosophy.

My attitude isn't a result of the form of critique that claims to be a methodological examination in order to reject all possible solutions except for the one valid one [as the polemicist would do]. It is more on the order of "problematization"—which is to say, the development of a domain of acts, practices, and thoughts that seem to me to pose problems for politics. (DE342.2, 114)

So these indications, at the very opening of the 1978 course, delineate a movement and trajectory that brings the ethical into the field of power relations, in terms (especially the final term, "polemics") that will be further clarified as late as 1983.

Though beginning from an analysis of power, Foucault explicitly indicates that such an analysis cannot stand alone and constitutes just a piece of a larger social analysis. That larger analysis has to be reciprocally grounded in a normative context—even if in 1978 what seems immediately possible in that context is merely aesthetic and not yet ethical. Nevertheless, this inescapable imperative discourse pulls us (and Foucault) toward the deeper, fundamental philosophical relations between struggle and truth, in other words, toward the ethical.

Of course, Foucault often recast earlier work in terms of his current preoccupations—we saw in Chapter 2 how in the 1974 Collège de France course he recast *History of Madness* as "really about power." But the opening to the ethical through—beginning in—the analysis of power that Foucault introduces here (and his characterization of it as an "indication of choice" is revealing) is not exactly the same kind of move: it is much more speculative. He doesn't yet know where this arc or trajectory will take him; he can only indicate its underlying or framing elements. Foucault is still focused on understanding power relations—and they will remain present, sometimes even central, in his later analyses (as is only appropriate, since ethics emerges within a framework of power relations)—but the dawn is rising on a new horizon.

Further, these opening pages suggest not only *that* a concern for ethics is on Foucault's horizon but also an important insight into *how* to approach ethical questions or problematics in a Foucauldian way. And this key—that ethics is not outside of (as a Habermasian might characterize it) but essentially and intensively embedded within power relations—helps us see how Foucault's various subsequent ethical strands of inquiry (aesthetic self-fashioning, friendships, sadomasochism, parrhesiastic courage, and the government of oneself and others) can be coherently integrated into an ethical vision.

So the second critical insight—interwoven with that first insight that power relations constitute a framework for ethics—is that this general analysis of power gives us *concrete resources* (as well as problems) for an ethics. As he characterizes his project in a later interview,

> I am attempting . . . to *open up* problems that are as *concrete* and *general* as possible, problems that approach politics from behind and cut across societies on the diagonal, problems that are at once constituents of our history and constituted by that history. (DE341.1, 375–376)

Along his ethical itinerary, Foucault will develop a number of specific resources—possibilities and sites of resistance emerging from the particular domains under analysis, for example, sexuality. Indeed, most of Foucault's initial ethical forays are explorations of this kind of specific resource. And just as his overarching understanding of modern power had to evolve, so will the strategies and tactics that he explores as ethical possibilities. We have already heard the first of these specific resources at the close of *La volonté de savoir*, when Foucault asserted that "the rallying point for the counterattack against the deployment of sexuality ought not to be sex-desire, but bodies and pleasures" (1976ET, 157). His exploration of "bodies and pleasures," particularly in the explicitly power-laden practices of sadomasochism, will lead him to a new set or source of specific resources, which would fall under the rubric of friendship or "care" (that fundamental feature of pastoral power).

But Foucault's development of these specific ethical resources is not unproblematic. Indeed, some of his most acute critics take him to task precisely because of these resources' or resistances' specificity: the challenge is how any ethical or normative stance that emerges from a contingent and specific situation could offer something broader than merely context-specific justification.

However, Foucault's analysis of power also gives us more general resources that authorize a response to these critics. The first of these is the insight that has already emerged, that the multiple vectors of micro and macro power relations guarantee a certain amount of play, so that there is always room for resistance, and power relations can never be absolutely fixed into permanent states of domination. Beyond that, and essentially, the very basic structure of power relations—that power is only possible on the presupposition of freedom (and hence, resistance)—provides the resources for normative justification. This justification will obtain even though, given the contingency of any particular situation and the ongoing nature of the struggle, any course of action will remain dangerous.

These two critical insights—that an analysis of power relations necessarily frames ethics and that it simultaneously provides resources for such an ethics—are both reflected in Foucault's own intellectual itinerary: it was only on the basis of his fully developed analysis of power that he was able to begin to speak explicitly about ethical concerns, without which his critical theory would remain incomplete. For as he noted in an 1978 interview with Duccio Trombadori, "I've never argued that a power mechanism suffices to characterize a society" (DE281.2, 293). Of course, Foucault always maintained a certain reticence about making proclamations—in the language of the first lecture of the 1978 course, he wanted his "imperatives" to be mere "tactical pointers," or, in Kantian language, mere hypothetical imperatives. What, then, is the content of these imperatives? What constitutes the itinerary or trajectory of a Foucauldian ethics? Answering these questions, understanding Foucauldian ethics—its framework and the trajectories that emerge from this engagement with power—will be the work of our next chapter.

Freedom's Critique:
The Trajectories of a Foucauldian Ethics

Robert Nye observes about Foucault's history of sexuality that "his scholarly hermeneutic made it possible for him to be both the object and the subject of his investigations, providing him with a way of understanding the discursive influences that shaped his identity as well as the tools for an active self-transformation" (Nye 1996, 225). What is generally characterized as Foucault's shift from an emphasis on power to an emphasis on ethics is marked by a shift from analysis of the subject as object of power relations to analysis of the subject as an agent. Nye's insight is that, in fact, both approaches are copresent, even in Foucault's analyses of sexuality, psychiatry, prisons, and power in the 1970s. Foucault's ethics clearly emphasizes, as Nye notes, "active self-transformation." And so, if we wish to understand the evolution of Foucault's ethical thought, we must look for its roots in his analysis of power.

And we find that Foucault's ethical emphases evolved along with his understanding of the operation of power precisely because that ethics emerges and is articulated within his then-current understanding of power. Foucault's ethical thinking can thus be recognized at each stage of his development. The task of this chapter is to trace how his ethical impulses developed in parallel to the analyses of power that we traced up to this point. We shall begin at the end, however, looking at the "new theoretical basis" that he articulated for ethics in the Introduction to *The Use of Pleasure* (volume 2 of *The History of Sexuality*, published in 1984, weeks before his death). Just as did his new theoretical basis for analysis of power relations, which emerged only out of his empirical studies, this reconception of ethics, emerging out of his own ethical explorations, will give us the framework in which to understand Foucault's ethical development. Ethics is, fundamentally, for Foucault, a practice.

In the process of recognizing or discovering this new framework for "what constitutes ethics," Foucault's ethical thought developed along four principal trajectories. The first was already telegraphed in the closing pages of *La volonté de savoir*—the exploration of "bodies and pleasures" as sites of resistance to the disciplinary production of sexuality and desire. This exploration emerged explicitly as an attempt to resist the totalizing effects of disciplinary power, and it came to a focus in Foucault's engagement with sadomasochism, a site where power is explicitly thematized as an element of pleasure and where pleasure is not reducible to sexuality. This first trajectory serves to authorize speaking about—and exploring—kinds of relations other than power. Thus the second trajectory emerges, again beginning in sexual relationships between men. But what interests Foucault in homosexual relations is not sex but the friendship and caring that emerge within them and that can be transformative for the relations themselves and for larger social norms. Here we can recognize the "active self-transformation" that Nye identified, which will be the springboard for Foucault's next ethical trajectory.

Both of these first two trajectories, however, draw directly from the micropractices of very personal experience—sexual practices and practices of friendship. But Foucault's ethical trajectories are not exclusively personalist. The last two trajectories that I will outline are both much more general (and macro) in their scope and significance—these latter trajectories allow Foucault to give an account of ethical validity or justification from within these practices.

The third trajectory is an exploration of "critique" as an attitude. As an attitude, critique begins in the personal (as had the first two trajectories), but critique's scope encompasses how one ought to be governed in the most general sense, including societies' norms and states' techniques as well as individuals' self-government. Kant's "What Is Enlightenment?" is a key text for Foucault's articulation of this attitude. And very interestingly, Foucault took up this theme in his last years (especially the 1983 and 1984 Collège de France courses) but also in 1978, just after he had completed the elaboration of his expanded analysis of power in terms of governmentality. There he even proposes that we should understand "the critical attitude as virtue in general" (OT-78-01ET, 383).

A critical attitude would be an essential virtue precisely because "everything is dangerous" (DE326.4, 256), and everything is dangerous because the myriad power relations within which we are inescapably situated themselves necessarily presuppose freedom. Understanding the ethical import of this ontological freedom constitutes the fourth and final trajectory that I will trace in Foucauldian ethics. Foucault's argument here, which is most developed in the 1984 interview on "The Care of the Self as a Practice of Freedom" and is very close to a line of argumentation that Simone de Beauvoir develops in *The Ethics of Ambiguity*, gives a Foucauldian ethics the resources to ground context-transcendent justifications, answering his most significant critics.

APPROACHING ETHICS FROM A NEW THEORETICAL BASIS

One of Foucault's most important contributions to social theory is the reconceptualization of power that he articulated in the 1970s, which we've traced in this book's earlier chapters. We see a parallel reconceptualization in his ethical thinking, too: not only must we understand ethics from *within* power relations, but we must also reimagine what constitutes "doing ethics," just as Foucault had reimagined what constitutes "using power." And just as Part 4 of *La volonté de savoir* was the key text for his articulation of his new theory of power, the Introduction to the second volume of *The History of Sexuality*, *The Use of Pleasure* (1984a) gives us his clearest elaboration of how ethics is to be reconceived.

The second and third volumes of *The History of Sexuality* appeared in the spring of 1984—months before his death and eight years after the first volume had appeared. These two volumes were nothing like what had been originally projected for the series. It was to have been a six-volume study of sexuality in the eighteenth through twentieth centuries, historically parallel to his study of prisons in *Discipline and Punish*. Instead, the last two volumes discuss classical Greek and Roman practices of self-formation—practices in which sex is often less important than dietetics and marriage. "I had to choose: either stick to the plan I had set . . . or reorganize the whole study around the slow formation, in antiquity, of a hermeneutics of the self" (1984a, 6). Clearly, the questions that were most urgent in Foucault's thinking, as well as the historical periods in which he oriented his studies, had shifted—which we saw heralded even in the 1978 Collège de France course. This means that the final two volumes of *The History of Sexuality* pose certain hermeneutical challenges. They attempt to do justice to two different projects—the original and the new—which now have been superimposed, rendering both partial and incomplete. Rather than a study of sexual discourse in modernity or of practices of self-formation in antiquity, we get a study of sexual discourses in antiquity. This "overlapping segment" does not fairly represent either the original study of sexuality nor the later study of antiquity.

Foucault's introduction to *The Use of Pleasure* begins by explicitly acknowledging these lacunae. This introduction is of critical importance because it articulates an important theoretical reorientation that has emerged from his work in the intervening years—a reorientation with respect to both the constitution of the subject, individual, or self and the development of an ethics. Just as Foucault had remade the theoretical landscape when he began his explicit analysis of power in the mid-1970s, he does the same here. Arnold Davidson observed that Foucault's "conceptualization of ethics . . . is as potentially transformative for writing the history of ethics as, to take the strongest comparison I can think of, John Rawls's *A Theory of Justice* is, in its cultural context, for articulating the aims of political philosophy" (Davidson 1994, 115). We shall begin with a discussion of this new theoretical approach to ethics and then turn in the next sections to trace the development of Foucault's ethical thinking in the last decade of his life.

In this reconception, Foucault frames ethics as a kind of practice that presupposes (or requires as a condition for its possibility) both a critical attitude toward oneself and a certain kind of freedom. First, ethics must be understood not as being about "moral codes," nor even the evaluation of particular behaviors, but rather a practice of "self-fashioning." Thus, ethics is about practices of the self upon the self—practices that are thus orthogonal or eccentric relative to the power relations that are exercised upon the self. And so "ethics is a practice; ethos is a manner of being" (DE341.1, 377). As such, ethics is fundamentally a practice that demands a critical attitude toward oneself (as well as toward others, external powers, those that govern, etc.). Ethics is also a fundamentally a practice that presupposes a certain kind of freedom (a freedom to change, to resist, not being entirely determined by the grid of power relations in which one is situated—in part because one is situated in other types of relations as well). Elaborating these last two fundamental attributes of the practice of ethics constitute the final two trajectories that I will discuss.

In "Morality and Practice of the Self," the third chapter of the Introduction to *The Use of Pleasure*, Foucault begins, as with his retheorization of power, by couching his shift in perspective as a series of "methodological considerations" (1984aET, 25).

> A theoretical shift had also been required in order to analyze what is often described as the manifestations of "power." . . . It appeared that I now had to undertake a third shift, in order to analyze what is termed "the subject." It seemed appropriate to look for the forms and modalities of the relation to self by which the individual constitutes and recognizes himself *qua* subject. (1984aET, 6)

To identify these forms and modalities, the first things to note are the different senses—Foucault will delineate three, which collapse to two—of the term "morality." First, "morality" refers to a code, "a set of values and rules of action that are recommended to individuals through the intermediary of various prescriptive agencies" (1984aET, 25); second, the term "also refers to the real behavior of individuals in relation to the rules and values that are recommended to them" (1984aET, 25). These two senses can in fact be merged, since particular sorts of behaviors will be closely wed to the codes by which they are judged. Third and finally, "morality" can refer to ethical self-fashioning. "Another thing still is the manner in which one ought to form oneself as an ethical subject acting in reference to the prescriptive elements that make up the code" (1984aET, 26). This third sense (self-fashioning) is broader or deeper than the second sense (behavior)—it is a question that goes beyond mere activity and points to the creation of ethical subjectivity.

In these three definitions, Foucault notes, we can recognize two basic orientations toward moral problems and problematizations: one emphasizes the codes and behaviors, and from this view "subjectivation occurs basically in a quasi-juridical form" (1984aET, 29); another emphasizes "the forms of subjectivation and the practices of the self" (1984aET, 30).

This first orientation, comprising the first two elements (code and behavior), will be present, broadly speaking, in every morality. This is not to say that the relationship between code and behavior or even between different aspects of code will necessarily be straightforward or simple: it is often the case that "far from constituting a systematic ensemble, they form a complex interplay of elements that counterbalance and correct one another, and cancel each other out on certain points, thus providing for compromises or loopholes" (1984aET, 25). Examples of this interplay, and of the domination of this first orientation, can be readily recognized—the sixteenth-century formalization and codification of the practice of penitence following the Council of Trent and the subsequent development of minutely negotiated casuistry are perhaps paradigmatic; certain neo-Kantian or utilitarian approaches to morality may also share this basic orientation. Moreover, this first orientation uses the same kind of language as, and hence could be reduced to, an analysis in terms of power relations. For example, Foucault had noted in *Discipline and Punish* how the new disciplinary techniques of power were promulgated through "the formulation of explicit, general codes and unified rules of procedure" (1975ET, 7).

The second general orientation emphasizes the third definition, in which practice of the self on the self, ascesis, ethical self-fashioning, is the dominant theme. Foucault characterizes this orientation as "ethics oriented," and it may be useful thus to distinguish between ethics and morality. (This distinction, obviously, is not the same as the Habermasian distinction between ethics and morality.) Just as the code-oriented morality will provide some account of subjectivity (but subjectivity would be a secondary or derivative concern), adopting an ethical orientation does not entail that codes are unimportant. Rather, from this view, the codes will be secondary, and the question of how one produces one's subjectivity as an ethical subjectivity becomes the encompassing or framing context in which codes must be situated and assessed. It is clear that Foucault wants to adopt this second orientation in his approach to ethical and moral problems. This shift holds out the possibility that ethics conceived along the second orientation would not be reducible to power relations—though modern punitive methods had constructed or fashioned the "delinquent" as a correlate of certain kinds of power relations, this approach seeks to transcend particular arrangements of power. It is also important to note that a shift from a code-oriented morality to an ethics- or subjectivity-oriented morality marks a certain revolution in moral thinking and will require a rethinking of the demands of justification.

Foucault discovered examples (perhaps themselves paradigmatic) of this ethics orientation in the ancient Greek attitudes and practices with respect to what we would anachronistically call "sexuality." What Foucault termed a "male ethics"

> spoke to them concerning precisely those conducts in which they were called upon to exercise their rights, their power, their authority, and their liberty. . . . These themes of sexual austerity should be understood, not as an expression of, or commentary on, deep and essential prohibitions, but as the elaboration and stylization of an activity in the exercise of its power and the practice of its liberty. (1984aET, 23)

We can recognize a shift paralleling Foucault's retheorization of power here: as with power, the conducts are not the expression of "deep and essential" prohibitions. Further, as Foucault understands these practices, the power that one does exercise and the liberty that, given Foucault's analysis, that very power presupposes, are situated within elements of a larger framework of aesthetico-ethical activity and practice. And so the articulation and elaboration of these examples became the new task of his reconceived *History of Sexuality* series.

> It thus seemed to me that a whole recentering was called for. Instead of looking for basic interdictions that were hidden or manifested in the demands of sexual austerity, it was necessary to locate the areas of experience and the forms in which sexual behavior was problematized, becoming an object of concern, an element for reflection, and a material for stylization. (1984aET, 23–24)

Note how in this "recentering" Foucault is now interested in "sexuality" not as the correlate of and hinge between various micro and macro power relations (interdictions, codes, normalizations) but as an area of experience. This experience is an object of concern—that is, the object (the construct or correlate) of practices of caring; it is an element for reflection—that is, it is something to be critically assessed and evaluated; last, it is a material for stylization—that is, it can be taken up aesthetically, as part of one's self-fashioning according to an art of existence.

Foucault's emerging analysis of this ethical practice of self-fashioning is built around four distinct aspects of its "relationship to oneself" (DE326.4, 263)—and he articulates these four aspects in both *The Use of Pleasure* and a 1983 interview with Paul Rabinow and Bert Dreyfus, "On the Genealogy of Ethics" (DE326). These four aspects are ethical substance, a mode of subjectivation, the ethical work ("self-forming activity" or "asceticism"), and the telos toward which the work aims. "Ethical substance" is "the aspect or the part of myself or my behavior which is concerned with moral conduct" (DE326.4, 263). This framework is schematic and adaptable: these substances could be one's acts or one's intentions, thoughts, or desires, etc. The "mode of subjectivation" is "the way in which people are invited or incited to recognize their moral obligations" (DE326.4, 264), "the way in which the individual has to constitute this or that part of himself as the prime material of his moral conduct" (1984aET, 26). Here, too, a number of modes are possible. And the Stoic idea of an "aesthetics of existence" has been displaced by a Kantian "idea that we must do such and such things because we are rational beings—as members of the human community, we must do them" (DE326.4, 264). "Ethical work" is "the means by which we can change ourselves in order to become ethical subjects" (DE326.4, 265); it is the ascetic (in the broad sense) practice of self-fashioning. Finally, ethical subjects will have a "telos": "the kind of being to which we aspire when we behave in a moral way" (DE326.4, 265), for "an action is not only moral in itself, in its singularity; it is also moral in its circumstantial integration and by virtue of the place it occupies in a pattern of conduct" (1984aET, 27–28).

This four-part analysis of what constitutes ethical self-fashioning both emerged from and served to guide Foucault's historical research into ancient, Hellenistic, and early Christian practices. In the last two volumes of *The History of Sexuality*, he discusses four particular areas or domains in which the aphrodesia (or "pleasures") became problematized in these practices. These domains include one's body (tied to questions of health, life, and death), relations to the other sex (especially one's spouse and the familial and social institutions thus produced), relations to members of one's own sex (and questions about who were appropriate sexual partners), and one's relations to truth (and what spiritual conditions were necessary for wisdom) (1984aET, 23). So the final two volumes of *The History of Sexuality* are framed around a series of key questions:

> Why was it in those areas—apropos of the body, of the wife, of boys,
> and of truth—that the practice of pleasures became a matter for debate?
> . . . How did sexual behavior, insofar as it implied these different types
> of relations, come to be conceived as a domain of moral experience?
> (1984aET, 24)

I will not go into a detailed discussion of these domains nor how they illustrate the four aspects that organize Foucault's analysis. This brief outline serves to show, however, "that every morality, in the broad sense, comprises the two elements . . . : codes of behavior and forms of subjectivation; . . . [and that] they can never be entirely dissociated, though they may develop in relative independence from one another" (1984aET, 29), and that the latter was primary in these ancient cultures. In the pre-Christian practices, Foucault argues, "more important than the content of the law and its conditions of application was *the attitude* that caused one to respect them" (1984aET, 31, my italics). This notion of an attitude at the core of the practice of ethical self-fashioning is an important one that will allow Foucault to connect this analysis to his analysis of modern power relations.

Nevertheless, there are important limitations to Foucault's (and our) use of the ancient Greek practices. First of all, we cannot simply import these ancient practices as some sort of "solution" for our contemporary challenges: "you can't find the solution of a problem in the solution of another problem raised at another moment by other people" (DE326.4, 256). Second, even if we could, we shouldn't want to do so. For even though the ancient Greek practices reveal a reprioritization in which things we take for granted in modernity are explicitly rejected (and thus help us imagine ourselves differently), many of the ancient Greek values were themselves very troubling. It was a misogynistic culture that embraced slavery, among many other dissymmetries. Foucault puts his rejection of these values quite bluntly: "All that is quite disgusting!" (DE326.4, 258). So, even if the particular Greek practices are merely reference points, not "solutions," the general framework that they reveal is nevertheless not foreclosed to us—and in particular, it might give us resources to resist a certain kind of negative "subjectification" in terms of "desire" and "sexuality."

There is, to many philosophers' ears, a tension between Foucault's uses of the terms "ethical" and "aesthetic" to describe these practices: is "the ethical" merely "aesthetic"? Part of our resistance to this stems from a presupposition that ethical or moral norms or codes should be universal whereas the aesthetic seems "merely" preferential. But Foucault is quite clear that we cannot expect to find transcendental universals—all of our norms (even if we can justify their general acceptance) emerge from historically contingent circumstances and remain subject to reconsideration and alteration. Thus, for Foucault, the term "aesthetic" serves to remind us of the historically contingent and tentative character of our values and norms, our ethics. Indeed, Foucault made this point in the prefatory remarks that open his 1978 Collège de France course:

> However, in the theoretical domain, the imperative discourse that consists in saying "love this, hate that, this is good, that is bad, be for this, beware of that," seems to me, at present at any rate, to be no more than an aesthetic discourse that can only be based on choices of an aesthetic order. (CdF78ET, 3)

Interestingly, his caveat that it seems so "at present at any rate" holds out the possibility that some other basis could be found. I'll suggest that for Foucault, the fact of freedom can provide something like such a basis. In any case, this is the rationale for his bringing together of the ethical and the aesthetic. On the one hand, "ethics" need not be reduced to codes and normalization: "I don't think one can find any normalization in, for instance, the Stoic ethics . . . the principal aim, the principal target of this kind of ethics, was an aesthetic one" (DE326.4, 254). This claim that there was no normalization in the Stoics is frankly problematical; nevertheless, it illustrates the important shift in which the ethical/aesthetic is not reducible to normalizing techniques of power. On the other hand, this insight has implications for our contemporary situation, in which much of our self-understanding and subjectivity has been constituted through power relations: "From the idea that the self is not given to us [as an *a priori*], I think there is only one practical consequence: we have to create ourselves as a work of art" (DE326.4, 262). And we can only effect this self-creation or self-fashioning through a ethical practice: "No technique, no professional skill can be acquired without exercise; neither can one learn the art of living, the *tekhne tou biou* without an *askesis* which must be taken as a training of oneself by oneself" (DE326.4, 273). There are two important and related ideas here. First is the idea that one's life or *bios* can be taken "as a material for an aesthetic piece of art" (DE326.4, 260), but it is connected to another important insight: "that ethics can be a very strong structure of existence, without any relation with the juridical per se, with an authoritarian system, with a disciplinary structure" (DE326.4, 260). Foucault gives a concise definition of these "arts of existence" in *The Use of Pleasure*:

> What I mean by the phrase are those intentional and voluntary actions
> by which men not only set themselves rules of conduct, but also seek to

transform themselves, to change themselves in their singular being, and to make their life into an *oeuvre* that carries certain aesthetic values and meets certain stylistic criteria. (1984aET, 10–11)

Foucault then gives us a sense of the historical itinerary that he outlined in the 1978 Collège de France course, when he immediately adds that

These "arts of existence," these "techniques of the self," no doubt lost some of their importance and autonomy when they were assimilated into the exercise of pastoral power [*pouvoir pastoral*] in early Christianity, and later, into educative, medical, and psychological types of practices. (1984aET, 11; trans. mod.)

So a certain kind of self-fashioning, a certain kind of ethical practice, was transformed and displaced with the introduction and rise of pastoral power into Rome—the very root of the modern modes of disciplinary power and biopower. And thus, understanding this ancient ethical practice could help us grasp the possibilities for reimagining ourselves—constituting a source of resistance to the ways that modern power serves to construct our subjectivities. As Sandra Bartky incisively argues, "there is nothing in Foucault's account of the social construction of the subject that threatens the concept of agency or compels us to abandon, in principle, the idea of a subjectivity free enough to build a freer society" (Bartky 1995, 32).

This reconception of ethics as a practice also allows Foucault to redefine philosophy as philosophical activity. In his 1978 Collège de France course, he had defined philosophy (which, he added, was "what I am doing") as "the politics of truth" (CdF78ET, 3). Here, in *The Use of Pleasure*, he further specifies, in the form of a rhetorical question, that "philosophy today—philosophical activity, I mean— . . . [is] the critical work that thought brings to bear upon itself" (1984aET, 8–9). Thus, philosophy is "an 'ascesis,' an exercise of oneself in the activity of thought" (1984aET, 9). In a 1982 interview, Foucault notes that "this transformation of one's self by one's own knowledge is, I think, something rather close to the aesthetic experience" (DE336.3, 131). He adds in a 1984 interview that this gives us the means to "speak the truth": the truth is spoken by "free individuals who establish a certain consensus, and who find themselves within a certain network of practices of power and constraining institutions" (DE356.4, 297). This language, recalling Foucault's earlier analysis of power, reminds us that the philosophical activity of critique is not merely focused on oneself, however.

It is also oriented toward the power relations (practices and institutions) in which one is immersed—up to and including the contemporary macro forms of the state and biopower: "the role of philosophy is also to keep watch over the excessive power of political rationality" (DE306.4, 328).

This philosophical—ethical, political—project is inherently dangerous. Most of all, it recognizes that it works in a field devoid of certainties. It means that he (and we) must be willing "to work hard, to begin and begin again, to attempt and be mistaken, to go back and rework everything from top to bottom, and still find reason to hesitate from one step to the next— . . . in short, . . . to work in the midst of uncertainty and apprehension" (1984aET, 7). These uncertainties do not mean that the project is doomed to failure—on the contrary, Foucault explicitly denies that view[1]—but rather that it is an ongoing challenge, and we must always maintain a sense of our own limitations, frailties, and humility. We can give answers right now, but we may have to revise those answers in light of new evidence tomorrow. This also means that ethical prescriptions will always be tentative and contingent—as he put it in 1978, these imperatives will always be hypothetical, aesthetic, "tactical pointers" (CdF78ET, 3). And so he notes in a 1982 interview that:

> It is one of my targets to show people that a lot of things that are a part of their landscape—that people think are universal—are the result of some very precise historical changes. All my analyses are against the idea of universal necessities in human existence. They show the arbitrariness of institutions and show which space of freedom we can still enjoy and how many changes can still be made. (DE362.1, 11)

This "politics of truth" is, at its core, a pragmatic, fallibilist philosophy. "The object was to learn to what extent the effort to think one's own history can free thought from what it silently thinks, and so enable it to think differently" (1984aET, 9). We might add that this has been Foucault's object all along, and we can hear this effort to "free thought from what it silently thinks" even in the closing pages of the first volume of *The History of Sexuality*, eight years earlier.

"BODIES AND PLEASURES"

In a November 1976 interview, Foucault explained that "Sex is the hinge between anatomo-politics and bio-politics, it is at the intersection of disciplines and regulations" (DE297.1, 162). So if we want to resist these hinged mechanisms of power, if, in other words, we want to "enable [ourselves] to think differently" (1984aET, 9), we might want to start with sexuality. Indeed, this is what Foucault did, in the first of the four ethical trajectories that we shall trace. And though it begins from within the analyses of power that he has constructed—sexuality is, after all, the hinge where the micro and macro forms are conjoined—it also begins in an area that will lead Foucault toward his reconceptualization of ethics as a practice of self-fashioning.

This project comes into focus in the closing pages of *La volonté de savoir*:

> By creating the imaginary element that is "sex," the deployment of sexuality established one of its most essential internal operating principles: the desire for sex. . . . And it is this desirability of sex that attaches each one of us to the injunction to know it, to reveal its law and its power; it is this desirability that makes us think we are affirming the rights of our sex against all power, when in fact we are fastened to the deployment of sexuality . . . (1976ET, 156–157)

"Sex" and the desire for sex bind us to certain kinds of truth discourses (the "injunction to know it") through confessional practices (which are themselves, as Foucault will later show us, the legacy of earlier forms of pastoral power). "Sex" and the desire for sex "fasten" us to deployments of power, to what in *Discipline and Punish* he termed "mechanisms of 'incarceration'" (1975ET, 308), even as they give us a false consciousness of liberating ourselves. "Sex" and the desire for sex are thus the linchpins as well as the hinge of these power relations—how then could it be challenged and resisted? Foucault's answer comes in a famous passage:

> It is the agency of sex that we must break away from, if we aim— through a tactical reversal of the various mechanisms of sexuality—to counter the grips of power with the claims of bodies, pleasures, and knowledges, in their multiplicity and their possibility of resistance. The rallying point for the counterattack against the deployment of sexuality ought not to be sex-desire, but bodies and pleasures. (1976ET, 157)

There are several things to note in Foucault's phrasing here. First, what he gives us is explicitly a hypothetical imperative—we should do this only *if* we share a certain aim or goal of countering the grips of power. Next, these are, as he would note in 1978, only "tactical pointers"—a "tactical reversal," not necessarily a solution for all people or all time. Finally, we can recognize all four elements of ethical self-fashioning implicit in this characterization: we have an aim or telos, our bodies themselves constitute the ethical substance, our mode of subjection will be manifest in a resistance to sex-desire, and the development of bodies' pleasures will constitute the ethical work.

Robert Nye situates this vision explicitly in terms of Foucault's own homosexuality:

> He was not willing to engage in narrow or confrontational identity
> politics, which offended him both personally and philosophically. On
> the other hand, he had no desire to repudiate his own (homo)sexual self,
> and so he applied himself to the delicate task of reconfiguring a new
> kind of identity out of the wreckage of the one he had spent a consider-
> able part of his life trying to escape. The famous passages at the end of
> *La Volonté de Savoir* about "bodies and pleasures" were his first efforts to
> deal with this problem intellectually. (Nye 1996, 235)

Nye's reading of these passages is not incorrect—questions of reconstructing identities and embracing his own homosexuality are present in Foucault's evocation of "bodies and pleasures," and (as we shall see) Foucault will draw from his own experience of homosexual relationships in his exploration of ethics. But Nye's assessment does not appreciate the full depth of Foucault's concern with either bodies or pleasures: Foucault's ethical itinerary begins with bodies precisely because bodies are the locus or material upon which disciplinary power operates to construct subjectivities. For "deployments of power are directly connected to the body—to bodies, functions, physi-ological processes, sensations, and pleasures; far from the body having to be effaced, what is needed is to make it visible" (1976ET, 151–152). So looking to bodies themselves—and to their pleasures, something that might be (in some sense) prior to bodies' immersion within the particular power relations that condition them in ways we want to resist—give Foucault, at the very least, an opening, a possibility for a kind of practice or relation that would not be reducible to power.

But as David Halperin (a much stronger reader of Foucault than Nye) reminds us,

> The very possibility of pursuing such a body- and pleasure-centered
> strategy of resistance to the apparatus of sexuality disappears, of course,
> as soon as "bodies" and "pleasures" cease to be understood merely as

handy weapons against current technologies of normalization and attain instead to the status of transhistorical components of some natural phenomenon or material substrate underlying "the history of sexuality" itself. (Halperin 1998, 95)

Halperin's worry is warranted because Foucault's evocation of "bodies and pleasures" here is immediately followed by what could well be characterized as a "utopian vision" (indeed, one that recalls the closing lines of *The Order of Things*):

> Perhaps one day people will wonder at this. . . . Moreover, we need to consider the possibility that one day, perhaps, in a different economy of bodies and pleasures, people will no longer quite understand how the ruses of sexuality, and the power that sustains its organization, were able to subject us to that austere monarchy of sex, so that we became dedicated to the endless task of forcing its secret, of exacting the truest of confessions from a shadow. (1976ET, 157, 159)

This vision is utopian in part because Foucault will refuse to prescribe how this "different economy" is to be brought about. (He explains in a 1981 interview that "the idea of a program of proposals is dangerous. As soon as a program is presented, it becomes a law, and there's a prohibition against inventing" [DE293.3, 139].) But, it is also utopian in that it could be read as reifying bodies and pleasures, in contrast to sex, in precisely the ways Halperin warns against. However, even if we constantly recall that even these "bodies and pleasures" are themselves contingent constructs, they can still function as the site and material for resistance, invention, and transformation. Foucault explains in a 1975 interview that "once power produces this [contingent] effect [of bodies and pleasures], there inevitably emerge the responding claims and affirmations, those of one's own body against power, of health against the economic system, of pleasure against the moral norms of sexuality, marriage, decency" (DE157.1, 56).

Indeed, the roots of "bodies and pleasures"—contingent constructs that they are—nevertheless go quite deep as a possible source and route forward for resistance to power. Foucault had, for example, highlighted pleasure's complicated relationship to power at least as early as the 1973–1974 Collège de France course. There are, in fact, many kinds of pleasure that go far beyond sex. In developing his treatments for "the mad," the psychiatrist François Leuret had "identified something in his patient that had three forms: the pleasure of the asylum, the pleasure of being ill, and the pleasure of having symptoms" (CdF74ET, 162). Pleasure is something that power (such as the psychiatrist's attempt to effect a cure of madness) must grapple with; pleasure can also become a source of resistance to power: "the cure must not only work at the level of reality, but also at the level of pleasure, and not only at the level of the pleasure the patient takes in his madness, but at the level of the pleasure the patient takes in his own treatment" (CdF74ET, 163).

What, then, is the significance of Foucault's quasi-utopian evocation of "bodies and pleasures"? Though he says very little (and, for him, necessarily little) about how to go forward, "bodies and pleasures" are posited as the site where such a way forward could begin, a locus for resistance, for what he will later describe (and we have discussed in the preceding section) as an ethical practice. Thus, "bodies and pleasures" represent Foucault's first ethical trajectory, as he attempts to explore what kind of an ethics could emerge in the face of modern power. As Foucault elaborates in a 1977 interview, "the monarchy of sex," as he characterized it both in this interview and *La volonté de savoir*, can be resisted by "inventing other forms of pleasures, of relationships, coexistences, attachments, loves, intensities" (DE200.3, 116).[2] And in a 1978 interview, Foucault explicitly identified homosexuality (as an activity and a community) as a means to develop this ethical trajectory: "Today, homosexuality can become intelligible to itself by thinking of itself simply as a certain relationship between bodies and pleasures" (BdS-B46, 34). He continues that "For several years now, [in homosexuals' practices] we have been witnessing a kind of enlargement of the economy of pleasure" (BdS-B46, 35). Foucault explored these possibilities for invention: "You find emerging in places like San Francisco and New York what might be called laboratories of sexual experimentation" (DE317.4, 151). Foucault will take on this ethical work of inventing pleasures, relationships, intensities—in ways that yield theoretical fruit—in a practice that at least appears to be all about sex and desire: sadomasochism (S&M).[3]

(Though Foucault had begun his initial articulations of biopower in *La volonté de savoir*, at that point he still understood modern power as essentially disciplinary. So it is not at all surprising that he would look for resistance to discipline and the possibility of an ethics that cannot be reduced to power relations in micropractices. And given the pattern of Foucault's "Hobbesian hypothesis," in which he uses modus tollens to justify positing something positive of which he would otherwise have to be doubtful, it is not at all surprising that Foucault would begin in a microrelation that appears to be the sexualization of power.[4])

Foucault's exploration of S&M accomplishes three things. It will explore a relationship that appears to be thoroughly defined in terms of power relations and show that in fact those power relations are subordinate to other relations of pleasure. It will demonstrate that bodies' pleasures are *not* all about sex. So S&M shows us that bodies and pleasures take us beyond the scope of sex-desire and can even serve as a(n ethical) frame for relations of power. And finally, in exploring what those relations of pleasure demand, S&M will move Foucault's ethical itinerary forward, from its initial starting point in pleasure relations to the broader category of caring relations.

First, Foucault's discussion of sadomasochistic practices suggests that there is a relation more important than power in these practices: pleasure. Foucault explicitly notes that power plays an important role in practices of S&M—for most people uninitiated in these practices, in fact, S&M seems to revolve around the exercise of power—but Foucault explains that power relations are not the most important element in these practices. Rather, pleasure, distinct from power, is the most important element. Though S&M is a practice that very explicitly employs power relations—prima facie, in inflicting pain or asserting discipline, the "top" or "master" exercises power upon and against the "bottom" or "slave"—the exercise of power plays a situated role within these practices. "One can say that S&M is the eroticization of power. . . . What strikes me with regard to S&M is how it differs from social power" (DE358.2, 169). Rather, the organizing relations in S&M are relations of pleasure. "The practice of S&M is the creation of pleasure, and there is an identity with that creation. . . . S&M is the *use* of a strategic relationship as a source of pleasure (physical pleasure)" (DE358.2, 169–170).

Power relations are present in the practice of S&M but are situated within the practice as a means for the creation of physical pleasure. But S&M is *identified with* the creation of this pleasure. The important relation in the practice of S&M is the creation of pleasure. Power relations are only an aspect of these relations. Further, power relations do not delineate the possibilities for these relations of pleasure because the power relations themselves are altered in the course of the practice. "Sometimes the scene begins with the master and slave, and at the end the slave has become the master. Or, even when the roles are stabilized, you know very well that it is always a game" (DE358.2, 169). The power relations and their transformations are subordinate to the relations of pleasure creation, and it is these pleasure-creating relations that are of most importance in the analysis of practices of S&M.

In Foucault's analysis of S&M, then, an analysis of the power relations involved in the practice is insufficient for an understanding of the practice. But could these relations of pleasure creation be reducible to power relations? Foucault's discussions of the relationship between pleasure and power in *La volonté de savoir* indicate that it is not: there he discusses the family as "a network of pleasures and powers linked together at multiple points and according to transformable relationships" (1976ET, 46). This suggests not a reduction of pleasure relations to power relations but rather that two distinct, mutually irreducible kinds of relations, both immanent in the social relations of the family, interact in various ways dependent upon the contexts in which they arise. In a context of S&M, the relations of pleasure are the more important organizing relations, and power relations are subordinated to them.

Foucault also notes that "what interests the practitioners of S&M is that the relationship is at the same time regulated and open" (DE317.4, 151). This openness is interesting—Foucault explains that since S&M is a game, either the master or the slave could "lose" the game if he or she "is unable to respond to the [partner's] needs and trials" (DE317.4, 152). He continues that

> This mixture of rules and openness has the effect of intensifying sexual relations by introducing a perpetual novelty, a perpetual tension and a perpetual uncertainty, which the simple consummation of the act lacks. The idea is also to make use of every part of the body as a sexual instrument. (DE317.4, 152)

As he speaks of making "every part of the body" into a sexual instrument, Foucault means that every part of the body can be explored as a source of pleasure in S&M—that pleasure is not restricted to the genitalia. Homosexual practices in general and S&M in particular provide opportunities "for inventing oneself, for making one's body a locus for the production of extraordinarily polymorphous pleasures, and at the same time moving away from emphasis upon the sex organ and particularly the male sex organ" (BdS-B46, 34). "By taking the pleasure of sexual relations away from the area of sexual norms and its categories, and in so doing making the pleasure the crystallizing point of a new culture—I think that's an interesting approach" (DE313.2, 160). Though he is still speaking in terms of sex, in fact, S&M

moves pleasure beyond sex toward something that Foucault characterizes as "mythical relations" (DE317.4, 151) since it involves the assumption of identities and roles. And so "sexuality is something that we ourselves create—it is our own creation, and much more than the discovery of a secret side of our desire" (DE358.2, 163). S&M is better understood as

> a creative enterprise, which has as one of its main features what I call the desexualization of pleasure. The idea that bodily pleasure should always come from sexual pleasure as the root of *all* our possible pleasure—I think *that's* something quite wrong. (DE358.2, 165)[5]

Bodies and their pleasures cannot be reduced to sex, just as pleasure cannot be reduced to power—all of this emerges from Foucault's experiments with S&M. Sex is just one aspect of pleasure (indeed, he catalogued other pleasures in his 1973 discussion of Leuret's treatment of "the mad"), and the exploration of pleasure constitutes "a possibility for creative life" (DE358.2, 163). Ladelle McWhorter nicely summarizes Foucault's argument:

> Pleasure figures prominently, then, in Foucault's understanding of power as normalization, but it also figures prominently in his excursions into discourses and practices having to do with shaping an ethos, with leading a good or beautiful life. . . . Pleasure, like power, is creative. . . . Foucault advocates the use of pleasure and the expansion of our capacities for pleasure as a means of resisting sexual normalization and creating different lives for ourselves. (McWhorter 1999, 177)

McWhorter brings out both sides of this first trajectory. On the one hand, as she notes, pleasure functions as a means of *resisting* sexual normalization and the power relations and deployments of sexuality that are involved in that normalization. On the other hand, bodies and pleasures also open up new possibilities for the creation of "a good or beautiful life," "an ethos." As Foucault notes:

> Still, I think we have to go a step further. I think that one of the factors of this stabilization will be the creation of new forms of life, relationships, friendships in society, art, culture, and so on through our sexual, ethical, and political choices. (DE358.2, 164)

This "step further"—from bodily pleasures to relationships, friendship, and society—brings us to Foucault's second ethical trajectory.

FRIENDSHIP AS A PRACTICE OF CARE

In the game of S&M, both partners must be attentive to the other's pleasure, because the other's pleasure is necessarily a constitutive element of their own pleasure. As Leo Bersani characterizes this fact, "the practice of S/M depends on a mutual respect generally absent from the relations between the powerful and the weak, underprivileged, or enslaved in society" (Bersani 1995, 87). Looked at from the outside, this may seem surprising; nevertheless, this notion of mutual respect is at the heart of S&M—without it, none of S&M's possibilities for pleasure or creation can be realized. And this insight led Foucault to a new problem and a new question, which he articulated in the 1983 interview "On the Genealogy of Ethics":

> What I want to ask is: Are we able to have an ethics of acts and their pleasures which would be able to take into account the pleasure of the other? Is the pleasure of the other something that can be integrated in our pleasure, without reference either to law, to marriage, to I don't know what? (DE326.4, 258)

These questions raise several issues. First, and importantly, Foucault explicitly links pleasures with ethics—one's pleasures ought to take into account the other's pleasures. (The second question here highlights Foucault's desire to create such an ethics without recourse to laws or institutions.) But implicit in this orientation—taking an other's pleasure into account *as part of* one's own pleasures—are notions of responsiveness, reciprocity, and mutual recognition. (Practices of S&M, Foucault's analysis suggests, presuppose this kind of responsiveness and recognition, for neither role—master or slave—can achieve its own pleasure without taking the other's into account. They are, we might say, constitutive values of the practice.) These notions emerging out of Foucault's engagement with S&M—these values of responsiveness, reciprocity, and recognition—will direct Foucault to another kind of relationship that homosexual men may be in a privileged position to explore and develop: friendship. And friendship will, in its turn, serve as a bridge from pleasures (the starting point of this ethical itinerary) to a broader conception of caring—practices of *epimeleia heautou*, "care of the self," which in ancient cultures were understood as a prolegomena to caring for and governing others, but also a contemporary development of caring practices within feminist ethics.

The connection between S&M and friendship is not haphazard. For Foucault, homosexuals, who have been explicitly excluded from the normalization of institutions like courtship and marriage, are thereby freed to explore a variety of alternative kinds of relationships. In an interview published in 1981, "Friendship as a Way of Life" (DE293), Foucault notes:

> Another thing to distrust is the tendency to relate the question of homosexuality to the problem of "Who am I?" and "What is the secret of my desire?" Perhaps it would be better to ask oneself, "What relations, through homosexuality, can be established, invented multiplied, and modulated?" The problem is not to discover in oneself the truth of one's sex, but, rather, to use one's sexuality henceforth to arrive at a multiplicity of relationships. (DE293.3, 135)

This characterization of the value of homosexuality—that it is a means through which one can invent oneself and one's relationships—closely mirrors Foucault's later characterization of "the dandy" in "What Is Enlightenment?" (DE339):

> The dandy . . . makes of his body, his behavior, his feelings and passions, his very existence, a work of art. Modern man, for Baudelaire, is not the man who goes off to discover himself, his secrets and his hidden truth; he is the man who tries to invent himself. (DE339.2, 312)

"The development toward which the problem of homosexuality tends is the one of friendship," which Foucault defines as "the sum of everything through which they can give each other pleasure" (DE293.3, 136). Homosexual men, excluded from traditional rituals and institutions of courtship and marriage (and their accompanying normalization), have no codes to guide or determine how they will relate to each other. On the contrary, "they have to invent, from A to Z, a relationship that is still formless, which is friendship" (DE293.3, 136). Foucault could just as well have said "they get to invent" as "they have to invent," for this exclusion also produces a freedom for creation. What is threatening about homosexuality for "normal" society, Foucault suggests, is not that men have sex with each other. It is rather that they would walk down the street hand in hand. "To imagine a sexual act that doesn't conform to law or nature is not what disturbs people. But that individuals are beginning to love one another—there's the problem" (DE293.3, 136–137). Moreover, as Marilyn Friedman notes: "No consanguineous or legal connections establish or maintain ties of friendship" (Friedman 1989, 286), so these relations of friendship are external to the institutions of law. This kind of love, of creation of oneself and one's relationships, can be a potent source of resistance to power, for it brings with it

> everything that can be troubling in affection, tenderness, friendship, fidelity, camaraderie, and companionship, things that our rather sanitized society can't allow a place for without fearing the formation of new alliances and the tying together of unforeseen lines of force. (DE293.3, 136)

Indeed, Foucault hypothesizes, the two issues are historically conjoined. "The disappearance of friendship as a social relation [in the eighteenth century] and the declaration of homosexuality as a social/political/medical problem are the same process" (DE358.2, 171). Thus, Foucault's exploration of friendship continues along two dimensions: a contemporary one, in which the creative possibilities of homosexual friendships are explored and developed, and a historical one, in which Foucault will investigate the much richer institutional framework for friendship in ancient Greece and Hellenistic Rome.

Richard White notes that "the ideal of friendship had a privileged place in the ancient world" (White 1999, 19), in an essay that highlights some of the key differences between ancient and modern conceptions of friendship and identifies some of the essential characteristics that constitute an "ethical" friendship. White notes two complementary dangers that confront any attempt to define friendship. On the one hand, "we must avoid simply legislating the nature of friendship in the absence of any empirical support" (White 1999, 21). On the other hand, however, "the discussion of friendship cannot be merely empirical or 'value-free.' The account of friendship that emerges . . . must be critical and self-questioning" (White 1999, 22). We can note that Foucault's account circumnavigates between both of these dangers. He was able to draw on rich (if anecdotal) empirical support for his conclusions from his experience of friendship in the homosexual community, and he certainly was not interested in legislating particular forms but rather in the creation of new possibilities for friendship. And as we shall see, the values of critical self-questioning are at the heart of Foucault's ethics as well as of his understanding of friendship.

White identifies three key differences that distinguish modern from ancient conceptions of friendship. First, friendship has declined or disappeared as an ideal in modernity, replaced by romantic love. Foucault notes how romantic or "courtly love" is itself a kind of "strategic relation in order to obtain sex" (DE358.2, 170), and, by contrast, gay men's relationships displace this game—strategic games emerge "inside sex" in the case of S&M, but more generally questions of what affection one partner will have for another often only arises after the consummation of sexual acts. "Now, when sexual encounters become extremely easy and numerous, as is the case with homosexuality nowadays, complications are only introduced after the fact" (DE317.4, 151). Thus, Foucault suggests, it is possible for friendship to re-emerge as an ideal in a homosexual practice that displaces the rituals and strategies of courtly love.

White's second key difference between modern and ancient friendship is precisely its "essentially moral aspect" in the ancient tradition, for "from a contemporary perspective friendship is not obviously about virtue in the first instance" (White 1999, 20). Foucault's renewed interest in friendship, however—and his interests in investigating ancient conceptions as well as contemporary practices of friendship—is as an ethical practice. Our friendships, he suggests, are practices that contribute to our self-fashioning; what is more, friendship, like S&M, carries within it certain substantive ethical commitments—such as a "concern for the pleasures of the other" rooted in a responsiveness, reciprocity, and recognition of the other.

The third distinguishing mark between ancient and modern accounts of friendship, White argues, is that the ancient account "is a very limited and ideologically burdened account" bound up with other ancient practices and norms that would no longer be acceptable (20). Here, too, I think Foucault is in agreement with White. This is why Foucault insists that many of the ancient Greek values (in particular, nonreciprocity) were "quite disgusting!" and that those ancient practices cannot be a "solution" for contemporary problems (DE326.4, 256–258). Nevertheless, White finds Aristotle's account of friendship to be worth exploring—Books VIII and IX of the *Nicomachean Ethics* are, after all, still the canonical discussion of friendship. A key problem emerges from his reading of Aristotle:

> The question that emerges from all this is whether friendship really is based upon an absolute concern for my friend as an unconditional end [an end-in-itself], or whether friendship is, on the contrary, just another (albeit higher) manifestation of self-concern that only accepts the friend in a conditional sense. (White 1999, 25)

(On White's reading, Aristotle seems to argue for the latter position.) This tension within friendship is an important element for Foucault's discussion, for it brings to light a dialectical balance between concern for one's self and concern for the other—precisely the kind of concern that Foucault's study of S&M highlighted. And as Foucault examines and appropriates the ancient concepts of *epimeleia heautou* ("care for oneself"), it will be interwoven with concern for the other. Concern for oneself is not in contradiction with concern for others. White concludes that

> What is most basic here is that friendship involves caring about the well-being of another person and cherishing this [caring] as an end in itself. This involves a more or less profound *knowledge* of who each is and an awareness of what each seeks and values, as well as a willingness to reflect upon oneself and to overcome any inner obstacles. (28)

We can recognize several key Foucauldian elements in this summary. First, the connection of these practices of caring with knowledge, both of oneself and the other and what we value, brings this into a framework that can fit within Foucault's analysis of power. Second, friendship as caring about another entails a commitment to critical self-reflection and a willingness to refashion oneself—central elements of Foucault's understanding of ethics as a practice of self-fashioning.

White is thus able to define friendship as "a relationship that is grounded in recognition" (29) and to identify four essential features—implicit ethical commitments—of friendship. They are equality, reciprocity, solidarity, and alterity. The last is perhaps most surprising—we must recognize that our friend is different from ourselves, as part of that friendship. "These four conditions," White concludes, "must be regarded as the essential conditions for recognition which must therefore be present in order for friendship to exist" (30). He adds that "the most intimate knowledge and involvement with another that is offered by friendship is more likely to provoke a deeper level of self-awareness and self-esteem; hence, it is productive of autonomy itself" (33). Thus, White's analysis nicely articulates the ethical substance within Foucault's discussion of friendship—we can see how this rich account of friendship could emerge in marginalized homosexual communities and how it would become a source for autonomy, for the construction of subjectivity not entirely conditioned by the normalizing power relations that Foucault wants to resist. Correspondingly, gay communities would be optimal laboratories for the development of friendship, since (as both White and Foucault note and has been well documented elsewhere) heterosexual men often have very few genuine friendships (cf. White 1999, 32n17). These four key ethical values, as well as the constitutive tension between caring for oneself and caring for others, are important elements of Foucault's ethical trajectory.

Relations of friendship for Foucault, then, are framed in terms of reciprocity and concern for the other. We will return to the theme of reciprocity shortly, but first I would like to examine more carefully the notion of concern for the other. This moral commitment has been theorized in feminist ethics of care, the foundational works of which are Nel Noddings's *Caring* (1984) and Carol Gilligan's *In a Different Voice* (1983), which were published at the same time that Foucault's own work was shifting to questions of care of oneself and others. Just as Foucault has argued that homosexuals may have a privileged access to relations of friendship precisely because of their exclusion from heterosexual institutions and norms of courtship, Noddings and Gilligan have argued that women may have had a privileged access to the moral orientation of caring because of their exclusion from the institutions and norms of what they characterize as an ethic of justice. Indeed, these feminists' articulation of the principles of an ethics of care are consistent with, and can be integrated into, Foucault's larger critical theory of society.

An ethics of care, Noddings notes, occurs between at least two parties, the one caring and the cared for. As such, the ethics of care takes "*relation* as ontologically basic" (Noddings 1984, 4), paralleling, we can add, Foucault's reframed understanding of power as, in essence, a relation rather than a thing. She continues that "the ethic to be developed is one of reciprocity" and that in it the "focus of our attention will be upon how to meet the other morally" (4). We can hear this focus in the question Foucault asked: "Are we able to have an ethics of acts and their pleasures which would be able to take into account the pleasure of the other?" (DE326.4, 258). Joan Tronto, whose 1993 book *Moral Boundaries* moved the discussion forward, specifies four "elements of care"—caring about, taking care of, care giving, and care receiving—to each of which corresponds an ethical commitment: "attentiveness, responsibility, competence, and responsiveness" (Tronto 1993, 127). She thus describes "care as a practice" that "requires a deep and thoughtful knowledge of the situation, and of all of the actors' situations, needs and competencies" (136). This is how Foucault will describe *epimeleia heautou*, "which means 'working on' or 'being concerned with' something . . . ; it describes a sort of work, an activity; it implies attention, knowledge, technique" (DE326.4, 269). For

Noddings, the ethics of care will reject "principles and rules as the major guide to ethical behavior" as well as "the notion of universalizability" (Noddings 1984, 5). This parallels Foucault's reframing of ethics as primarily a practice of self-fashioning—not in the first instance concerned with codes, rules, or universals. And he finds an example of this in the ancient care of the self: "In antiquity, this work on the self with its attendant austerity is not imposed on the individual by means of civil law or religious obligation, but is a choice about existence made by the individual" (DE326.4, 271).

Of course, there is an important divergence between these two accounts of an ethics of care: the feminists' account has emphasized caring for *others* while the ancient practices that Foucault explores are explicitly cases of caring for *oneself*. These are not, however, diametrically opposed orientations. Indeed, as Gilligan articulates an arc of moral development and maturity from within women's ethical language, what she discovers is that a fully developed ethic of care demands both care for others *and* care for oneself. A simple illustration of this fact would be a woman who is so devoted to caring for others that she neglects to care for herself: over time, this neglect will render her ill, exhausted, or otherwise unable to give proper care to others. Gilligan summarizes that "responsibility now includes both self and other, viewed as different but connected, rather than as separate and opposed" (Gilligan 1983, 147). This brings us back to what Richard White described as a constitutive tension within friendship, between concern for the other as an end in itself and concern for the other as an especially noble manifestation of concern for oneself. Clearly, there is a delicate balancing act that has to be maintained between caring for oneself and caring for others—they are, however, not opposed but intertwined and mutually dependent practices: we cannot care for others without caring for ourselves, and vice versa.

Tronto maintained that "to take moral arguments more seriously . . . we have to understand them in a *political* context" (Tronto 1993, 3). And discussion of care ethics within feminism has steadily moved from personal contexts toward larger social, political, and even international contexts—even Noddings has moved in this direction (cf., for example, Noddings 2002). For Tronto, this means "that we need to take seriously the political context, and the inherent power relationships, within moral theories and situations" (Tronto 1993, 5). Thus within feminism, care ethics has had to begin to grapple with the issues of its integration within myriad institutions and power relations—precisely the direction that a Foucauldian would anticipate and a project for which the Foucauldian framework of ethics within power can be a great resource. To be sure, this movement toward direct engagement with the political has shown that an ethics of care is not a simple panacea for all problems. Indeed its value and its dangers are still a subject of considerable debate (cf. Narayan 1995 and Beasley and Bacchi 2005, for just two examples). Tronto poses one of the questions at the heart of these debates:

> What would it mean in late twentieth century American society [or, we could amend this, in twenty-first century global societies] to take seriously, as part of our definition of a good society, that values of caring—attentiveness, responsibility, nurturance, compassion, meetings others' needs—traditionally associated with women and traditionally excluded from public consideration? (Tronto 1993, 2–3)

Her answer is that it "requires a radical transformation in the way we conceive of the nature and boundaries of morality, and an equally radical rethinking of structures of power and privilege in this society" (3). This radical reconception is precisely what Foucault has been trying to effect—and he has given us a framework for both sides of this task in his retheorizations of "structures of power" (and subjectivity) as fundamentally relational and of "the nature and boundaries of morality" and ethics as a practice.[6]

This is why Foucault's "interest in friendship has become very important" (DE293.3, 137). For gay men, Foucault observes, "one doesn't enter a relationship simply in order to be able to consummate it sexually, which happens very easily" (DE293.3, 137). Rather, these relationships, born on the other side of the threshold of sex, are an opportunity to develop friendships that are undefined by larger (and heterosexual) cultural institutions and norms. This leads Foucault to ask: "Is it possible to create a homosexual mode of life?" (DE293.3, 137). He continues:

> A way of life can be shared among individuals of different age, status, and social activity. It can yield intense relations not resembling those that are institutionalized. It seems to me that a way of life can yield a culture and an ethics. To be "gay," I think, is . . . to try to define and develop a way of life. (DE293.3, 138)

A way of life can lead to an ethics—through a practice of ascesis: "Yet it's up to us to advance into a homosexual ascesis that would make us work on ourselves and invent—I do not say discover—a manner of being that is still improbable" (DE293.3, 137). Though this new ethics must be invented, not discovered, Foucault did find useful (if not unproblematic) examples of ascetic ethical practice that were not conditioned by modern forms of normalizing power in the ancients' forms of *epimeleia heautou*, or care of the self.

The practice of taking care of oneself "does not mean simply being interested in oneself, nor does it mean having a certain tendency to self-attachment of self-fascination" (DE326.4, 269)—which again underscores the connection between caring for oneself and caring for others. Indeed, this term was used in a number of political or power-laden contexts: agricultural management, doctors' care of patients, and a monarch's responsibility to his or her citizens. In the adoption of certain ascetic themes, ancient practitioners of *epimeleia heautou* "acted so as to give to their life certain values. . . . It was a question of making one's life into an object for a sort of knowledge, for a *tekhne*—for art" (DE326.4, 271).

The ancient practice of caring for oneself, at least in authors like Seneca, Foucault notes, "can be, if not a care for others, at least a care of the self which will be beneficial to others" (DE356.4, 289). Foucault notes in an 1984 interview that despite the limitation and problems inherent in the ancient practice of *epimeleia heautou*—and despite the fact that it cannot be a "solution" but merely an alternative perspective that may help us produce something new: "I would very much like to come back to more contemporary questions to try to see what can be made of all this in the context of the current political problematic" (DE356.4, 294). One of the ways that it could be particularly useful is that this care of the self serves to create limitations upon power:

> In fact, it is a way of limiting and controlling power. . . . In the abuse
> of power, one exceeds the legitimate exercise of one's power and im-
> poses one's fantasies, appetites, and desires on others . . . such a man is
> the slave of his appetites. And the good ruler is precisely the one who
> exercises his power as it ought to be exercised, that is, simultaneously
> exercising his power over himself. And it is the power over oneself that
> thus regulates one's power over others. . . . But if you take proper care
> of yourself . . . you cannot abuse your power over others. (DE356.4, 288)

Thus, in this ancient schema, "care for oneself is ethically prior [to care for others] in that the relationship to oneself is ontologically prior" (DE 356.4, 287).[7] This ancient practice thus illustrates one side of the woman's dialectic that Gilligan had described, that caring for oneself is a prerequisite for caring well for others. It also marks a clear line by which caring for oneself and for others is directly associated with the good exercise of political power.

"Care of the self enables one to occupy his rightful position in the city, the community, or interpersonal relationships, whether as a magistrate or a friend" (DE356.4, 287)—this care of the self is important for both friendship and governing well. Foucault adds here that "the man who cares about others . . . is the particular position of the philosopher" (DE356.4, 287). This suggests another connection with the present, for as he put it in the 1979 Tanner Lectures (and again, verbatim, in 1982), "since Kant . . . the role of philosophy has also been to keep watch over the excessive powers of political rationality" (DE291.4, 299 = DE306.4, 328).

And so, in our contemporary context, Foucault argues, a new variation of this ascesis, this concern for the self, can contribute to the kind of "radical rethinking of structures of power" that Tronto advocated. As such, a contemporary concern for the self will be situated within relationships such as friendship, within newly constructed "cultural forms" (DE313.2, 157): "Because it seems to me that the 'we' must not be previous to the question; it can only be the result—and the necessarily temporary result—of the question as it is posed in the new terms in which one formulates it" (DE342.2, 114–115). Our "we"s, our identities, are themselves in part a function of the questions that we pose, and they, too, are transformable. Thomas Brennan, a gay Jesuit, acutely observes in his own life how the recognition and the integration of different "we"s within oneself (oneself as gay man, oneself as celibate priest, etc.) is part of a practice of freedom—freedom for oneself and for others: "Only by recognizing this ongoing play of identities—and the need to negotiate among them—can we then experience freedom ourselves and empower others to take on the same work" (Brennan 2006, 184).

Tom Roach recognizes the connections for Foucault between ancient practices of care for oneself and contemporary homosexual friendship: "friendship becomes not merely a relation but a *practice*: part of a regimen of self-care through which one can attain an immanent salvation" (Roach 2012, 34). And this practice of friendship also brings out the critical—politically critical— elements of a Foucauldian ethic. This practice, and the communities that are built through the practice of friendship, were put to the test in the face of AIDS. In the preface to the French edition of his *Saint Foucault*, David Halperin observes that a "Foucauldian political model could be seen in action at each ACT-UP meeting that I attended, where those who were normally objects of expert's discourse—the homosexuals, the seropositive, PWAs—reversed the power/knowledge *dispositif* and gave themselves the means to powerfully resist the authorized discourses of doctors and politicians" (Halperin

2000, 16; cited and translated by Roach 2012, 82). Andrew Sullivan, an HIV-positive gay man who survived the AIDS crisis (and who brings a quite different political perspective than Halperin), concurs about the central importance of friendship and the impact of AIDS on the gay community:

> The deepest legacy of the plague years is friendship. The duties demanded in a plague, it turned out, were the duties of friends. . . . In this sense, gay men were perhaps oddly well prepared for the trauma, socially primed more than many others to face the communal demands of plague. Denied a recognized family, often estranged from their natural one, they had learned in the few decades of their free existence that friendship was the nourishment that would enable them to survive and flourish. (Sullivan 1998, 175)

Sullivan's impressions—based upon his own first-hand experience of the ongoing crisis and surviving as HIV-positive—are confirmed in Randy Shilts's history of the early phases of the AIDS epidemic, *And the Band Played On.* (Shilts's history ends before the establishment of ACT-UP.) Shilts reports that Jim Foster, a major figure in San Francisco gay politics who had founded the Alice B. Toklas Memorial Democratic Club in 1972,

> certainly had not helped build a gay community so that his generation would spend its middle age in death vigils. Yet, through the ordeal, Foster had seen the incredible courage of people like Larry [Ludwig, his lover of twelve years, who died of AIDS on January 29, 1985], and he had experienced the compassion with which gay men were helping each other through this collective trauma. Foster sensed that there was a new community emerging from the AIDS tragedy. It was not the community of politicians or radicals talking about bathhouses, but of people who had learned to take responsibility for themselves and for each other.
>
> This is what a community really is, Foster thought. And ultimately, that is what he had been fighting for in all those years of gay politicking: the opportunity for gay people to enjoy their own community. Now, against this backdrop, that community was being forged. (Shilts 1988/2007, 523–524)

Echoing Foucault's understanding of homosexuality as a development toward friendship (DE293.3, 136), Sullivan argues throughout his reflections that "the trajectory of a homosexual life often places, in a way unique to itself, a focus on friendship that many heterosexuals, to their great loss, never quite attain" (Sullivan 1998, 230). He continues that "What gay culture really is, before it is anything else, before it is a culture of desire or a culture of subversion, or a culture of pain, is a culture of friendship" (Sullivan 1998, 231). We can recognize these three alternatives to friendship in Foucault's own analyses, too: his originally conceived *History of Sexuality* project was designed as a critique of the "culture of desire," his work on power and resistance is an exploration that goes well beyond mere "subversion," and his own analysis of the interior dynamics of sadomasochism show that it is not best framed as a culture of pain.

The friendship at the heart of the gay community, for Sullivan, embodies the four ethical commitments that White had identified—equality, reciprocity, solidarity, and alterity. He and his friends discovered "a new kind of solidarity—not one of painful necessity, but of something far more elusive. Hope, perhaps? Or merely the shared memory of hopelessness?" (Sullivan 1998, 63). And central to the community created through homosexual friendship was responsibility:

> But with AIDS, responsibility became a central, involuntary feature
> of homosexual life. Without it, lovers would die alone, or without
> proper care. Without it, friends would contract a fatal disease because
> of lack of education. Without it, nothing would be done to stem the
> epidemic's wrath. In some ways, even the seemingly irresponsible
> outrages of ACT-UP were the ultimate act of responsibility. They come
> from a conviction that someone had to lead, to connect the ghetto to
> the center of the country, because it was only by such a connection that
> the ghetto could be saved. (Sullivan 1998, 65)

Sullivan recognizes that this constitutes a kind of "new politics," an inversion of stereotypical expectations:

> Before AIDS, gay life—rightly or wrongly—was identified with free-
> dom *from* responsibility, rather than its opposite. Gay liberation was
> most commonly understood [by others, from the outside] as liberation
> from the constraints of traditional norms, almost a dispensation that
> permitted homosexuals the absence of responsibility in return for an
> acquiescence in second-class citizenship. (Sullivan 1998, 65; my italics)

The key point to note however is that in Sullivan's reflections upon friendship in the face of AIDS, the act of assuming responsibility toward others *and* toward oneself, taking care of oneself and others, is enabled and supported through a community and a "way of life . . . shared among individuals of different age, status, and social activity" (DE293.3, 138). For both Sullivan and Foucault, "to be 'gay,' I think, is not to identify with the psychological traits and the visible masks of the homosexual but to try to define and develop a way of life" (DE293.3, 138).

Sullivan's observations about freedom and responsibility bring us back to Foucault's view of the nature and role of rights (which the feminist ethics of care has often been cast against), in conjunction with the theme, which we discussed above, of reciprocity in friendship. Foucault suggests that "if what we want to do is to create a new way of life, then the question of individual rights is not pertinent" (DE313.2, 158). He makes this claim—discounting the importance of individual rights[8]—because he wants to emphasize the development of relationships:

> We live in a relational world that institutions have considerably impoverished. Society and the institutions which frame it have limited the possibility of relationships because a rich relational world would be very complex to manage. We should fight against the impoverishment of the relational fabric. (DE313.2, 158)

This fits with a distancing from rights that can be heard in the feminist ethics of care, too:

> This conception of morality as concerned with the activity of care centers moral development around the understanding of responsibility and relationships, just as the conception of morality as fairness ties moral development to the understanding of rights and rules. (Gilligan 1983, 19)

But we should not read these remarks to mean that Foucault is against rights in any sense at all. On the contrary, "in the serious play of questions and answers, in the work of reciprocal elucidation, the rights of each person are in some sense immanent in the discussion. They depend only on the dialogue situation" (DE342.2, 111). These relational rights emerge from the relationship and situation—the rights of each role in S&M, the rights of each interlocutor in dialogue, and the rights of each person in friendship. Foucault adds—recalling his own "categorical imperative" never to engage in polemics, from the 1978 Collège de France course—that "the polemicist, on the other hand, proceeds encased in privileges that he possesses in advance and will never agree to question" (DE342.2, 112). So polemics is, at root, a denial or violation of the relational rights immanent in dialogue.[9] Thus "we should consider the battle for gay rights as an episode that cannot be the final stage" because, importantly, "a right, in its real effects, is much more linked to *attitudes* and patterns of behavior than to legal formulations" (DE313.2, 157; my italics). Foucault will have much more to say about what constitutes these attitudes, but we can already note that they can constitute part of the ethical substance upon which ethics will practice. And the new possibilities, the new cultural forms and ethics, that could be created through a homosexual ascesis of friendship, Foucault suggests, "would create relations that are, at certain points, transferable to heterosexuals" (DE313.2, 160). Thus, "by proposing a new relational *right*, we will see that nonhomosexual people can enrich their lives by changing their own schema of relations" (DE313.2, 160).[10] Thus, "the problem of relationships with others is present throughout the development of the care of the self," for the "care of the self is ethical in itself; but it implies complex relationships with others insofar as this ethos of freedom is also a way of caring for others . . . It is also the art of governing" (DE356.4, 287).

In just a few short years, Foucault's thought has undergone a profound reorientation: from "politics as the continuation of war" to "caring for oneself and others as the art of governing." Foucault's movement is perhaps nicely captured in a remark by the fictional founder of the utopian community "Walden Two" in B. F. Skinner's novel: "We are only just beginning to understand the power of love because we are just beginning to understand the weakness of force and aggression" (Skinner 1948, 97). Foucault's observation about the role of philosophy since Kant (in the 1982 version only) is prefaced by noting that "what we need is a new economy of power relations" (DE306.4, 328), paralleling his call in *La volonté de savoir* for "a different economy of bodies and pleasures" (1976ET, 159). Consistent throughout these shifts is the view that "the question of what kinds of institutions we need to create is an important and crucial issue. . . . I think that we have to try to build a solution" (DE358.2, 172). Foucault adds, in closing this interview, that many such exploratory movements—like civil rights, the student revolts in France, second-wave feminism, and gay liberation—"have really changed our whole lives, our mentality, our attitudes, and the attitudes and mentality of other people—people who do not belong to these movements. And that is something very important and positive" (DE358.2, 173). Understanding the critical importance of attitudes is the third trajectory in Foucault's ethical itinerary.

CRITIQUE AS ATTITUDE AND VIRTUE

> A human being lives out not only his personal life as an individual, but
> also, consciously or subconsciously, the lives of his epoch and con-
> temporaries; and although he may regard the general and impersonal
> foundations of his existence as unequivocal givens and take them for
> granted having as little intention of ever subjecting them to critique as
> our good Hans Castorp himself had, it is nevertheless quite possible that
> he senses his own moral well-being to be somehow impaired by the lack
> of critique. (Mann 1924, 31)

At several points I have cited Foucault's remark about philosophy's role
after Kant. The full passage reads thus:

> Since Kant, the role of philosophy is to prevent reason from going
> beyond the limits of what is given in experience. But from the same
> moment—that is, since the development of the modern state and the
> political management of society—the role of philosophy is also to
> keep watch over the excessive powers of political rationality. (DE291.4,
> 298–299 = DE306.4, 328)

For Kant, philosophy's role in demarcating reason's metaphysical limits is
what he calls *Kritik*, critique. But, Foucault argues, keeping watch over excessive power in politics is also critique. He traces a direct linkage between
these two senses of the term in Kant's 1784 essay "What Is Enlightenment?"—
and Foucault discussed this text, which, he rightly notes, "is not always
very clear despite its brevity" (DE339.2, 305), on several occasions. His
four major engagements with this text were a May 1978 lecture, "What Is
Critique?"(OT-78–01, given just a few months after he had completed that
year's Collège de France course but unpublished until 1990 and thus excluded from *Dits et écrits*), more briefly in a 1979 book review (DE266),
again in the opening lecture of his 1983 Collège de France course (excerpts
of which were published as DE351), and in a 1984 text "What Is Enlightenment?" (DE339), which Foucault selected especially for inclusion in Paul
Rabinow's *The Foucault Reader*, one of the first comprehensive anthologies
of Foucault's work. I will focus on the first and last of these four texts.

Foucault begins by summarizing Kant's understanding of Enlightenment as

the moment when humanity is going to put its own reason to use, without subjecting itself to any authority; now, it is precisely at this moment that critique is necessary, since its role is that of defining the conditions under which the use of reason is legitimate in order to determine what can be known, what must be done, and what may be hoped. (DE339.2, 308)

What intrigues Foucault about Kant's definition of Enlightenment is that it explicitly "raised the philosophical question of the present day" (DE339.2, 305). This philosophical question of the present raises the second task that Foucault highlighted above—keeping watch over political rationality—and underscores a view of philosophy that Foucault had held since at least 1967: "philosophy's function is diagnosis. In effect, philosophy is no longer about what exists eternally. It has the much more difficult and much more elusive task of describing what happens in the present" (DE047, I-581). Indeed, the first chapter of *Discipline and Punish* closes with the note that what Foucault is trying to do is a "history of the present" (1975ET, 31)—underlining its philosophical and critical import. In his other engagements with this text, Foucault will speak of it as at the juncture between philosophy and journalism, between critically drawing the limits of (political) reason and critical engagement with the events of the current day (DE266.2, 443; OT-78-01ET, 386).

As Foucault's summary highlights, "the 'way out' which characterizes Enlightenment is a process that releases us from the status of 'immaturity.' And by 'immaturity,' he [Kant] means a certain state of our will which makes us accept someone else's authority to lead us in areas where the use of reason is called for" (DE339.2, 305). Kant goes on to discuss the conditions that would make possible this release from immaturity; these conditions are, Foucault notes, "at once spiritual and institutional, ethical and political" (DE339.2, 306). These conditions constitute, as Foucault characterizes them, "a point of departure: what one might call the attitude of modernity" (DE339.2, 309). This notion of an *attitude* as the condition for, indeed the embodiment of, a critical exit from immaturity is key for Foucault's reading of Kant's text.

Foucault goes on to define and develop this notion of "modernity as an attitude":

And by "attitude," I mean a mode of relating to contemporary reality; a voluntary choice made by certain people; in the end, a way of thinking and feeling; a way, too, of acting and behaving that at one and the same time marks a relation of belonging and presents itself as a task. No doubt, a bit like what the Greeks called an *ethos*. (DE339.2, 309)

No doubt. Indeed, we should recognize here the core of what Foucault defined in the introduction to *The Use of Pleasure* as ethics as a practice of self-fashioning. We should also recognize it in the spirit of ongoing self- and community fashioning that Foucault explored in homosexual friendship.

These connections become clear as Foucault goes on to illustrate this notion of modernity as an "attitude" in the next parts of this essay. His example here is Charles Baudelaire's "man of modernity," the dandy. For Baudelaire, as Foucault reads him, the "deliberate, difficult attitude" (DE339.2, 310) of modernity—a characterization that parallels his description decades earlier of the "much more difficult and much more elusive task" of philosophy—

> is an exercise in which extreme attention to what is real is confronted with the practice of a liberty that simultaneously respects this reality and violates it. . . . However, modernity for Baudelaire is not simply a form of relationship to the present; it is also a mode of relationship that must be established with oneself. The deliberate attitude of modernity is tied to an indispensable asceticism. (DE339.2, 311)

This attitude thus is constituted through a relationship to oneself and the exercise of a practice of liberty. Though he does not make the link to his larger conception of ethics explicit here, it is quite apparent. This attitude of modernity, of Enlightenment, is an ethical practice, and like the ancient *epimeleia heautou*, and all imperatives (as Foucault described them in 1978 [CdF78ET, 3]), it is an aesthetic and ascetic practice of self-fashioning. This is what Foucault finds in "the dandy who makes of his body, his behavior, his feelings and passions, his very existence, a work of art. . . . This modernity . . . compels him to face the task of producing himself" (DE339.2, 312). (In the 1984 Collège de France course, Foucault will also link this spirit with the ancient school of Cynicism.[11])

In short, Foucault tells us, "the thread which may connect us with the Enlightenment is not faithfulness to doctrinal elements but, rather, the permanent reactivation of an attitude—that is, of a philosophical ethos that could be described as a permanent critique of our historical era" (DE339.2, 312). As a permanent reactivation, this attitude will be constantly in the process of being reinvented, reinvigorated, and reassessed. In the course of such a project, we will not necessarily be committed to any particular doctrinal element—be it Kant's or Foucault's, for that matter—but rather an attitude of critical assessment of our era.

Foucault did some work to elucidate the content of this attitude in his 1980 course at the Collège de France, *On the Government of the Living*. The initial lecture of this course begins with themes of "raison d'état" (from the 1978 and 1979 courses) but then introduces a significant shift—looking instead at the relations that obtain between practices of government and truth: "So there are two successive shifts if you like: one from the notion of dominant ideology to that of knowledge-power, and now, a second shift from the notion of knowledge-power to the notion of government by the truth" (CdF80ET, 11). He then devotes the course's next three lectures to an interpretation of Sophocles' *Oedipus Rex* in order to highlight several key themes in the relationship between power and truth.[12] And this is where he introduces the concept of an "attitude." In the fourth lecture (30 January 1980), he asks: "What does the systematic, voluntary, theoretical and practical questioning of power have to say about the subject of knowledge and about the bond with the truth by which, involuntarily, this subject is held?" (CdF80ET, 77). His answer is that "it is the movement of freeing oneself from power that should serve to reveal the transformations of the subject and its relations with the truth. . . . *This form of analysis . . . rests much more upon an attitude than upon a thesis*" (CdF80ET, 77; trans. mod., my italics; cf. CdF80, 76). We can hear here an early formulation of what he will speak of as an ethical "relationship of the self to the self"; we can even understand Foucault to be speaking of his own work when he discusses "this form of analysis."

He goes on to specify that this attitude "consists, first, in thinking that no power goes without saying, that no power, of whatever kind, is obvious or inevitable, and that consequently no power warrants being taken for granted" (CdF80ET, 77). This attitude that no particular power has to be accepted as a given is an ethical attitude, not an ontological thesis, that ought to be at the basis of our judgments. And this attitude is fundamentally a critical one: no power is justified in advance, we must examine each case, and we must look beyond each case. He continues:

> Let us say that if the great philosophical approach consists in establishing a methodical doubt that suspends every certainty, the small lateral

approach on the opposite track that I am proposing consists in trying to bring into play in a systematic way not the suspension of every certainty, but the non-necessity of all power of whatever kind. (CdF80ET, 78)

This "non-necessity of power" is another (admittedly awkward) way of describing freedom.

Foucault here echoes Viktor Frankl's experience as a survivor of the Holocaust. In his memoir, *Man's Search for Meaning*, Frankl asks, "But what about human liberty? Is there no spiritual freedom . . . ?" (Frankl 1946, 65). He responds unambiguously:

> The experiences of camp life show that man does have a choice of action. . . . Man *can* preserve a vestige of spiritual freedom, of independence of mind, even in such terrible conditions of psychic and physical stress. . . . Everything can be taken from a man but one thing: the last of the human freedoms—to choose one's attitude in any given set of circumstances, to choose one's own way. (Frankl 1946, 65–66)

Frankl continues that "there is also purpose in that life which is almost barren of both creation and enjoyment and which admits of but one possibility of high moral behavior: namely, *in man's attitude to his existence*, an existence restricted by external forces" (Frankl 1946, 67; my italics). To paraphrase Frankl's experience in Foucauldian language, this choice of attitude is an ethical self-fashioning by which one makes one's life into a work of art—and this ethical practice is available even in the absence of creation or pleasure, even in the depths of despair in a death camp. "It is this spiritual freedom—which cannot be taken away—that makes life meaningful and purposeful" (Frankl 1946, 67). The adoption of a critical attitude is a practice, an enactment, of spiritual freedom—it is the assertion, not as a thesis but as an attitude, of the "non-necessity of power."

Foucault notes that this attitude toward the "non-necessity of power" is akin to anarchism and regrets that anarchism is so badly misunderstood and held in such low esteem. This leads him to the second feature of this attitude—in the description of which Foucault makes a surprisingly frank comment about his own ethical project or attitude:

> One can define anarchy by two things: [a] first, the thesis that power is essentially bad; and [b] second, the project of a society in which all relations of power would be abolished and annulled. What I propose is clearly different from this. [A] The point is not to have a society free

of power relations, but rather to make the non-power, or the non-acceptability of power, at the beginning of work in the form of a calling into question of all the forms in which power is in actual fact accepted. [B] Second, it does not suffice to say that power is bad, but one must say, or at least start from the point, that no power, in whatever form, has the right to be acceptable or is absolutely, necessarily inevitable. (CdF80ET, 78; trans. mod. based on audio recordings; cf. CdF80, 76–77, BdS-C62, cass. 4, side A)

In other words, we cannot simply say "power is bad," but we will be able to say that "everything is dangerous" (DE326.4, 256). And we start from a position that will be (at least initially) suspicious and critical of all forms of power—we start from an attitude that questions and critiques all these forms of power. This "philosophical ethos that could be described as a permanent critique of our historical era" is "the thread which may connect us with the Enlightenment" (DE339.2, 312).

In "What Is Enlightenment?" Foucault notes that this critique is both negative and positive. In its negative aspect, it is a "mode of reflective relation to the present" that "will be oriented toward the 'contemporary limits of the necessary,' that is, toward what is not or is no longer indispensable for the constitution of ourselves as autonomous subjects" (DE339.2, 313). It will therefore be wary and suspicious of supposed necessities—including demands that one must be either "for" or "against" Enlightenment (we could be both, in different respects) and the claims of humanism, which is "in itself too supple, too diverse, too inconsistent to serve as an axis for reflection" (DE339.2, 314). Hence the suspicion voiced in *Discipline and Punish* toward humanist and humanitarian explanations of the shift from torture to imprisonment.

On the other hand, this critique must also have some positive content—what are the values or norms that it would advocate? Foucault suggests that this critical attitude

is no longer going to be practiced in the search for formal structures with universal value but, rather, as a historical investigation into the events that have led us to constitute ourselves and to recognize ourselves as subjects of what we are doing, thinking, saying. (DE339.2, 315)

Discipline and Punish and *La volonté de savoir* are both apt illustrations of this sort of historical investigation—they indicate directions to be explored ("bodies and pleasures," in the latter example, which as we have seen led him to a number of emergent values), even if they will not assert that these directions have a universal or eternal validity. In a May 20, 1978, conversation, Foucault described the positive content of *Discipline and Punish* like this:

> It's true that certain people, such as those who work in the institutional setting of the prison—which is not quite the same as being in prison—are not likely to find advice or instructions in my books that tell them "what is to be done." But my project is precisely to bring it about that they "no longer know what to do," so that the acts, gestures, discourses that up until then had seemed to go without saying become problematic, difficult, dangerous. This effect is intentional. (DE278.5, 235)[13]

This fits with his 1980 Collège de France description of an attitude that announces the "non-necessity of power." And it anticipates language he will use one week later, in "What Is Critique?," when he defines this critical attitude as "the art of not being governed, or the art of not being governed like that and at this price" (OT-78-01ET, 384).

For critique is also historically tied to that "*ars artium*," the art of arts, "the art of governing men" (OT-78-01ET, 383). Critique and a critical attitude arises in opposition to this art, as a counterart, so to speak:

> as at once partner and adversary of the arts of governing, as a way of suspecting them, of challenging them, of limiting them, of finding their right measure, of transforming them, of seeking to escape these arts of governing or, in any case, to displace them, as an essential reluctance, but also and in that way as a line of development of the arts of governing (OT-78-01ET, 384)

As he put it in describing homosexual friendship, this art of not being governed this way is expressed as a "No!": "'No! Let's escape as much as possible from the type of relations that society proposes for us and try to create in the empty space where we are new relational possibilities'" (DE313.2, 160). But it also points to several positive ways of resisting, which serve as "historical anchoring points" (and various historical forms) for this critical attitude. Foucault mentions three: spiritual resistance, which took the form of alternative biblical hermeneutics as ways of challenging "the ecclesiastical magisterium"; the use of "universal and indefeasible" or natural rights as a source of resistance to tyranny; and finally Kantian maturity, "not accepting as true what an authority tells you to be true. . . . Rather, it is to accept it only if one thinks oneself that the reasons for accepting it are good" (OT-78-01ET, 385). And so the positive content of this critical attitude may vary, and it emerges from its context of origin, whose frameworks have been the target of Foucault's own inquiries: "The focus of critique is essentially the cluster of relations that bind the one to the other, or the one to the two others, power, truth, and the subject" (OT-78-01ET, 385–386).

But Foucault also gave us a radically different illustration of how positive content can emerge in a critical attitude and practice, in an example from antiquity that he discussed on numerous occasions—the evening examination that Seneca describes in *De Ira*, Book III, Chapter 36.[14]

Seneca tells us that before retiring to sleep, one should ask oneself, "What evils have I cured today? What vices have I cured? In what respects am I better?"—thus examining and criticizing all of the day's activities. "I spoke too brusquely with so-and-so, so that they were more offended than enlightened by my comments," etc. Thus, tomorrow, I will be able better to respond in a similar situation. This kind of concern for oneself, Foucault tells us in the 1980 Collège de France course, is

> not a question of judging acts in terms of a code, but of developing,
> exercising, ascesis, to make oneself stronger, better adapted to deal with
> situations. So the point is to discover the rational principles in the soul
> that will better adapt one to deal with such situations. An autonomous
> conduct, and therefore a rational conduct, is the goal of this examina-
> tion. This has virtually nothing to do with the exploration of the secrets
> of the heart, or the origins of one's faults. It is a question of an exami-
> nation of oneself insofar as one is a rational subject, inasmuch as one
> proposes one's proper ends, and can only achieve these ends through
> an autonomous activity. (CdF80, March 12; my transcription of audio
> recordings. Cf. CdF80ET, 245–246; BdS-C62, cass. 10, side B)

This critical attitude toward oneself thus leads one to positive content, in the question "How can the subject act as she should, how can she be as she ought to be?" It thus functions, Foucault notes in 1982, "as a test of the reactivation of the fundamental rules of action, of the rules we should have in mind, and of the means we should employ to achieve these ends and the immediate objectives we may set ourselves" (CdF82ET, 483). Two points in Seneca's discussion are particularly relevant in illustrating the positive content of critique. First, the ethical problem of which "rational principles" or norms one should adopt is explicitly raised in these questions; second,

Foucault characterizes this care of oneself as a tactic to be adopted within the play of power and resistance that frames his discussions of modern society. Seneca's self-examination is a tactic, but it is centered within a practice of self that reveals an underlying attitude or *ethos*. At the heart of creating one's subjectivity and practicing this care for oneself, then, is an attitude, a preparation for and orientation toward the moral demands of one's culture, its codes, and one's behavior.

In sum, this critical attitude (which does *not* simply follow Kant's *doctrine*) "is not seeking to make possible a metaphysics that has finally become a science; it is seeking to give new impetus, as far and wide as possible, to the undefined work of freedom" (DE339.2, 316) that, as Frankl noted, "makes life meaningful and purposeful" (Frankl 1946, 67). As such, "this historico-critical attitude must also be an experimental one" (DE339.2, 316). Finally, it constitutes a "philosophical ethos appropriate to the critical ontology of ourselves as a historico-practical test of the limits we may go beyond, and thus as work carried out by ourselves upon ourselves as free beings" (DE339.2, 316).

Consider what this experimental attitude entails. First, "we have to give up hope of ever acceding to a point of view that could give us access to any complete and definitive knowledge of what may constitute our historical limits" (DE339.2, 316). This means that we will never achieve a "God's-eye" view "from nowhere"; our knowledge will never be "complete and definitive." Second, "the theoretical and practical experience we have of our limits, and of the possibility of moving beyond them, is always limited and determined; thus, we are always in the position of beginning again" (DE339.2, 316–317). Because our knowledge is necessarily incomplete, and because it is determined in part by our position within the matrices of power relations, we are always in the position of starting over, of calling our own presuppositions into question just as we call external structures of power into question.

This is a pragmatist epistemology.[15] Louis Menand succinctly characterizes pragmatism in his description of William James's view of belief: "there is no noncircular set of criteria for knowing whether a particular belief is true, no appeal to some standard outside the process of coming to the belief itself. For thinking just *is* a circular process, in which some end, some imagined outcome, is already present at the start of any train of thought" (Menand 2001, 353). As Otto Neurath puts it, "for those who are of the opinion that complete insight can never be reached [i.e., both Neurath and Foucault], these preliminary rules [a critical attitude] become definitive ones" (Neurath 1913, 2). He continues that this is the necessary condition of science:

> we do *not* arrive at "*one*" system of science that could take the place of the "real world" so to speak; everything remains ambiguous and in many ways uncertain. "*The*" *system is the great scientific lie*. . . . *Multiplicity* and *uncertainty* are essential. . . . The progress of science consists, as it were, in constantly changing the machine and in advancing on the basis of new decisions. (Neurath 1935, 116)

Or, as Foucault put it, "we are always in the position of starting over." In other words: "If everything is dangerous, then we always have something to do" (DE326.4, 256). And hence Foucault's much-reiterated refusal to "tell us what to do" (cf. DE157.1, 62; DE218.1, 144–145, etc.). Cornel West characterizes the pragmatic project like this:

> The community understands inquiry as a set of social practices geared toward achieving and warranting knowledge, a perennial process of dialogue which can question any claim but never all at once. This self-correcting enterprise requires neither foundations nor grounds. It yields no absolute certainty. The social or communal is thus the central philosophical category of this pragmatist conception of knowledge. It recognizes that in knowledge the crucial component is not intuition but social practice and communal norm. (West 1982, 21)

This "self-correcting enterprise" is a community undertaking and a "perennial process of dialogue"—which is exactly what Foucault was describing as he discussed the possibilities for the "creation of cultural forms" through the practice of friendship. Neurath continues: "Still, the result in fact is far-reaching unity that can *not* be deduced logically" (Neurath 1935, 116). For Foucault, this unity takes the form of a "work carried out by ourselves upon ourselves as free beings" (DE339.2, 316). And thus, he tells us, the critical attitude "is undergirded by a more general sort of imperative—more general still than that of warding off errors. . . . What I wanted to speak to you about was the critical attitude as virtue in general" (OT-78-01ET, 383).

PARRHESIA AND PRAGMATIC JUSTIFICATION

This means that this attitude, this virtue, this practice of "critique is the movement through which the subject gives itself the right to question truth concerning its power effects and to question power about its discourses of truth" (OT-78-01ET, 386). The subject gives itself the right to question and challenge—this is an act of freedom, which freedom is present in the situation to be questioned and challenged. Recall Foucault's observations about dialogue and polemics: "the rights of each person are in some sense immanent in the discussion. They depend only on the dialogue situation" (DE342.2, 111). ("I will therefore propose only one imperative, but it will be categorical and unconditional: Never engage in polemics" [CdF78ET, 4].) What emerges as immanent in discussion is, in effect, the right to engage in critique—the enactment of a critical attitude, which can question both truth and power. This questioning of truth and power constitute another illustration of this critical attitude in practice: parrhesia. Foucault introduces this illustration in his 1982 Collège de France course, *The Hermeneutics of the Subject*; it then emerges as the central theme of Foucault's last two courses, *The Government of Self and Others* (1983) and *The Courage of Truth* (1984).

Here is how Foucault frames his discussion of parrhesia, in the first lecture of *The Courage of Truth*:

> With the notion of *parrhesia*, originally rooted in political practice and the problematization of democracy, then later diverging towards the sphere of personal ethics and the formation of the moral subject, with this notion with political roots and its divergence into morality, we have, to put things very schematically—and this is what interested me, why I stopped to look at this and am still focusing on it—the possibility of posing the question of the subject and truth from the point of view of the practice of what could be called the government of oneself and others. And thus we come back to the theme of government which I studied some years ago. It seems to me that by examining the notion of *parrhesia* we can see how the analysis of modes of veridiction, the study of techniques of governmentality, and the identification of forms of practice of self interweave. Connecting together modes of veridiction, techniques of governmentality, and practices of the self is basically what I have always been trying to do. (CdF84ET, 8)

Parrhesia, "frank speech" or "truth telling," is both an attitude and a dialogical practice—one speaks the truth to an interlocutor who is affected by this truth, affirming that one is committed to this truth as a personal conviction. In so speaking, one puts oneself at risk, minimally of disrupting the relationship (of trust, friendship, vassalage, etc.) in which one is speaking, maximally risking one's own life (CdF84ET, 10–11). It is, as it were, "speaking truth to power." Or, we could say, it is "the right to question truth concerning its power effects and to question power about its discourses of truth" (OT-78-01ET, 386). This "fundamental philosophical attitude" (CdF84ET, 67; trans. mod.; cf. CdF84, 64) of parrhesia thus commits one to a frank and critical assessment of what the truth is, both with respect to oneself and to one's interlocutor and to the subject at hand (whatever norms or practices are being spoken about). This *ethos*, seeking to speak the truth, thus also seems to commit one (at least provisionally) to whatever forms of rationality are the binding ones in one's culture or discourse—perhaps even if one wishes to criticize frankly the currently practiced norms or rationalities.

Parrhesia is an ascesis—it is "both the moral quality, the moral attitude or the *ethos*, if you like, and . . . the technical procedure or *tekhne*" (CdF82ET, 372). This practice of parrhesia is also intimately interwoven with what Foucault described as the care of the self, in ways that facilitate a shift from speaking of ancient practices to our contemporary situation. For, first, the critical practice upon oneself of care of the self must be broadened. It does not suffice simply to question one's actions according to a given set of moral or ethical norms and principles—rather, these norms and principles must themselves be subjected to the same critical examination, as must the actions that follow and the ends they serve. These actions must be carefully scrutinized, too, at the level of their consequences, because an action may not lead to the desired end, or may lead toward other, unanticipated and undesirable ends, and the ends themselves may need to be reconsidered. Further, the deployment of strategic relations of power institutionalized in one's society should also come under this critical gaze. Thus, we have a critical attitude, an *ethos*, and it is in this attitude that the moral and ethical quality of one's practices inheres. (Taking up the ancient distinction between friendship and flattery, Foucault gives the practice of friendship as an example in which parrhesia is a distinguishing characteristic.) And so this critical examination stems from and is oriented toward the complex interrelationships that constitute one's social roles, position, and responsibilities. This brings us to the cusp of "the arts of governing," the proper direction and guidance of oneself and others, exactly what a parrhesiastic critical ethos of care for the self should equip one to do.

Let me try to pull all of this together with an extended quotation (the last part of which I cited in Chapter 3) from the 1982 Collège de France course:

And in this series of undertakings to reconstitute an ethic of the self, in this series of more or less blocked and ossified efforts, and in the movement we now make to refer ourselves constantly to this ethic of the care of the self without ever giving it any content, I think we may have to suspect that we find it impossible today to constitute an ethic of the self, even though it may be an urgent, fundamental, and politically indispensible task, if it is true after all that there is no first or final point of resistance to political power other than in the relationship one has to oneself.

In other words, what I mean is this: if we take the question of power, of political power, situating it in the more general question of governmentality understood as a strategic field of power relations in the broadest and not merely political sense of the term, if we understand by governmentality a strategic field of power relations in their mobility, transformability, and reversibility, then I do not think that reflection on this notion of governmentality can avoid passing through, theoretically and practically, the element of a subject defined by the relationship of self to self . . . the analysis of governmentality—that is to say, of power as the ensemble of reversible relations—must refer to an ethics of the subject defined by the relationship of self to self. Quite simply, this means that in the type of analysis I have been trying to advance for some time you can see that power relations, governmentality, the government of the self and others, and the relationship of self to self constitute a chain, a thread, and I think it is around these notions, that we should be able to connect together the question of politics and the question of ethics. (CdF82ET, 251–252; trans. mod.; cf. CdF82, 241–242)

In other words, we must adopt an ethical orientation, a critical relationship to ourselves, rather than a code-oriented moral orientation, if, on Foucault's view, we will be able to articulate, and to think, politics and ethics. And the critical attitude that we adopt will always be situated within practices, practices already inflected by relations of power, which may themselves be the very object of critique.

This orientation—and the critical attitude at its core—gives us certain resources for a pragmatic justification of the values that we embrace. In moving toward this different orientation, we'll have to give up certain notions that traditionally constitute our understanding of what justification entails. These would include both universality and the idea of transcendental foundations or grounding. All moral and ethical norms of behavior (or codes) are situated within particular practices and hence are themselves necessarily provisional—this provisional character was an element of the pragmatic epistemology of the critical attitude. Even the ethical subjectivity, or identity, which frames our orientation to these practices is so limited: "We must not think of identity as an ethical universal rule" (DE358.2, 166).

Giving these up, however, does not mean that we lose the capacity to claim that ethical evaluations or moral norms are justified—rather, it means that justification itself must be reconceived as provisional and, as it were, "deflated." Let me give you a very rough sketch of what justification will entail:

The ethical orientation and the critical *ethos* that Foucault seeks to excavate from antiquity—and from his contemporary exploration of pleasures and friendships—can be seen as one level removed from any particular (coded) claim that "x is right" or "p is wrong." One must take a critical attitude towards oneself and the codes and norms that one adopts (following the example of Stoics such as Epictetus: challenging one's motivations, the ends that one seeks, one's position in society, one's behavior toward others) as well as a critical attitude toward society (following the example of the ancient Cynics: challenging the networks of power relations that are institutionalized, the intended and unintended consequences of political decisions, etc.), in order to allow oneself to act toward whatever one will affirm, as a result of this critique, as "a good" or "a better."

Now, as we have seen, Foucault has explicitly refused to specify a program by which to define this "good." Such a program, too, emerges out of the critical practices of one's orientation. (We've seen how certain "goods" emerge for Foucault out of, for example, the practices of S&M and friendship. Of course, these "goods" themselves remain necessarily provisional.) Thus, each moral actor will define this term herself through her decisions and actions, as well as her interactions with others, and will have to adopt the same critical, challenging attitude with respect to this definition as she has done with respect to herself and society. Our critical *ethos* must be at once Janus faced—oriented forward toward the actions guided by the norms and oriented backward toward the norms themselves. Thus, an ethical norm or vision of the good will be prima facie justified after it has passed a certain number of such challenges (and this norm or vision will be perpetually subject to revision or rejection in light of the next challenge—hence provisional and nonuniversalizable—no matter how many such challenges it has met).

One of John McDowell's characterizations of what it means to be rational fits this Foucauldian view of justification very well—where he speaks of reasons, add "and norms or values":

> Being at home in the space of reasons includes a standing obligation
> to be ready to rethink the credentials of the putatively rational link-
> ages that constitute the space of reasons as one conceives it at any time.
> This leaves exactly as much room for innovation as there is. (McDowell
> 1996, 186)

McDowell's phrase "exactly as much room for innovation as there is" is, to be sure, tautological. But it is also liberating, for the space for innovation is not delimited in advance. Hence Foucault's suggestion in "What Is Enlightenment?" that "this philosophical ethos may be characterized as a *limit-attitude* . . . we have to be at the frontiers. . . . The point, in brief, is to transform the critique conducted in the form of necessary limitation into a practical critique that takes the form of a possible crossing-over" (DE339.2, 315). Thus, justification will emerge not from "formal structures with univer- sal value" but from historical investigations that are "genealogical in [their] design and archaeological in [their] methods" (DE339.2, 315)—the very crit- ical work from which this view of justification has emerged.

In a certain sense, this altered conception of justification may not be completely satisfying—it may take some getting used to. This may indi- cate some of the critical work to be done in our relationships to ourselves. As Otto Neurath observes for the doing of science, "One's back is *never* completely free, and working with 'dubious' statements has to be learned" (Neurath 1935, 118). Such a Foucauldian ethics remains ungrounded and seems unable to address all of the different difficulties with which it might be confronted. But this is precisely what I think we have to see: *no* ethics ever will be justified or grounded in an absolute sense, but difficulties can *still* be addressed. It simply won't be possible to express in advance what one should do in any imaginable situation. No ethic could be complete in this fashion without becoming empty. Hence, our standard of justification must be altered because demands for more than this now appear unreasonable.

One consequence of the inherently provisional nature of ethical and moral norms is that, since every norm's claim to validity may later turn out to be unwarranted, everything is dangerous. "My point is not that every- thing is bad, but that everything is dangerous, which is not exactly the same as bad. If everything is dangerous, then we always have something to do"

(DE326.4, 256). So all of our actions will remain "dangerous" in two senses: they may or may not achieve their intended aim (since there are always un-anticipated effects), and, in the end, the aim itself may not prove to be an ethically laudable one. This double danger does not mean that we should not act on the norms that have been prima facie justified (for this suffices to justify our action *now*); it reiterates the continuing importance of the criti-cal, challenging attitude that Foucault put forth as an ethical orientation, as we find ourselves constantly "work[ing] in the midst of uncertainty and apprehension" (1984aET, 7).

In sum, then, a new ethical orientation is realized when one fashions oneself such that one can critically, parrhesiastically, confront oneself *and* others and speak truly about the practices and discourses that condition and norm our behavior. We have come full circle: parrhesiastic justification as part of a critical attitude constitutes a practice that Foucault identified as ethical. So this ethical orientation becomes the basis, as it were—or better, the delimiting context—for justification. All justified claims are "for now" and cannot be universalized in anything like a "permanent" or "eternal" sense. This, in fact, doesn't seem all that radical or new. An obvious his-torical antecedent suggests itself—and this should not be a surprise, given Foucault's interest in the ancients—the Aristotelian conception of *phronesis*. And as in a pragmatist view of truth, all such claims are fallible, subject to being discarded, perhaps for something radically different (as well, Foucault suggests, as should be our very conceptions of ourselves), and we shall never achieve an endpoint where the constant inquiry could cease. I think that this pragmatic attitude and approach toward justification can also explain a puzzle in Foucault that Charles Taylor has pointed out. For Taylor, one of the disconcerting features of Foucault's work is that he never quite comes out and affirms what seem to be his implicit goods, his implicit critical metersticks—in Foucault, everything that we could apparently affirm as a good, upon subsequent analysis, disappears and seems to be replaced by another, which itself in turn disappears (Taylor 1984, 152). Given this prag-matic view of justification as dynamic and unmoored, the problematization of each preceding "solution" is precisely to be expected, and one cannot affirm any of these goods except in the provisional way that I've tried to describe.

Difficulties can still be addressed, and values can still be asserted, even though those values remain provisional. As Thomas Nagel has argued, "prog-ress in particular areas of ethics and value theory need not wait for the discovery of a general foundation (even if there is such a thing)" (Nagel 1977, 137). On the contrary, "there can be good judgment without total justification, either explicit or implicit" (134). For Nagel, "provided one has taken the process of practical justification as far as it will go in the course of arriving at the conflict, one may be able to proceed without further justification, but without irrationality either" (135). For Neurath, "there is no *tabula rasa* for us that we could use as a safe foundation on which to heap layers upon layers" (Neurath 1935, 118). This means, of course, that "we always have work to do" (DE326.4, 256). For we must always critically and parrhesiastically assess ourselves—have we really taken the process as far as it can go?—and the conflict of values itself. "What makes this possible," Nagel suggests (a connection that will sound familiar), "is *judgment*—essentially the faculty Aristotle described as practical wisdom" (Nagel 1977, 135) and that Foucault has described as the virtue of critique. Nagel continues that this view "does not imply that we should abandon the search for more and better reasons and more critical insight in the domain of practical decision" (135). This means, as Foucault has noted, that the process will be ongoing, that even when we have justification "for now" we must continue critically to reevaluate those reasons.

In a 1979 book review (which he opened by citing Kant's "What Is Enlightenment?" as straddling philosophy and journalism), Foucault praised Jean Daniel's *L'ere des ruptures* [*The Age of Ruptures*] as an example of this critical attitude of reevaluation. (Daniel was one of the founders of *Le Nouvel Observateur*, and this book critically engaged the French Left of the early 1970s.) What Foucault finds compelling in Daniel's work is that "his whole book is a quest for those subtler, more secret, and more decisive moments when things begin to lose their self-evidence" (DE266.2, 447). This moment of losing one's self-evidence is a moment that opens up spaces of freedom "on the frontier," when gestalt shifts become possible. He closes the review by invoking Merleau-Ponty and "what was for him the essential philosophical task: never to consent to being completely comfortable with one's own presuppositions" (DE266.2, 448). This remark is both epistemological and ethical: it is epistemological in that we must recognize the provisional nature of our presuppositions and hence not become too comfortable with them. It is ethical because to become comfortable with one's own presuppositions is to become polemical—and this is exactly what transcendental justifications would seem to allow us to do. Rather, we must always "be mindful that everything one perceives is evident only against a familiar and little-known horizon, that every certainty is sure only through the support of a ground that is always unexplored" (DE266.2, 448). For as he notes in "What Is Critique?": "Bringing out the conditions of acceptability of a system and following the lines of rupture that mark its emergence are two correlative operations" (OT-78-01ET, 395). And hence, "no founding recourse, no escape into a pure form—that is no doubt one of the most important and most contestable points of this historicophilosophical approach" (OT-78-01ET, 395)—that is one of the main dangers of Foucault's ethics. But "if it is necessary to pose the question of knowledge in its relation to domination, it would be first and foremost on the basis of a certain decisive will not to be governed, this decisive will, an attitude at once individual and collective of emerging, as Kant said, from one's immaturity" (OT-78-01ET, 398). And "ethics is the considered form that freedom takes when it is informed by reflection" (DE356.4, 284), that is, critique.

BOOTSTRAPPING FREEDOM

Foucault's critics would likely reply that this notion of pragmatic justification does not yet address their central worries. However, I think that Foucault's account of ethics emerging within power relations has additional resources that can in fact answer the most compelling objections. Mark Bevir has characterized most criticism of Foucault as "highlight[ing] two main aporias that bedevil his work" (Bevir 1999, 357).

> The first aporia is: if the subject is a product of a regime of power, how can he act innovatively, and if he cannot act innovatively, how can we explain changes within a regime of power? The second aporia is: if all claims to truth merely hide a will to power, if we reject all notions of objectivity, then on what grounds can we assert the superiority of our preferred theories and values? (357–358)

Both of these aporias, in fact, dissolve. Enough has been said here for us to see how to answer the first:[16] subjects are not *exclusively* the products of a regime of power even as they are never exempt from regimes of power. And those very regimes, themselves fundamentally relational, are themselves necessarily subject to resistance, transformation and change.

The second aporia that Bevir identifies is, I think, the more serious one. Indeed, I think the most important criticisms of Foucault's ethical project revolve around this second aporia. Charles Taylor's worry, discussed above, speaks to this concern; Jürgen Habermas's central criticisms of Foucault, too, drive at this aporia.[17] Foucault himself recognizes the concern behind this aporia: "Recent liberation movements suffer from the fact that they cannot find any principle on which to base the elaboration of a new ethics" (DE326.4, 255–256). He goes on: "They need an ethics, but they cannot find any other ethics than an ethics founded on so-called scientific knowledge of what the self is, what desire is, what the unconscious is, and so on" (DE326.4, 256). An ethics founded on any particular constructs of power relations, as Bevir rightly notes, would be ungrounded and problematical. An ethics founded on the principle of freedom, however, which itself must be posited for power relations to obtain, would avoid this trap.

The ethical values that have emerged from Foucault's ethical trajectories—reciprocity, responsiveness, concern for the other—have all emerged out of the logic of the relationships in which they obtained. But, to rephrase Bevir's second aporia, couldn't we look to dissymmetrical or unresponsive relationships to justify other kinds of values? How are we to determine which relationships ought to be valorized? Part of the answer to this question reflects Foucault's pragmatism: we'll never have a final answer and may in fact have chosen poorly right now. So we must maintain the vigilance of our critical attitude, and we have to be always willing to abandon the values we currently embrace. This is analogous to the point that John Stuart Mill makes in *On Liberty*, that

> Complete liberty of contradicting and disproving our opinion, is the very condition which justifies us in assuming its truth for purposes of action. . . .
>
>   The steady habit [or, Foucault would call it, attitude] of correcting and completing his own opinion by collating it with those of others, so far from causing doubt and hesitation in carrying it into practice, is the only stable foundation for a just reliance on it. . . .
>
>   The beliefs which we have most warrant for, have no safeguard to rest on, but a standing invitation to the whole world to prove them unfounded. . . . This is the amount of certainty attainable by a fallible being, and this the sole way of obtaining it. (Mill 1859, 23–24)

But, as the analogy with Mill suggests, there is another important part of the answer, which has to do with the essentially relational character of power and its presupposition of freedom: the second part of the answer brings freedom forward as a basis for evaluation. And this is also the reason for Foucault's insistence on a distinction between "power relations" and "domination" (DE356.4, 299)—"domination" suggests a complete absence of freedom, which Foucault calls "intolerable:"

> the important question here . . . [is] whether the system of constraints in which a society functions leaves individuals the liberty to transform the system. . . . [A] system of constraint becomes truly *intolerable* when the individuals who are affected by it don't have the means of modifying it. (DE317.4, 147–148; my italics)

Systems are intolerable precisely when they eliminate freedom, the freedom that must be presupposed for power relations to obtain. Foucault had used this word "intolerable" before, in the early 1970s during his work with the Groupe d'Information sur les Prisons (GIP), to describe prisoners' conditions. "Let what is intolerable, imposed by force and silence, cease to be accepted. Our inquiry is not done in order to accumulate information, but to heighten our intolerance and to make it an engaged intolerance" (DE087, II-176). In the GIP, we could say, the task of Foucault's philosophy-journalism was to "keep watch over the excessive powers of political rationality" (DE306.4, 328) within French prisons: "It is a matter of alerting public opinion and keeping it on the alert" (DE086, II-175).

Nevertheless, the strongest, most direct statement of Bevir's second aporia was made by Nancy Fraser in 1981. (Indeed, both Taylor and Habermas, whose respective critiques were published in 1984, essentially echo Fraser's argument. Likewise, Charles Scott's argument that Foucault's work "put[s] in question the normative status of the values that find expression in his thought" [Scott 1990, 52] is but another variation on Fraser's critique.) However, there is a coherent and satisfying resolution to this second aporia, and Fraser's criticism in particular, *within* Foucault's own work. The key concept that I'll use to explain how Foucault can resolve this aporia is "bootstrapping"—defined in the *Oxford English Dictionary* as "To make use of existing resources or capabilities to raise (oneself) to a new situation or state; to modify or improve by making use of what is already present." To be clear, I do not mean by this term something like the Horatio Alger myth of a "self-made" man who pulls himself up by his bootstraps.[18] On the contrary, I am drawing on the notion as it is used in developmental and linguistic psychology: young children "bootstrap" more complex linguistic functions and learn entirely new grammatical forms by building them out of the linguistic experience they have already acquired.

What emerges from Foucault's ethical trajectories (we have already seen ethical values and norms emerging from the practices of S&M and friendship)—and what he explicitly clarifies in the January 1984 interview "The Ethics of the Care of the Self as a Practice of Freedom" (DE356)—is a conceptual bootstrapping, where the grounding for ethical evaluative and normative judgments are found within the critical attitude and social practices themselves. More particularly, ethical content can emerge from and be grounded in the conditions of possibility for power relations, namely, from freedom.

Nancy Fraser's critique that Foucault is "normatively confused" is, I find, one of the most compelling and difficult to address of the various criticisms of his work. Nancy Fraser famously criticized Foucault for being guilty of "normative confusion," of "inviting questions that [his work] is structurally unequipped to answer" (Fraser 1981, 27). Foucault is guilty, she argues, of implicitly appealing to normative standards that he cannot justify (and sometimes even seems to reject), in particular the liberal framework built around the notion of freedom. In the absence of an explicitly articulated criterion according to which he can distinguish between "good" and "bad" forms of power, Fraser argues, "it follows, in his view, that one cannot object to a form of life simply on the ground that it is power-laden. Power is productive, ineliminable, and therefore normatively neutral" (31). She concludes that "clearly, what Foucault needs, and needs desperately, are normative criteria for distinguishing acceptable from unacceptable forms of power" (33). This is the essence of Bevir's second aporia.

Though she offered this critique over thirty years ago, I find that Fraser's remains one of the most significant criticisms of Foucault's project, one for which I have not yet seen an entirely adequate and direct answer. Ultimately, however, I think Fraser's analysis is mistaken—Foucault's project does provide the normative resources to justify a critique of domination and other "evils." It is in his discussion of freedom that the internal "bootstrapped" resources for normative and ethical judgments become clear.

I want to show here how ethical or normative claims can emerge in a justified or "grounded" way, *given* Foucault's structural analysis of power. The key for this development is Foucault's claim that freedom and power relations are mutually constitutive for each other, a claim that we have seen emerging throughout my argument.

Before we look at how bootstrapping works in Foucault, I find it's quite helpful to look at another, remarkably similar, ethical bootstrapping project—Simone de Beauvoir's in *The Ethics of Ambiguity*. Her argument aims to establish freedom as the basis and justification for normative judgments. She begins from an existential analysis of the human condition—thrown into the world with others, we are necessarily free to choose how we shall act in that world—and uses this fact of freedom as a source for valuation and moral judgment: "Freedom is the source from which all significations and all values spring" (de Beauvoir 1947, 24). "To will oneself free is to effect the transition from nature to morality by establishing a genuine freedom on the original upsurge of our existence" (25). Like Foucault, de Beauvoir recognizes that an ethics cannot make universal precepts but rather offers a method, one that is constantly subject to error and revision. Given the inherent ambiguity of the human condition, this ethics is necessarily provisional: "Ethics does not furnish recipes. . . . It is impossible to determine this relationship between meaning and content abstractly and universally: there must be a trial and decision in each case" (134). As such, this ethics is, like Foucault's, an always ongoing project; it does not and cannot offer a "final" verdict. Finally, here in contrast to Foucault, de Beauvoir's presentation directly and explicitly confronts the justification problem: Our normative judgment "*has* no reason to will itself. But this does not mean that it can not justify itself, that it can not *give itself* reasons that it does not *have*" (12). And, she continues, "this justification requires a constant tension. My project is never founded, it founds itself" (26). This "founding itself" is the bootstrapping moment in de Beauvoir.

Two strikingly important parallels emerge between Foucault's and de Beauvoir's ethical projects. First, both owe a profound debt to Kant, even as they both explicitly reject Kant's attempts to ground morality on a universal basis in reason. As Kant observes in his essay "To Perpetual Peace,"

> To be sure, if neither freedom nor the moral law that is based on it exist, and if everything that happens or can happen is mere mechanism of nature, then politics (as the art of using that mechanism to govern men) would be the whole of practical wisdom, and the concept of right would be a contentless thought. (Kant 1795, 128; Ak. 8:372)[19]

Kant notes in the *Grounding for the Metaphysics of Morals* that "It is not enough to prove freedom from certain alleged experiences of human nature (such a proof is indeed absolutely impossible, and so freedom can be proved only a priori)" (Kant 1785, 50). Nevertheless, Kant continues, "we must presuppose it [freedom]" (51). Foucault's (and de Beauvoir's) bootstrapping project shows us not only that we must presuppose freedom but that this presupposition is both necessary and justified. Its logic is as follows: Begin with an account that does not presuppose but rather denies freedom. This account proves unable to account for the world as we find it. Therefore, we cannot deny freedom but must posit it. Indeed, as I have tried to demonstrate in the earlier chapters, this is what Foucault's extended analysis of power relations has shown us. So Foucault's refutation of the "Hobbesian hypothesis" is in effect an argument to show the Kantian point that freedom must be presupposed. (This insight also does much to explain Foucault's continuing fascination with Kant and with the particular Kantian texts that most intrigued him—the texts that emphasized the interface with actual, empirical life rather than a priori deductions—the *Anthropology*, which Foucault translated, and "What Is Enlightenment?")

Foucault's articulation of an ethical framework, too, is already situated in his prior analyses of power—the linchpin of the ethical shift is the concept of freedom at the structural core of Foucault's understanding of power. All power relations do—and, significantly, *must*—presuppose freedom: these relations are only possible on the hypothesis that resistance to the initial force, a kind of freedom, is possible. This concept provided the basis for Foucault's refutation of what I have called the "Hobbesian hypothesis"; it also becomes the basis for ethical or moral action (which, initially framed within power relations, now is able to become the frame for relations of power and government).

This is the second parallel between Foucault's and de Beauvoir's projects: they share a structural core, and as such, they each must employ what I call a "bootstrapping" technique—to effect the move from, as Kristina Arp puts it, an "ontological" account of freedom (in power relations, or in humans' "thrown" condition) to a "moral," normative, notion of freedom.[20] Both projects draw upon *internal* resources—namely freedom as a necessary precondition of social relations or the human condition—with which they can "pull themselves up by the bootstraps" to generate normative criteria.

When I talk about "bootstrapping" in Foucault's ethical thinking, there are really two senses in which this is going on. First, there is what we could call "theoretical" bootstrapping—this is the project, which we've seen quickly sketched in de Beauvoir, of constructing ethical freedom from ontological freedom, of a project "founding itself" from within its own resources. This is by far the most important sense and is what I generally mean when I say "bootstrapping." But there is a second sense, call it "discovery" bootstrapping, which is the process of adopting a concept as a central organizing or framing lens for one's analyses, discovering its inadequacies through its articulation and use, and then revising or recasting that concept in favor of another "framing" lens—one that was perhaps itself also already employed in one's earlier analyses. This process of "discovery" bootstrapping was Foucault's modus operandi throughout his career, and it accounts, in part, for his constant "recasting" of earlier work in his presently current terms—for example, in the 1970s recasting his work on madness as "always having been about power" and, on the very first page of an 1984 interview, "The Care of the Self as a Practice of Freedom," recasting his 1970s work on power relations as "always concerned with subjectivity and truth" (DE356.4, 281).

So let's look at how Foucault's ethics "pulls itself up by the theoretical bootstraps" in this January 1984 interview. It is especially helpful because it synthesizes ideas from throughout the last decade of Foucault's work and thus gives us an important overview of the arc of his entire project. He begins with certain general claims about power relations (claims that were clarified in 1975 and 1976), moves to situate his more recent (since 1981)[21] discussions of "the subject" within the framework of power relations, and pulls these two strands of thought together through the related concepts of "governmentality" and "ethics as a practice of freedom."

Early in the interview Foucault makes a quite striking claim: "Freedom," he says, "is the ontological condition of ethics" (DE356.4, 284). Ethics is built upon freedom, in other words—ethics constructs itself, or founds itself, upon resources that are internal to it, normative resources that are interwoven in the ontological fabric of the world. For indeed, we might add that freedom is the ontological condition of power relations. As he says several pages later, "power relations are possible only insofar as the subjects are free" (DE356.4, 292). And he reiterates, "if there are relations of power in every social field, this is because there is freedom everywhere" (DE356.4, 292). This is not a new idea for Foucault—these are core tenets of the theory of power that he had laid out in 1975 and 1976, particularly, as we have seen, in *La volonté de savoir*. He elaborates:

> When I speak of *relations of power* I mean that in human relationships, whether they involve verbal communication such as we are engaged in at this moment, or amorous, institutional, or economic relationships,

power is always present: I mean a relationship in which one person tries to control the conduct of the other. (DE356.4, 291–292)

Note what he's included in this list—institutional and economic relationships but also amorous relationships. Even if he would later say that "sex is boring" (DE326.1, 229), we have seen how amorous relationships have been a site for his analysis of both power (think S&M) and ethics (think friendship) for at least the last decade—here we can see more of the "discovery" bootstrapping at work. The point, however, is clear enough: power is omnipresent because freedom is omnipresent.

At the very end of the interview, Foucault pulls these two strands—freedom as the basis of ethics and as the condition of possibility for power relations—together in the concept of "governmentality" (used in the broader sense that emerged in 1978):

> I am saying that "governmentality" implies the relationship of the self to itself, and I intend this concept of "governmentality" to cover the whole range of practices that constitute, define, organize, and instrumentalize the strategies that individuals in their freedom can use in dealing with each other. Those who try to control, determine, and limit the freedom of others are themselves free individuals who have at their disposal certain instruments they can use to govern others. Thus, the basis for all this is freedom, the relationship of the self to itself and the relationship to the other. (DE356.4, 300)

Let me stress the "thus" here. Freedom is the condition that makes power relations possible, the basis in an ontological sense. But it is also—simultaneously—the criterion by which we reflectively evaluate those power relations, the basis in a moral sense. Foucault adds:

> I believe that this problem [that is, abuses of power, or "bad" power] must be framed in terms of rules of law, rational techniques of government and *ethos*, practices of the self and of freedom. (DE356.4, 299)

It is an interesting conjunction here: rules of law *and* practices of the self—certainly not what we're used to hearing from Foucault, and almost recalling his discussion of "relational rights." But the important point is that an ethos of freedom is the frame for normative evaluation of "good" and "bad" exercises of power. The interviewer immediately follows up with another question:

Q: Are we to take what you have just said as the fundamental criteria of what you have called a new ethics? It is a question of playing with as little domination as possible . . .

MF: I believe that this is, in fact, the hinge point of ethical concerns and the political struggle for respect of rights, of critical thought against abusive techniques of government and ethical research that makes it possible to ground individual freedom. (DE356.4, 299; trans. mod.)

Freedom is the hinge point, the (as the interviewer put it) "fundamental criterion." The very last phrase in Foucault's response I find particularly striking, and I've altered the English translation: "la recherche éthique qui permet de fonder la liberté individuelle" (DE356, IV-728)—"ethical research that makes it possible to ground individual freedom." What I understand this to suggest is that our individual freedom—subjects' freedom, our individual choices and actions, even given an understanding of our "selves" as in part socially constructed—is grounded in ethical reflection, which itself begins in the (ontologically necessary) space of freedom, just as our selves are in part constituted through relations of power (which themselves begin in a space of freedom). In other words, freedom is the criterion for ethical evaluation. (Here we are very close to what de Beauvoir was saying, too.) I'll happily concede that I'm stretching and pushing what is literally said here—but I'll also insist that this move is within the spirit and trajectory of the larger Foucauldian ethical project. Much earlier in the interview (near its beginning and, in fact, at the point from which our discussion began), Foucault had asked, "for what is ethics, if not the practice of freedom, the conscious practice of freedom?" (DE356.4, 284). After a quick interjection from his interviewer,[22] Foucault continued, "Freedom is the ontological condition of ethics. But ethics is the considered form that freedom takes when it is informed by reflection" (DE356.4, 284). "What is ethics but the conscious practice of freedom" and "ethics is the considered form that freedom takes"—as I understand these remarks, freedom is the criterion, the content, for ethical reflection and judgment. And note that Foucault characterizes it in this way immediately after his stipulation that it is the "ontological condition" of ethics—just as it is for power relations. We have in these two sentences the "bootstrapping moment" by which Foucault can provide justification for freedom as a norm without merely "positing" it or uncritically adopting it from the Western liberal tradition. The ethical resources are in fact implicit in the very conditions of possibility of power relations, and they give us a criterion with which we can evaluate others' and our own exercises of power. As such, Foucault's ethical project is profoundly Kantian in character: the normative resources are *internal* to the project, and they turn out to be the very conditions of possibility for the social relations that are to be normatively evaluated.

So how does this help us answer Nancy Fraser's criticism? In her view,

> He fails to appreciate the degree to which the normative is embedded in and infused throughout the whole of language at *every* level and the degree to which, despite himself, his own critique has to make use of modes of description, interpretation, and judgment formed within the modern Western normative tradition. (Fraser 1981, 30–31)

On the contrary, I think we see in this interview precisely *how* Foucault *does* appreciate that the normative is embedded in and infused throughout the social relations that frame and define our selves. Indeed, "freedom is the ontological condition" of power relations *and* ethics. Furthermore, that Foucault's critique makes use of elements formed within the Western tradition should be unsurprising and uncontroversial—for the essence of any bootstrapping project is to make use of the resources that are available to it at a given moment. Foucault (and we) can make use of concepts while simultaneously subjecting them to critique and even suspicion—indeed, any pragmatist project would do so. What I find so fascinating is that the Foucauldian ethical project simultaneously fuses both this pragmatic, provisional, bootstrapped facet *and* a Kantian quasi-transcendental facet—not merely taking us beyond Fraser's criticism but also, perhaps, showing us a new face for embodied, engaged ethical thinking that avoids the Scylla and Charybdis of universalism and relativism.

With this understanding of freedom, Foucault's ethical trajectories have come full circle: initially arising spontaneously from resistance to power, from "not wanting to be governed like this," through caring for oneself and others to governing oneself and others, this ethics is embodied in a critical attitude that always remains aware of its own situated provisionality, its own dangerousness, revealed and justified in the freedom for resistance that is a necessary condition for the very existence of power, and it also gives us the tools to evaluate the exercise of that power. In the end, this ought not surprise us. For, as Foucault described it, "the care of the self is ethical in itself; but it implies complex relationships with others insofar as this *ethos* of freedom is also a way of caring for others. . . . It is also the art of governing" (DE356.4, 287, trans. mod.). This critical ethics of freedom, this art of governing, is a practice we are all called to engage in, even as Foucault will steadfastly refuse to tell us precisely how or what we should do. We cannot rely on Foucault to do our thinking for us but rather must act in accord with the motto of Enlightenment—"Sapere aude!" or, as he entitled his final course at the Collège de France, the "courage of truth"—if we are actively to create a Foucauldian ethics.

Conclusion

To Struggle with Hope

Lift ev'ry voice and sing,
Till earth and heaven ring,
Ring with the harmonies of liberty;
Let our rejoicing rise,
High as the list'ning skies,
Let it resound loud as the rolling sea.
Sing a song full of the faith that the dark past has taught us,
Sing a song full of the hope that the present has brought us;
Facing the rising sun of our new day begun,
Let us march on till victory is won.

    —James Weldon Johnson

James Weldon Johnson's "Lift Ev'ry Voice and Sing," written to celebrate Abraham Lincoln's birthday, came to be known as the "Negro National Anthem." Its first stanza, the epigraph for this chapter, speaks of African Americans' rejoicing hope, even though, as is clear in the stanza's last line, "victory" is not yet won and the struggle for liberty continues. (Johnson himself later served as a national organizer for the NAACP.) But in Johnson's poem, this hope was not guaranteed. The second stanza recalls the institution of slavery: "Bitter the chast'ning rod/Felt in the days when hope unborn had died" (Johnson 1900, 768–769). Johnson's poem captures the dialectic between hope and despair that has framed the legacy of slavery in African Americans' experience, a dialectical struggle between hope and despair that also shaped the gay community's responses to the crisis of AIDS (for one poignant example, see Shilts 1988/2007, 356–357). And this dialectical struggle is an underlying theme in my interpretation of Foucault's work. I think that this hope lies at the root of what Foucault described as his "hyper- and pessimistic activism" (DE326.1, 232). For, he explains, "if everything is dangerous, then we always have something to do" (DE326.1, 231–232). Without hope, after all, why do anything at all?

We can, as I have attempted to show, hear this hope running throughout Foucault's work. We can even hear this hope in the closing lines of *Discipline and Punish*, arguably at the nadir of a seeming bleakly despairing portrayal of our society:

> In this central and centralized humanity, the effect and instrument
> of complex power relations, bodies and forces subjected by multiple
> mechanisms of "incarceration," objects for discourses that are in them-
> selves elements for this strategy, we must hear the distant roar of battle.
> (1975ET, 308)

After this presentation of humanity as bodies that have seemingly been entirely enclosed in a complex strategy of incarceration, what significance should we give to the final phrase (in fact, the main clause) of this sentence, that "we must hear the distant roar of battle"? It is, I think, a harbinger of hope: this bleak portrait is not intended to induce despair but to rally the forces, for a battle approaches—a battle that might inaugurate new modes of relating to others and to ourselves. Indeed, Foucault's first ethical itinerary in 1976 was to look at these bodies and their pleasures as sites of resistance to the incarcerating forms of power.

A quite different example poignantly captures the hopeful spirit of Foucault's remark that "we always have something to do." Closing the 1997 "Afterword" to his 1983 history of Jackie Robinson and the integration of baseball, Jules Tygiel notes:

> We remain engrossed in the great social experiment that he [Jackie Rob-
> inson] began. But, as with all incomplete experiments, we must periodi-
> cally reassess its progress and reinvigorate its promise. We must reinforce
> those strategies that work, reject those that have failed, and assay new
> initiatives. (Tygiel 1997, 355)

This process—of reassessment and reinvigoration, reinforcement and rejection, and of beginning anew—is the critical work that follows from Foucault's claim that everything is dangerous, that we always have work to do. Tygiel continues:

> The Jackie Robinson saga, whether in myth or reality, has always appealed to "the better angels of our nature." Today, fifty years after he first graced us with his pride, his courage, his passion, and his vision, our nation, amidst our current failures, disappointments, and dispiriting political drift, has yet to produce a more compelling prophecy of a just, interracial society than that which we envision when we invoke the memory of Jackie Robinson. (Tygiel 1997, 355)

Tygiel's point is that, despite our current failures, Jackie Robinson's story nevertheless continues to inspire our hope. (One might legitimately ask, is it appropriate to cite the example of a baseball player here? Indeed it is, for Jackie Robinson's experience demonstrated the quotidian face of resistance and the multiply interwoven layers of racism that he had to circumnavigate.)

Foucault spoke explicitly about the place of hope in an unpublished April 1983 interview. There, Leo Löwenthal challenged Foucault, noting that "I [Löwenthal] cannot discover thus far in your [Foucault's] argumentation about distrust any kind of theoretically argued possibility to overcome this hopelessness, this defeatism, this distrust" (BdS-D250[07], 10), to which Foucault responded:

> I don't think that to be suspicious means that you don't have any hope. Despair and hopelessness are one thing; suspicion is another. And if you are suspicious, it is because, of course, you have a certain hope. The problem is to know which kind of hope you have, and which kind of hope it is reasonable to have in order to avoid what I would call not the "pessimistic circle" you spoke of, but the political circle which reintroduces in your hopes, and through your hopes, the things you want to avoid by these hopes. (BdS-D250[07], 11)

Foucault had described his attitude as one of "hyper- and pessimistic activism." His suspicion and pessimism, but also his hyperactivity, are present precisely because he has "a certain kind of hope." As J. Joyce Schuld notes—and her two adjectives are well chosen—this interview reminds us that "he has been inspired by something that is both more promising and more dangerous [than pessimism]—hope" (Schuld 2003, 1). Later in this conversation, Foucault clarified:

It's not a circle, a vicious circle from hope to despair, or from hope
to complete disappointment. All it is is strategic features, and hope is
totally essential to our political life. . . . And we don't have to renounce
our hope because we are suspicious, or renounce our suspicion because
we have hope. (BdS-D250[07], 14)

Looking back, we can hear that hope quite clearly in a famous 1977
remark:

It seems to me that power *is* "always already there," that one is never
"outside" it, that there are no "margins" for those who break with the
system to gambol in. But this does not entail the necessity of accepting
an inescapable form of domination. . . . To say that one can never be
"outside" power does not mean that one is trapped and condemned to
defeat no matter what. (DE218.1, 141–142)

Though power is everywhere, though it inflects and shapes all of our relationships and even frames our ethical possibilities, we are not "condemned
to defeat." On the contrary, this means that resources for freedom are everywhere and that "we always have something to do."

And the challenge, always, involves determining what one ought to
do. Consider again a few passages from Foucault's 1978 Collège de France
course—that pivotal course in which the final architectural structures of
Foucault's analysis of power were articulated and in which the ethical stakes
of the "art of governing" were clarified. He notes, in his description of biopower, that

risks are not the same for all individuals, all ages, or in every condition, place or milieu. There are therefore differential risks that reveal,
as it were, zones of higher risk and, on the other hand, zones of less or
lower risk. This means that one can thus identify what is dangerous.
(CdF78ET, 61)

This process of evaluating dangers is linked to the exercise of power in governing. As Foucault notes in discussing Machiavelli's *The Prince*:

On the one hand, [Machiavelli's analysis] involves the identification of
dangers: where they come from, in what they consist, and their com-
parative severity; what is the greater danger, and what is the lesser? The
second aspect is the art of manipulating relations of force that enable the
Prince to protect his principality. (CdF78ET, 92)

However, Foucault continues, the contemporary anti-Machiavellian literature showed that that analysis should not be restricted to "preserving one's
principality" but rather to a much broader "art of government" encompassing three levels: "the government of oneself, which falls under morality; the
art of properly governing a family, which is part of economy; and finally, the
'science of governing well' the state, which belongs to politics" (CdF78ET,
93–94). Foucault's analysis of power gives us the resources to integrate these
three levels and to recognize (and hence manipulate) the kinds of force relations (sovereign, disciplinary, and biopolitical) at play within them. Foucault's ethical trajectories serve to identify and evaluate the concomitant
dangers, giving us grounds upon which to act, and criteria for evaluating
that action, however tentatively, for "we always have something to do."

Indeed, we must always bear in mind the contingency and provisionality of our maxims—this gives us a sense of humility that might avert
or resist a hubristic tendency to totalizing (if not totalitarian) or utopian
visions—even as we articulate these maxims as "imperatives." Thus, his 1977
remark that

> the role for theory today seems to me to be just this: not to formulate the
> global systematic theory which holds everything in place, but to analyse
> the specificity of mechanisms of power, to locate the connections and
> extensions, to build little by little a strategic knowledge. (DE218.1, 145)

Or, as he put it in a 1975 interview, "But as for saying, 'Here is what you
must do!,' certainly not" (DE157.1, 62). This brings us back to the 1978
course. At the very beginning of the first lecture, as he was outlining how an
analysis of power entails ethical commitments, he noted:

> Since there has to be an imperative, I would like the one underpinning
> the theoretical analyses we are attempting to be quite simply a condi-
> tional imperative of the kind: If you want to struggle, here are some
> key points, here are some lines of force, here are some constrictions and
> blockages. In other words, I would like these imperatives to be no more
> than tactical pointers. (CdF78ET, 3)

After this precautionary note about the provisional nature of any such
claims, Foucault continued:

> Of course, it's up to me, and those who are working in the same direc-
> tion, to know on what fields of real forces we need to get our bearings

in order to make a tactically effective analysis. But this is, after all, the circle of struggle and truth, that is to say, precisely of philosophical practice. (CdF78ET, 3)

In other words, which bring us full circle (again, as it were), "the ethico-political choice we have to make every day is to determine which is the main danger" (DE326.1, 232). And so this "circle of struggle and truth"—of hope—thus constitutes "philosophical practice," which Foucault was to later define both (in 1982) as keeping "watch over the excessive powers of political rationality" (DE306.4, 238) and (in 1984) as "the critical work that thought brings to bear on itself" (1984aET, 9) at the heart of his ethics.

The tensions at play in this struggle between despair and hope are acutely presented in the theologian Paul Tillich's (whom Foucault positively cites in his 1984 Collège de France course [CdF84ET, 178–180]) discussion of utopia. In discussing the critical value of utopian thinking, Tillich notes that "utopia" is fruitful, powerful, and truthful (in that it "opens up possibilities" through "an anticipation of human fulfillment" in real possibilities) *and* unfruitful, impotent, and untruthful (insofar as utopias portray "impossibilities as real possibilities—and fails to see them for what they are, impossibilities"; thereby "utopia succumbs to pure wishful thinking") (Tillich 1951, 297, 300).

Faced with utopia's necessary failure (because it portrays impossibilities), its ultimate unrealizability, Tillich observes that we can respond to this frustration with fanaticism, disillusionment, or terror. But these are the kinds of responses that Foucault repeatedly, throughout his life, actively tried to avoid, when he suggested, for example in his very first remarks of the opening lecture of the 1978 Collège de France course, that "since there has to be an imperative, I would like the one underpinning the theoretical analysis we are attempting to be quite simply a conditional imperative . . . no more than tactical pointers" (CdF78ET, 3). Tillich's resolution of these paradoxes—embodying the attitude that a Foucauldian ethic invites—is to note that "every utopia, when actualized, stands as a transitory reality and is therefore preliminary and ambiguous," for "something *can* happen, something new, something realizable here and now, under present circumstances and conditions, with their unique possibilities" (Tillich 1951, 306). But to hold onto this resolution means to embrace utopia while simultaneously giving up something of the idea—its transhistorical, transcendental character. Thus Tillich speaks of vertical and horizontal dimensions within utopia, which coexist:

We have the vertical, where alone fulfillment is to be found, yet precisely where we are unable to see it but can only point to it; and the horizontal, actualization in space and time but for that very reason never full actualization but always partial, fragmentary, in this hour, in that form. (308)

An important aspect of Foucault's project is to bring us to recognize the impossibility of such a vertical axis while simultaneously understanding that that impossibility "does not entail the necessity of accepting an inescapable form of domination. . . . To say that one can never be 'outside' power does not mean that one is trapped and condemned to defeat no matter what" (DE218.1, 141–142).

The attitude that Tillich calls on us to adopt with respect to utopias is, I suggest, precisely the attitude that Foucault invites us to fashion within ourselves: an attitude of critique that recognizes its convictions are always preliminary but that also recognizes that it is free, and empowered, to alter reality, to realize new possibilities, and to resist the norms and power relations within which it is given. What this attitude gives us is *hope* in the face of our continuing, many-layered struggles: a hope that is realized through the very critical engagement, motivated by a kind of care, with others and with ourselves as we cultivate and practice this critical attitude—a hope rooted in the fruitfulness, power, and truth that Tillich found in utopia. (And so it should be unsurprising that these very themes, power and truth, constitute central foci of Foucault's work throughout his career.)

Perhaps hope does not need justifications in the same way that other normative concepts do. Perhaps that is the important lesson of the myth of Pandora. As Hesiod relates the story in *Works and Days*, hope itself is ambivalent: it is one of the evil "gift[s]—a scourge for toiling men" (Hesiod 1983, 69, l.83) inside Pandora's jar. Yet when she opens the lid to release its contents, "only Hope stayed under the rim of the jar and did not fly away from her secure stronghold, for in compliance with the wishes of cloud-gathering Zeus, Pandora put the lid on the jar before she could come out" (Hesiod 1983, 69, ll.97–100). As the translator notes in his commentary,

if Hope is entirely bad, she should have been released together with all the other ills that plague man. On the other hand, if Hope is entirely good, she should have no place in Pandora's jar. Perhaps she is treated differently because she can be both good and bad. (Athankassakis, in Hesiod 1983, 90)

In Hesiod's telling, hope is given to humans by the gods—without justification. And hope, like everything else, "can be both good and bad," which is to say that hope is dangerous. It can lead us away from despair, but by the same token, it can lead us into disappointment or even disaster. But even in the face of that risk, if we can't know with certainty that our actions today will create a better world (and we can never know that), hope can be sufficient to spur us to action—and perhaps even hyperactivity, especially if we are pessimistic. Hope motivates us to continue our struggles to fashion a better self and to forge a better world—in other words, to grapple with the demands of an art of governing, this art understood to encompass not only the governing both of oneself and of others but also the critique of government (one's own and others'), in an ongoing and unending cycle. Thus, Foucault asked in the introduction to the second volume of *The History of Sexuality*, one of his last published works, "But, then, what is philosophy today—philosophical activity, I mean—if it is not the critical work that thought brings to bear on itself?" (1984a, 14; 1984aET, 8–9). That *philosophical activity* is the ongoing work that, through disconcerting images and exhilarating analyses, Foucault calls us to do. This underlying hope—which remains "under the rim of the lid" but can be heard throughout his writings, even his most disconcerting—is why Foucault continues to inspire.

Acknowledgments

While I take full responsibility for the many shortcomings of this work, I owe a profound thanks to the friendship, wisdom, insights, and support of many people: Amy Allen, Meryl Altman, Louise Burchill, Rich Cameron, Scott Campbell, Janet Donohoe, Ellen-Marie Forsberg, Nancy Fraser, Devonya Havis, Marcelo Hoffman, Lynne Huffer, Ed McGushin, Margaret McLaren, Claudia Mills, Timothy O'Leary, David Rasmussen, Jana Sawicki, Sam Talcott, Helen Tartar, Dianna Taylor, Kevin Thompson, and many others—but above all to Jim Bernauer, without whose insistent encouragement this book would not have been achieved. Financial support for early research was provided by the Andrew W. Mellon Foundation and the Boston College Graduate School of Arts and Sciences; the Janet Prindle Institute of Ethics at DePauw University provided a wonderful setting for reflection and writing. I owe a special debt of gratitude to the welcoming people at the three different libraries that have held the Collection Michel Foucault: the Bibliothèque du Saulchoir, the Institut Mémoires de l'Édition Contemporaine, and the library of the Collège de France. Profound thanks go also to the students in my spring 2012 DePauw University seminar on Foucault—our conversations helped give this book its final form. My mother and my daughter, Evelyn Pope and Sophia Isabelle Lynch, both inspired me to bring this project to fruition. But this book is dedicated to my wife, Stacy Klingler, who has suffered through the long process of writing with me. Thank you.

A significantly abridged (and much altered) version of Chapter 1 appeared as "Michel Foucault's Theory of Power," in *Michel Foucault: Key Concepts*, ed. D. Taylor (Acumen, 2010), 13–26. Portions of Chapter 3 appeared as "A New Architecture of Power, an Anticipation of Ethics," *Philosophy Today* 53 suppl. (2009): 263–267; the section "The Importance of Population" draws upon an unpublished manuscript originally commissioned for *Biopolitics and Racism: Foucauldian Geneaologies*, ed. E. Mendieta and J. Paris (to date unpublished). Portions of Chapter 4 were originally presented at several conferences: "Foucault's Implicit Strategies of Normative Justification" at a conference on "History, Technology, and Identity After Foucault" (March 2000, Columbia, S.C.); and "Freedom's Justification: Foucault's and Beauvoir's as Complementary Ethical Projects," at the tenth annual Foucault Circle meetings (April 2011, Banff, Canada) and the Feminist Ethics and Social Theory conference (October 2013, Tempe, Ariz.). Chapters 1, 2, and 4 all draw on work initially published as "Is Power All There Is? Michel Foucault and the 'Omnipresence' of Power Relations," *Philosophy Today* 42, no. 1 (Spring 1998): 65–70.

Notes

INTRODUCTION: MICHEL FOUCAULT AS CRITICAL THEORIST

1. All citations shall be included parenthetically in the text, by last name and date of publication. Works by Foucault are cited by year only ("Foucault" is omitted) or by another designation; full details of this apparatus are included in the bibliography. For another allusion to Taylor's claim that "Foucault disconcerts," cf. Bernauer and Mahon (1994, 141).

2. The first essay in Sullivan (1998) is a very compelling discussion of the new personal and sociocultural landscape, both for HIV-positive gay men and for society as a whole.

3. The number of feminists inspired by Foucault is by now far too long to even pretend to provide an exhaustive list. Illustrative early examples include Bartky (1990), Butler (1991), Sawicki (1991), McNay (1992), and the essays collected in Diamond and Quinby (1988); examples of more recent engagements include the essays in Taylor and Vintges (2004) and Huffer (2010).

4. For a different analysis of ways in which Foucault resembles Socrates, cf. Nehamas (1998, 157ff.).

5. We can note (as an aside at this point) that this kind of freedom, the challengability and revisability of our interpretations as well as actions, which is what produces the "empowering danger" that Foucault describes, is closely related to the kinds of challengability that Jürgen Habermas sees at the core of communicative rationality and validity.

6. Her citation is from Marx's "Letter to A. Ruge, September 1843" (Marx 1843a, 209). Pages 206–209 of Marx 1843a and 1843b are two different translations of the same German text. In the second translation, this passage is rendered as "the work of our time to clarify to itself (critical philosophy) the meaning of its own struggle and its own desires" (Marx 1843b, 15).

7. Cf., for example, Habermas (1983) and Honneth (1992).

8. Benhabib's definition is a good representative. Consider one additional example, Raymond Geuss's definition of critical theory in *The Idea of a Critical Theory*: "A critical theory, then, is a reflective theory which gives agents a kind of knowledge inherently productive of enlightenment and emancipation" (Geuss 1981, 2). The key elements that he highlights—critical theory is (1) a form of knowledge, (2) which is reflexive, and (3) which serves as a guide to action, in particular, toward enlightenment and emancipation—correspond not only to Benhabib's definition but to Marx's as well.

9. McCarthy makes this point to distinguish "critical social theory," by which he means Frankfurt School approaches, from Foucauldian genealogy. While McCarthy does bring out several important similarities between Foucault and the Frankfurt school in this essay (which I'm emphasizing here), his main task is to highlight key differences. I think that on the whole, however, McCarthy has misread Foucault's project.

10. Machiavelli's analysis is given in *The Prince* (1532), and Foucault observes that "Machiavelli was among the few—and this no doubt was the scandal of his 'cynicism'—who conceived the power of the Prince in terms of force relationships, perhaps we need to go one step further, do without the persona of the prince, and decipher power mechanisms on the basis of a strategy that is immanent in force relationships" (1976ET, 97). Machiavelli is the key figure for Friedrich Meinecke (cf. Meinecke 1924), and Foucault draws on Meinecke in CdF1978 and DE291, when he turns to *raison d'état*. Hobbes's account, however, looms larger for Foucault's first articulations of his account of power, which emphasize disciplinary micropower and which will be our concern here.

11. We can recognize in Rousseau a theme that will loom large in Foucault's work: freedom as deviation from a rule, that is, freedom in resistance.

12. The theme of friendship, too, is one that Foucault will take up.

13. Lynch (2001) shows how Kojève misreads Hegel and how a more hopeful reading emerges from Hegel's text.

14. Joan Tronto's work (e.g., Tronto 1993) was pioneering in bringing care and politics together; others have also done so.

15. Because the English title is so unwieldy, I'll refer to this text throughout by its French title.

1. APPROACHING POWER FROM A NEW THEORETICAL BASIS

1. The French original is at 1976, 120: "en se donnant une autre théorie du pouvoir."

2. This and the next two paragraphs are drawn from Lynch (1998), which gives a much fuller discussion of Foucault's view of the omnipresence of power.

3. These are not necessarily the same relationships.

4. When Foucault articulates his new theoretical framework for ethics, he will again criticize the theoretical privilege of the "code"—this time in the form of a "moral code"—in the introduction to *The Use of Pleasure* (1984aET, 25).

5. More precisely, I should say not only "will guide" but also "has emerged out of." This theory of power was intended to guide his empirical investigation of nineteenth-century practices of sexuality, but it also emerged from earlier empirical investigations, in particular his studies of psychiatry and the prison. In this study, I begin by working backward from this theoretical articulation to the earlier empirical studies.

6. As, for example, some Vienna Circle philosophers sought to reduce all scientific languages (and disciplines) to a basic set of physicalist "protocol sentences," so that psychological claims could be reformulated as biological claims, biological as chemical, and chemical as physical. Cf. Neurath (1932).

7. In this passage, Foucault is making an observation about Boulainvilliers's eighteenth-century history of France. But his point here in reference to Boulainvilliers is, in fact, a general one. More precisely, it speaks to Foucault's own methodology.

8. To anticipate, I quote from a 1984 interview: "What I refused was precisely that you first of all set up a theory of the subject—as could be done in phenomenology and in existentialism—and that, beginning from the theory of the subject, you come to pose the question of knowing, for example, how such and such a form of knowledge was possible. What I wanted to know was how the subject constituted himself . . . through a certain number of practices which were games of truth, applications of power, etc. I had to reject a certain a priori theory of the subject in order to make this analysis of the relationships which can exist between the constitution of the subject or different forms of the subject and games of truth, practices of power, and so forth" (DE356.2, 10).

9. He explicitly suggests this inversion in the first lecture of his 1976 Collège de France course (CdF76ET, 15) and takes it up again in the third and seventh lectures (CdF76ET, 47–48, 165)—he very clearly uses this inversion to frame his analysis. I'll discuss this phrase and its significance further in Chapter 3.

10. In a 1977 interview, Foucault again apparently juxtaposes a Kantian view of the moral state, "the Kingdom of Ends," with his own analysis of power relations at the basis of social relations: "I believe the great fantasy is the idea of a social body constituted by the universality of wills. Now the phenomenon of the social body is the effect not of a consensus but of the materiality of power operating on the very bodies of individuals" (DE157.1, 55).

11. We've already seen one example of this continuity: resistance as consti- tutive of power relations, from "The Ethics of Care for the Self as a Practice of Freedom" (DE356), an interview given in 1984. Another late essay that reiter- ates this basic framework is 1982's "The Subject and Power" (DE306).

12. Halperin himself recognizes that the charge is not fair. Immediately after quoting it, he adds, "I would not write such a sentence today" (Halperin 1995, 5).

2. DISCIPLINARY POWER: TESTING THE HOBBESIAN HYPOTHESIS

1. That something, I think, is a sense of hope in the face of an otherwise bleak portrait of modern society. This hope is an important key to Foucault's ethical vision and is the very thing that provokes critics like Nancy Fraser. We will take these ideas up in the last sections of this chapter and in Chapter 4.

2. This and the next three paragraphs are adapted from Lynch (1998).

3. We can note that this understanding of power relations is very Kantian in structure—although Foucault is quite clear that these power relations are not transcendental but contingent. In this respect, Foucault's analysis of power relations as an empirically grounded enabling constraint shares even more with Simone de Beauvoir's similarly detranscendentalized Kantian understand- ing of freedom: "Freedom is the source from which all significations and all values spring. It is the original condition of all justifications of existence. . . . But this justification requires a constant tension. My project is never founded; it founds itself" (de Beauvoir 1947, 24, 26). Indeed, a certain kind of freedom is necessarily presupposed in Foucault's account of the interplay between power and resistance, and it will play an important role in his ethics, too. This insight is the basis of what I will call "bootstrapping" in Foucault's ethics.

4. For the date that the interview was conducted, see Eribon (1989, 356n10). For more information about the circumstances of this interview, see also Miller (1993, 262–263).

5. As Foucault notes in the second lecture of the course (CdF74ET, 19, 28–29).

6. He makes this suggestion in the 1976 Collège de France course (CdF76ET, 15). I will discuss the course and the remark in more detail below.

7. In fact, George III did relapse, twice, in 1810, three years after Wil- lis's death. This episode thus also illustrates disciplinary psychiatric power's troubled relationship to discourses of truth, which Foucault takes up in the lecture of 12 December 1973 (esp. CdF74ET, 128–139).

8. Foucault here follows the analyses of Ernst Kantorowicz in *The King's Two Bodies* (1957). He also takes up Kantorowicz in *Discipline and Punish* (1975ET, 28–29), where he suggests that the body of the prisoner may be the analogue in disciplinary power to the king's body in sovereign power.

9. Foucault drew out certain similarities between his analyses of power and Marx's analysis in *Capital* in a 1976 lecture in Brazil. In this lecture, he summarizes his methodological guidelines (which we have discussed in Chapter 1), defines power as "forms of domination, forms of subjection, which function locally, for example in the workshop, in the army, in slave-ownership or in a property where there are servile relations," and notes that "we must speak of powers and try to localize them in their historical and geographical specificity" (DE297.1, 156). He also goes on to summarize the transformation from sovereign to disciplinary power in economic terms (esp. DE297.1, 258–259).

10. Foucault echoes this theme in the introductory lecture of the 1979 Collège de France course: "for, after all, what interest is there in talking about liberalism, the physiocrats, d'Argenson, Adam Smith, Bentham, and the English utilitarians, if not because the problem of liberalism arises for us in our immediate and concrete actuality?" (CdF79ET, 22).

11. We shall return to this quotation and its highlighting of "populations" below—it illustrates how Foucault in *Discipline and Punish* sees macro forms of power as reducible to the disciplinary micro forms.

12. "Is it surprising that prisons resemble factories, schools, barracks, hospitals, which all resemble prisons?" (1975ET, 228).

13. Indeed, Foucault will later identify other practices of individual-production that explicitly contrast with the disciplinary examination. See, for example, Foucault's discussion of the *hypomnemata* in "Self-Writing" (DE329).

14. *The Gulag Archipelago* was published in 3 volumes between 1973 and 1976.

15. This historical study will also provide illustrations of biopolitical techniques as well as of the ethical importance of freedom. Edward E. Baptist's *The Half Has Never Been Told* (2014), published after this manuscript was complete and therefore not discussed, also provides a rich catalog of the disciplinary techniques at the core of antebellum slavery. I do take one term from Baptist: "enslaver" in lieu of Stampp's more traditional but troublesome "master." Baptist's work is, in its style and power, reminiscent of *Discipline and Punish*; I highly recommend it.

16. Recall Foucault's discussion of soldiers as "natural" or "manufactured" at the beginning of Part 3 of *Discipline and Punish* (1975ET, 137), discussed above.

17. Shortly after reaching this nadir, Douglass notes that "You have seen how a man was made a slave; you shall see how a slave was made a man" (Douglass 1845, 50). Douglass recounts his resistance and eventual escape but refused until decades after the end of slavery to tell exactly how he escaped—so that those means of resistance would remain open to others.

18. This cautionary "or almost" is in fact quite important: it suggests that even in this "purest" manifestation of disciplinary power, the system is not "airtight," that there are other important elements of the subject's constitution that might allow for a subversion of or resistance to this discipline.

19. In, for example, the first lecture of the 1979 Collège de France course, *The Birth of Biopolitics*.

3. REFRAMING THE THEORY: BIOPOWER AND GOVERNMENTALITY

1. This is the third of three lectures that Foucault gave in Brazil in October 1974; they largely follow the lines of thinking that he had articulated in his 1974 Collège de France course. See my discussion of that course in Chapter 2.

2. Compare this with a passage from *La volonté de savoir* (part of which I quoted above): "If one can apply the term *bio-history* to the pressures through which the movements of life and the processes of history interfere with one another, one would have to speak of *bio-power* to designate what brought life and its mechanisms into the realm of explicit calculations and made knowledge-power an agent of transformation of human life" (1976ET, 143).

3. The second essay also includes a long list of "bibliographical suggestions," which were not included in 1976.

4. This is the title of Taylor (1977).

5. The theme of liberalism will be a central concern of Foucault's 1979 Collège de France course, *The Birth of Biopolitics*.

6. In *Discipline and Punish* (esp. 1975ET, 221–224).

7. Consider two examples from a recent issue of the *New York Times* to illustrate how this series continues to function: First, biopower's "global" reach has continued to expand, encompassing the entire ecological environment within its scope: "Disease, it turns out, is largely an environmental issue. Sixty percent of emerging infectious diseases that affect humans are zoonotic—they originate in animals. . . . Public health experts have begun to factor ecology into their models" (Robbins 2012). While on the one hand its scope has been becoming more global, it has also continued to insert itself into individual choices as well: "The current fascination with breast-feeding is also an extension of a society's efforts to control risk, including risk to our children" (Quart 2012).

8. These remarks suggest that Foucault would call for some sort of "total revolution." Indeed, a case could be made that he was tempted by such possibilities—hence his initial excitement for and close attention to the Iranian revolution in 1978–1979. But the lessons that he learned from the course of events in Iran—that he rather saw reconfirmed, since it had been the basis of his critiques of Maoists and Marxists throughout the 1970s—is that such

a "total" revolution is neither possible nor effective and that smaller, local engagements are a more productive direction forward. See, for example, the 1977 interview "Power and Strategies" (DE218).

4. FREEDOM'S CRITIQUE: THE TRAJECTORIES OF A FOUCAULDIAN ETHICS

1. Specifically, he says that "as to those [who think so] . . . all I can say is that clearly we are not from the same planet" (1984aET, 7).

2. Timothy O'Leary brought my attention to this passage (O'Leary 2002, 24).

3. Foucault discusses S&M in two interviews, both given in 1982, though they were published later: "Sexual Choice, Sexual Act" (DE317) and "Sex, Power, and the Politics of Identity" (DE358). For a very informative general introduction to S&M, I recommend Johnson Grey's "The soc.subculture.bondage-bdsm FAQ List" (Grey 1999). One will note, after reading the first frequently asked question (FAQ), that Foucault uses S&M as a generic term to refer to a variety of distinct practices, including (1) s&m—"sadism and masochism," the pleasures of giving and receiving pain; (2) b&d—"bondage and discipline," the pleasures of binding and otherwise regimenting the body; and (3) d&s—"dominance and submission," the pleasures of being in or under the control of another. To be strict about these distinctions, it is in d&s (and, to a lesser extent, b&d) rather than s&m where power relations are explicitly thematized (and eroticized) as such. However, since these distinctions are often merely analytic and since Foucault obviously has d&s and b&d relations in mind, as well as the pleasures of simple pain, I shall use S&M in this discussion in the generic way that Foucault does.

4. In a 1984 interview, Foucault again explains this pattern in reference to "the subject": "What I rejected was the idea of starting out with a theory of the subject—as is done, for example, in phenomenology or existentialism—and, on the basis of this theory, asking how a given form of knowledge was possible. What I wanted to try to show was how the subject constituted itself . . . I had to reject a priori theories of the subject in order to analyze the relationships that may exist between the constitution of the subject or different forms of the subject and games of truth, practices of power, and so on" (DE356.4, 290). Foucault won't begin by assuming what he wants to justify but rather will show that assuming its negation leads to a contradiction—thus justifying speaking of some sort of self-fashioned subject or of relations of pleasure that can't be reduced to power.

5. Leo Bersani notes that this passage "clearly echoes the call, at the end of the first volume of his *History of Sexuality*, for 'a different economy of bodies

and pleasures'" (Bersani 1995, 79). This is, of course, unsurprising, since Foucault's exploration of S&M constituted one of the experiments by which he developed the ethical resources in "bodies and pleasures." Several letters (IMEC-K.2, dating from 1979 and 1982) from Bersani to Foucault suggest that they may have explored these "laboratories of sexual experimentation" (DE317.4, 151) together.

6. Carol Gilligan's own intellectual trajectory has followed a seemingly Foucauldian arc, as suggested by the titles of her books after *In a Different Voice* (1982): *The Birth of Pleasure* (2002), *The Deepening Darkness: Patriarchy, Resistance and Democracy's Future* (2009—co-authored with David A. J. Richards, this book begins with a study of women's roles in ancient Rome), and *Joining the Resistance* (2011).

7. We will see this notion of ontological priority again, in the final section's discussion of freedom. And there is an analogy here, too, to Kant's vision of the role of the moral law in rational beings as legislators in the Kingdom of Ends (Kant 1785, 39–40).

8. Foucault does acknowledge, as we will see below, that individual rights have been an effective and important tool for a critical resistance to unjust power: "not wanting to be governed in this way is not to accept these laws because they are unjust. . . . From this point of view, critique is thus, in the face of the government and the obedience it demands, to oppose universal and indefeasible rights to which every government—whatever it might be, whether it has to do with the monarch, the magistrate, the educator, or the father of the family—will have to submit" (OT-78-01ET, 385).

9. For a further discussion of the ethics of dialogue, see Lynch (1993).

10. Two examples immediately come to mind: heterosexual men may find more avenues opening for intimacy and friendship with each other, and heterosexual couples may find new ways of creating reciprocal relations— particularly regarding communication about consensual and safer sex.

11. "We could therefore conceive of the history of Cynicism, not, once again, as a doctrine, but much more as an attitude and way of being, with, of course its own justificatory and explanatory discourse" (CdF84ET, 178).

12. Foucault had earlier discussed this play in his 1971 course at the Collège de France and in a series of lectures given in Rio de Janeiro, Brazil, in 1973 (DE139).

13. Ladelle McWhorter brought my attention to this passage (McWhorter 2003, 42).

14. Foucault discusses this text in *The Care of the Self* (the third volume of *The History of Sexuality*; 1984bET, 61–62); his 1983 course at Berkeley (*Fearless Speech*, OT-83-03ET, 145ff.), in both the 1980 (CdF80ET, 239–246) and

1982 Collège de France courses (CdF82ET, 481–484), and a 1982 lecture at the University of Vermont (DE363.2, 237).

15. Koopman (2013, esp. the final chapter) offers a more extensive discussion of the connections between Foucault's work and American pragmatism.

16. Bartky (1995) directly addresses this first aporia. Foucault himself is much more dismissive: "to depict this kind of research as an attempt to reduce knowledge to power, to make it the mask of power in structures, where there is no place for a subject, is purely and simply a caricature" (CdF84ET, 8–9).

17. Cf. Taylor (1984) and the two essays on Foucault in Habermas (1987). Both Taylor and Habermas ultimately misread Foucault, however. For example, Taylor reads Foucault to assert that "There is no escape from power into freedom, for such systems of power are co-extensive with human society" (Taylor 1984, 153). The problem is that, as we have seen quite clearly, freedom is not something found only "outside of power" but rather a very condition of possibility for power—freedom is present *within*, not outside, power relations. Since Amy Allen (2010) offers a succinct response to Habermas, I will not discuss him here.

18. Indeed, a typical Alger hero rises to financial success not merely through his or her own efforts but through a wide social support network and even wealthy benefactors—hardly "making use of what is already present" within him- or herself. The example I have in mind is *Ragged Dick*. Dick, a young bootblack and the hero, is told by just such a benefactor (the benefactor's own financial and moral support notwithstanding) to "Remember that your future position depends mainly upon yourself, and that it will be high or low as you choose to make it" (Alger 1868, 50)—a nice statement of the bootstrapping myth. My thanks to Debbie Geis for pointing out this potential confusion.

19. Foucault explicitly cites Kant's essay on perpetual peace in the January 24 lecture of his 1979 Collège de France course (CdF79, 58–60; CdF79ET, 57–58).

20. Kristana Arp (2001, 55) uses these terms in reference to de Beauvoir's ethics, and I find them apt.

21. Indeed, the interviewer explicitly references *The Hermeneutics of the Subject* (CdF82).

22. He says, "In other words, you understand freedom as a reality that is already ethical in itself" (DE356.4, 284).

Bibliography

I. Works by Michel Foucault

A. PUBLISHED WORKS NOT COLLECTED IN DITS ET ÉCRITS

Monographs and other uncollected works are cited in the text by publication
date. English translations (ET) are cited separately.

1961   *Histoire de la folie à l'âge classique.* Paris: Gallimard, 1972.

1961ET1 *Madness and Civilization: A History of Insanity in the Age of Reason.*
Trans. Richard Howard. New York: Vintage, 1988.

1961ET2 *History of Madness.* Trans. Jonathan Murphy and Jean Khalfa. New
York: Routledge, 2006.

1966   *Les mots et les choses: une archeology des sciences humaines.* Paris:
Gallimard.

1966ET *The Order of Things: An Archaeology of the Human Sciences.* New
York: Vintage, 1973.

1975   *Surveiller et punir: naissance de la prison.* Paris: Gallimard.

1975ET *Discipline and Punish: The Birth of the Prison.* Trans. Alan Sheridan.
New York: Vintage, 1977.

1976   *La volonté de savoir. Histoire de la sexualité 1.* Paris: Gallimard.

1976ET *The History of Sexuality: Volume 1: An Introduction.* Trans. Robert
Hurley. New York: Vintage, 1990.

1984a   *L'usage des plaisirs. Histoire de la sexualité 2.* Paris: Gallimard.

1984aET *The Use of Pleasure: Volume 2 of the History of Sexuality.* Trans. Robert
Hurley. New York: Vintage, 1990.

1984b   *Le souci de soi. Histoire de la sexualité 3.* Paris: Gallimard.

1984bET *The Care of the Self: Volume 3 of the History of Sexuality.* Trans. Robert
Hurley. New York: Vintage, 1988.

B. SHORTER WORKS COLLECTED IN DITS ET ÉCRITS

Most of Foucault's shorter (nonmonographic) works are collected in *Dits et écrits*, 4 vols. (Paris: Gallimard, 1994). These are cited in the text by the number assigned by the editors with the prefix "DE" (for example, DE233). Citations from the French will be indicated with the volume in Roman numerals and page in Arabic (for example, "DE233, III-562" would be a citation to "Sexualité et pouvoir" at volume 3, page 562). Citations from English versions include a decimal and number (for example, DE157.1); those texts are listed here. For a complete list of Foucault's shorter works in English, see Lynch (2013).

DE139.2   *"Truth and Juridical Forms."* In *Power*, ed. J. Faubion, trans. R. Hurley, 1–89. New York: New Press, 2000.

DE157.1   *"Body/Power."* In *Power/Knowledge: Selected Interviews and Other Writings, 1972–1977*, ed. and trans. C. Gordon, 55–62. New York: Pantheon, 1980.

DE168.1   *"The Politics of Health in the Eighteenth Century."* In *Power/Knowledge: Selected Interviews and Other Writings, 1972–1977*, ed. and trans. C. Gordon, 166–182. New York: Pantheon, 1980.

DE179.1   *"Bio-history and Bio-politics."* *Foucault Studies* 18 (October 2014): 128–130. [Trans. Richard A. Lynch.]

DE200.3   *"Power and Sex."* In *Politics, Philosophy, Culture: Interviews and Other Writings, 1977–1984*, ed. L. Kritzman, trans. D. J. Parent, 110–124. New York: Routledge, 1988.

DE218.1   *"Power and Strategies."* In *Power/Knowledge: Selected Interviews and Other Writings, 1972–1977*, ed. and trans. C. Gordon, 134–145. New York: Pantheon, 1980.

DE229.1   *"The Incorporation of the Hospital Into Modern Technology."* In *Space, Knowledge, and Power: Foucault and Geography*, ed. J. Crampton and S. Elden, trans. Edgar Knowlton Jr., William J. King, and Stuart Elden, 141–151. Aldershot: Ashgate, 2007.

DE257.1   *"The Politics of Health in the Eighteenth Century."* *Foucault Studies* 18 (October 2014): 113–127. [Trans. Richard A. Lynch.]

DE266.2   *"For an Ethic of Discomfort."* In *Power*, ed. J. Faubion, 443–448. New York: New Press, 2000.

DE278.5   *"Questions of Method."* In *Power*, ed. J. Faubion, 223–238. New York: New Press, 2000.

DE281.2   *"Interview with Michel Foucault."* In *Power*, ed. J. Faubion, trans. R. Hurley, 239–297. New York: New Press, 2000.

DE291.4   *"'Omnes et Singulatim': Towards a Critique of Political Reason."* In *Power*, ed. J. Faubion, trans. R. Hurley, 298–325. New York: New Press, 2000.

DE293.3   *"Friendship as a Way of Life."* In *Ethics: Subjectivity and Truth*, ed. P. Rabinow, trans. J. Johnston, 135–140. New York: New Press, 1997.

DE297.1   *"The Meshes of Power."* In *Space, Knowledge, and Power: Foucault and Geography*, ed. J. Crampton and S. Elden, trans. Gerald Moore, 153–162. Aldershot: Ashgate, 2007. [This is a translation of Foucault's lecture only (DE IV:182–194); a discussion that followed (DE IV:195–201) is not translated.]

DE306.4   *"The Subject and Power."* In *Power*, ed. J. Faubion, trans. R. Hurley, 326–348. New York: New Press, 2000.

DE313.2   *"The Social Triumph of the Sexual Will."* In *Ethics: Subjectivity and Truth*, ed. P. Rabinow, trans. B. Lemon, 157–162. New York: New Press, 1997.

DE317.4   *"Sexual Choice, Sexual Act."* In *Ethics: Subjectivity and Truth*, ed. P. Rabinow, trans. J. O'Higgins, 141–156. New York: New Press, 1997.

DE326.1   *"On the Genealogy of Ethics: An Overview of Work in Progress."* In *Michel Foucault: Beyond Structuralism and Hermeneutics*, by H. Dreyfus and P. Rabinow, 2nd ed., 229–252. Chicago: University of Chicago Press, 1983.

DE326.4   *"On the Genealogy of Ethics: An Overview of Work in Progress."* In *Ethics: Subjectivity and Truth*, ed. P. Rabinow, 253–280. New York: New Press, 1997.

DE329.2   *"Self-Writing."* In *Ethics: Subjectivity and Truth*, ed. P. Rabinow, trans. R. Hurley, 207–222. New York: New Press, 1997.

DE336.3   *"An Interview by Stephen Riggins."* In *Ethics: Subjectivity and Truth*, ed. P. Rabinow, 121–133. New York: New Press, 1997.

DE339.2   *"What Is Enlightenment?"* In *Ethics: Subjectivity and Truth*, ed. P. Rabinow, trans. C. Porter, 303–319. New York: New Press, 1997.

DE341.1   *"Politics and Ethics: An Interview."* In *The Foucault Reader*, ed. P. Rabinow, trans. C. Porter, 373–380. New York: Pantheon, 1984.

DE342.2   *"Polemics, Politics, and Problematizations."* In *Ethics: Subjectivity and Truth*, ed. P. Rabinow, 111–119. New York: New Press, 1997.

DE351.2   *"The Art of Telling the Truth."* In *Politics, Philosophy, Culture: Interviews and Other Writings, 1977–1984*, ed. L. Kritzman, trans. A. Sheridan, 86–95. New York: Routledge, 1988.

DE356.2 *"The Ethic of Care of the Self as a Practice of Freedom: An Interview with Michel Foucault, January 20, 1984, by Raúl Fornet-Betancourt, Helmut Becker, and Alfredo Gomez-Müller."* In *The Final Foucault*, ed. J. Bernauer and D. Rasmussen, trans. J. D. Gauthier SJ, 1–20. Cambridge, Mass.: MIT Press, 1998.

DE356.4 *"The Ethics of the Concern of the Self as a Practice of Freedom."* In *Ethics: Subjectivity and Truth*, ed. P. Rabinow, trans. P. Aranov and D. McGrawth, 281–301. New York: New Press, 1997.

DE358.1 *"Sex, Power, and the Politics of Identity: An Interview."* The Advocate 400 (August 7, 1984): 26–30, 58.

DE358.2 *"Sex, Power, and the Politics of Identity."* In *Ethics: Subjectivity and Truth*, ed. P. Rabinow, 163–173. New York: New Press, 1997.

DE361.2 *"Life: Experience and Science."* In *The Essential Foucault*, ed. P. Rabinow and N. Rose, 6–17. New York: New Press, 2003.

DE362.1 *"Truth, Power, Self: An Interview with Michel Foucault, October 25, 1982."* In *Technologies of the Self: A Seminar with Michel Foucault*, ed. L. Martin, H. Gutman, and P. Hutton, 9–15. Amherst: University of Massachusetts Press, 1988.

DE363.2 *"Technologies of the Self."* In *Ethics: Subjectivity and Truth*, ed. P. Rabinow, 223–251. New York: New Press, 1997.

C. SHORTER WORKS NOT INCLUDED IN DITS ET ÉCRITS

Certain of Foucault's other shorter works were not included in *Dits et écrits*. These are cited as "OT," with a two-digit number indicating the year of first appearance and a second accession number (for example, OT-78-01). A complete list of these texts is included in Lynch (2013).

OT-61-02   *L'anthropologie de Kant (thèse complémentaire).* T. I: *Introduction.* Paris: Bibliothèque de la Sorbonne.

OT-61-02ET *Introduction to Kant's Anthropology.* Ed. R. Nigro, trans. R. Nigro and K. Briggs. Cambridge, Mass.: Semiotext(e), 2008.

OT-78-01   *"Qu'est-ce que la critique? (Critique et Aufklärung)."* Bulletin de la Société française de Philosophie 84 (1990): 25–63 (communication à la Société française de philosophie, séance du 27 mai 1978).

OT-78-01ET *"What Is Critique?"* In *What Is Enlightenment? Eighteenth-Century Answers and Twentieth-Century Questions*, ed. J. Schmidt, trans. Kevin Paul Geiman, 382–398. Berkeley: University of California Press, 1996. [This translation does not include a Q&A session that followed the lecture.]

OT-78-07   *Interview with Jean Le Bitoux, conducted July 10, 1978*, published in two parts in *Mec*. "Le Gai Savoir (I)," *Mec* 5 (June 1988): 32–36; "*Le Gai Savoir (II)*," *Mec* 6–7 (July/August 1988): 30–33.

OT-78-07ET   "*The Gay Science*." *Critical Inquiry* 37, no. 3 (Spring 2011): 385–403. [Trans. Nicolae Morar and Daniel W. Smith.]

OT-83-03   *Six lectures at the University of California*, October and November 1983. [There is significant overlap between these lectures and the final two courses (1982–1983 and 1983–1984) at the Collège de France.]

OT-83-03ET   *Fearless Speech*. Ed. Joseph Pearson. New York: Semiotext(e), 2001.

D. COURSES GIVEN AT THE COLLÈGE DE FRANCE

Courses given at the Collège de France are cited in the text by CdF and the year of the lectures. Published lectures are cited by page number and listed below; unpublished lectures are cited by lecture date and are my own transcriptions and translations from the audio recordings.

CdF71   *Leçons sur la volonté de savoir: cours au Collège de France, 1970–1971*. Paris: Gallimard/Seuil "Hautes Études," 2011.

CdF74   *Le pouvoir psychiatrique: cours au Collège de France, 1973–1974*. Paris: Gallimard/Seuil "Hautes Études," 2003.

CdF74ET   *Psychiatric Power: Lectures at the Collège de France, 1973–1974*. New York: Palgrave MacMillan, 2006.

CdF75   *Les anormaux: cours au Collège de France, 1974–1975*. Paris: Gallimard/Seuil "Hautes Études," 1999.

CdF75ET   *Abnormal: Lectures at the Collège de France, 1974–1975*. New York: Picador, 2003.

CdF76   *«Il faut défendre la société»: cours au Collège de France, 1976*. Paris: Gallimard/Seuil "Hautes Études," 1997.

CdF76ET   "*Society Must Be Defended*": *Lectures at the Collège de France, 1975–1976*. New York: Picador, 2003.

CdF78   *Sécurité, territoire, population: cours au Collège de France, 1977–1978*. Paris: Gallimard/Seuil "Hautes Études," 2004.

CdF78ET   *Security, Territory, Population: Lectures at the Collège de France, 1977–78*. New York: Palgrave MacMillan, 2007.

CdF79   *Naissance de la biopolitique: cours au Collège de France, 1978–1979*. Paris: Gallimard/Seuil "Hautes Études," 2004.

CdF79ET   *The Birth of Biopolitics: Lectures at the Collège de France, 1978–79*. New York: Palgrave MacMillan, 2008.

CdF80   *Du gouvernement des vivants: cours au Collège de France, 1979–1980.*
           Paris: EHESS/Gallimard/Seuil "Hautes Études," 2012.
CdF80ET   *On the Government of the Living: Lectures at the Collège de France,
           1979–1980.* New York: Palgrave MacMillan, 2014.
CdF82   *L'herméneutique du sujet: cours au Collège de France, 1981–82.* Paris:
           Gallimard/Seuil "Hautes Études," 2001.
CdF82ET   *The Hermeneutics of the Subject: Lectures at the Collège de France,
           1981–1982.* New York: Palgrave MacMillan, 2005.
CdF83   *Le gouvernement de soi et des autres: cours au Collège de France,
           1982–1983.* Paris: Gallimard/Seuil "Hautes Études," 2008.
CdF83ET   *The Government of Self and Others: Lectures at the Collège de France,
           1982–1983.* New York: Palgrave MacMillan, 2010.
CdF84   *Le courage de la vérité (Le gouvernement de soi et des autres, II): cours
           au Collège de France, 1984.* Paris: Gallimard/Seuil "Hautes Études,"
           2009. I have also consulted an unpublished typescript prepared
           by Michael Behrent. Each chapter in that typescript is numbered
           separately, so I-19 refers to Lecture 1, page 19.
CdF84ET   *The Courage of Truth (The Government of Self and Others II):
           Lectures at the Collège de France, 1983–1984.* New York: Palgrave
           MacMillan, 2011.

E. ARCHIVAL DOCUMENTS

Archival documents are cited in the text by archive and catalogue num-
ber. BdS refers to the Bibliothèque du Saulchoir. IMEC refers to l'Institut
Mémoires de l'édition contemporaine.
BdS-B46   *"Le Gai Savoir (I)." Mec Magazine* 5 (June 1988): 32–36. The
               first of two parts of an interview with Jean Le Bitoux, con-
               ducted July 10, 1978. Cf. OT-78-07.
BdS-C62   *"Du gouvernement des vivants."* Lectures at the Collège de
               France, January–March 1980. *Audiotape recordings (12 cassettes).*
               Cf. CdF80.
BdS-D250[07]   *"Discussion with Michel Foucault"* (April 21, 1983), with Robert
               Bellah, Bert Dreyfus, Martin Jay, Leo Löwenthal, Paul Rabi-
               now, Charles Taylor. Unpublished typescript, 32 pp.
IMEC-K.2   *"Letters: Bernauer-Bersani-Brown"* [Letters from Bersani to
               Foucault include two handwritten notes (December 10, 1979,
               New York; and May 14, 1982) and a typed note (June 28, 1982,
               New York).]

II. Works by Other Authors

Works by other authors are cited in the text by author and publication date.

Agee, James, and Walker Evans. 1941. *Let Us Now Praise Famous Men.* New York: Houghton Mifflin.

Alger, Horatio. 1868. *Ragged Dick, or, Street life in New York with Bootblacks.* New York: Norton, 2008.

Allen, Amy. 2010. "*The Entanglement of Power and Validity: Foucault and Critical Theory.*" In *Foucault and Philosophy,* ed. T. O'Leary and C. Falzon, 78–98. Oxford: Wiley-Blackwell.

Arp, Kristiana. 1968. *The Bonds of Freedom: Simone de Beauvoir's Existentialist Ethics.* New York: Norton, 2008.

Baptist, Edward E. 2014. *The Half Has Never Been Told: Slavery and the Making of American Capitalism.* New York: Basic Books.

Bartky, Sandra Lee. 1990. *Femininity and Domination: Studies in the Phenomenology of Oppression.* Chicago: Open Court.

Bartky, Sandra Lee. 1995. "*Agency: What's the Problem?*" In "*Sympathy and Solidarity" and Other Essays,* 31–45. Lanham, Md.: Rowman and Littlefield, 2002.

Bartky, Sandra Lee. 2002. *"Sympathy and Solidarity" and Other Essays.* Lanham, Md.: Rowman and Littlefield.

Beasley, Chris, and Carol Bacchi. 2005. "*The Political Limits of 'Care' in Reimagining Interconnection/Community and an Ethical Future.*" *Australian Feminist Studies* 20, no. 46: 49–64.

Beauvoir, Simone de. 1947. *The Ethics of Ambiguity.* Trans. Bernard Frechtman. Secaucus, N.J.: Citadel, 1948.

Benhabib, Seyla. 1986. *Critique, Norm, and Utopia: A Study of the Foundations of Critical Theory.* New York: Columbia University Press.

Bentham, Jeremy. 1791. *The Panopticon Writings.* Ed. Miran Bozovic. New York: Verso, 1995.

Bernauer, James, and Michael Mahon. 1994. "*The Ethics of Michel Foucault.*" In *The Cambridge Companion to Foucault,* ed. Gary Gutting, 141–158. Cambridge: Cambridge University Press, 1994.

Bersani, Leo. 1995. *Homos.* Cambridge, Mass.: Harvard University Press.

Bevir, Mark. 1999. "*Foucault, Power, and Institutions.*" *Political Studies* 47, no. 2 (June 1999): 345–359.

Brennan, Thomas. 2006. "*A Tale of Two Comings Out: Priest and Gay on a Catholic Campus.*" In *Jesuit Postmodern: Scholarship, Vocation, and Identity in the Twenty-First Century*, ed. Francis X. Clooney, 181–194. Lanham, Md.: Lexington, 2006.

Butler, Judith. 1991. *Gender Trouble: Feminism and the Subversion of Identity.* New York: Routledge.

Butler, Judith. 1993. *Bodies That Matter: On the Discursive Limits of "Sex."* New York: Routledge.

Caraher, John. 2004. *Personal conversation*, September 17.

Clooney, Francis X., ed. 2006. *Jesuit Postmodern: Scholarship, Vocation, and Identity in the Twenty-First Century.* Lanham, Md.: Lexington.

Davidson, Arnold I. 1994. *"Ethics as Ascetics: Foucault, the History of Ethics, and Ancient Thought."* In *The Cambridge Companion to Foucault*, ed. Gary Gutting, 115–140. Cambridge: Cambridge University Press, 1994.

Davidson, Arnold I. 2003. *Introduction to* CdF76ET.

Davidson, Arnold I. 2006. *Introduction to* CdF74ET.

Diamond, Irene, and Lee Quinby. 1988. *Feminism and Foucault: Reflections on Resistance.* Boston: Northeastern University Press.

Douglass, Frederick. 1845. *Narrative of the Life of Frederick Douglass, an American Slave, Written by Himself.* New Haven, Conn.: Yale University Press, 2001.

Elden, Stuart. 2005. *"The Problem of Confession: The Productive Failure of Foucault's History of Sexuality."* *Journal for Cultural Research* 9, no. 1 (January 2005): 23–41.

Eribon, Didier. 1989. *Michel Foucault.* Trans. Betsy Wing. Cambridge, Mass.: Harvard University Press, 1991.

Falzon, Christopher, Timothy O'Leary, and Jana Sawicki, eds. 2013. *A Companion to Foucault.* Oxford: Wiley-Blackwell.

Flynn, Thomas R. 2005. *Sartre, Foucault, and Historical Reason. Vol. 2: A Poststructuralist Mapping of History.* Chicago: University of Chicago Press.

Frankl, Viktor E. 1946. *Man's Search for Meaning.* Boston: Beacon, 2006.

Fraser, Nancy. 1981. *"Foucault on Modern Power: Empirical Insights and Normative Confusions."* In *Unruly Practices: Power, Discourse, and Gender in Contemporary Social Theory*, 17–34. Minneapolis: University of Minnesota Press, 1989.

Fraser, Nancy. 1989. *Unruly Practices: Power, Discourse, and Gender in Contemporary Social Theory.* Minneapolis: University of Minnesota Press.

Fraser, Nancy. 2003. *"From Discipline to Flexibilization? Rereading Foucault in the Shadow of Globalization."* *Constellations* 10, no. 2: 160–171.

Friedman, Marilyn. 1989. *"Feminism and Modern Friendship: Dislocating the Community."* *Ethics* 99, no. 2: 275–290.

Gates, Henry Louis, and Nellie Y. McKay, eds. 1997. *The Norton Anthology of African American Literature.* New York: Norton.

Geuss, Raymond. 1981. *The Idea of a Critical Theory: Habermas and the Frank-furt School.* Cambridge: Cambridge University Press.

Gilligan, Carol. 1983. *In a Different Voice: Psychological Theory and Women's Development.* Cambridge, Mass.: Harvard University Press, 1993.

Gilligan, Carol. 2002. *The Birth of Pleasure.* New York: Knopf.

Gilligan, Carol. 2011. *Joining the Resistance.* Malden, Mass.: Polity.

Gilligan, Carol, and David A. J. Richards. 2009. *The Deepening Darkness: Patriarchy, Resistance, and Democracy's Future.* Cambridge: Cambridge University Press.

Grey, Johnson. 1999. "*The soc.subculture.bondage-bdsm FAQ List.*" Last updated April 21, 1999. http://www.unrealities.com/adult/ssbb/faq.htm.

Gutting, Gary, ed. 1994. *The Cambridge Companion to Foucault.* Cambridge: Cambridge University Press.

Habermas, Jürgen. 1983. *Moral Consciousness and Communicative Action.* Trans. Christian Lenhardt and Shierry Weber Nicholsen. Cambridge, Mass.: MIT Press, 1990.

Habermas, Jürgen. 1987. *The Philosophical Discourse of Modernity.* Cambridge, Mass.: MIT Press, 1987.

Halperin, David. 1986. "*Sexual Ethics and Technologies of the Self in Classical Greece.*" *American Journal of Philology* 107: 274–286.

Halperin, David. 1995. *Saint Foucault: Towards a Gay Hagiography.* New York: Oxford University Press.

Halperin, David. 2000. *Saint Foucault.* French ed. Trans. Didier Eribon. Paris: Epel, 2000.

Heidegger, Martin. 1924. *Plato's Sophist.* Trans. Richard Rojcewicz and André Schuwer. Bloomington: Indiana University Press, 1997.

Hesiod. 1983. *Theogony; Works and Days; Shield.* Trans. Apostolos N. Athanas-sakis. Baltimore, Md.: The Johns Hopkins University Press.

Hobbes, Thomas. 1651. *Leviathan.* Indianapolis, Ind.: Hackett, 1994.

Honneth, Axel. 1992. *The Struggle for Recognition: The Moral Grammar of Social Conflicts.* Trans. Joel Anderson. Cambridge, Mass.: Polity, 1995.

Horkheimer, Max, and Theodor Adorno. 1944. *Dialectic of Enlightenment.* Trans. John Cumming. New York: Seabury, 1972.

Huffer, Lynne. 2010. *Mad for Foucault: Rethinking the Foundations of Queer Theory.* New York: Columbia University Press.

James, William. 1907. *Pragmatism.* Indianapolis, Ind.: Hackett, 1981.

Johnson, James Weldon. 1900. "*Lift Ev'ry Voice and Sing.*" In *The Norton Anthology of African American Literature, ed.* Henry Louis Gates Jr. and Nellie Y. McKay, 768–769. New York: Norton, 1997).

Kant, Immanuel. 1784. "*An Answer to the Question: 'What Is Enlightenment?'*"

In *Political Writings*, 2nd enlarged ed., edited by Hans Reiss, translated by H. B. Nisbet, 54–60. Cambridge: Cambridge University Press, 1991.

Kant, Immanuel. 1784b. *"Idea for a Universal History with a Cosmopolitan Intent."* In *Perpetual Peace and Other Essays*, trans. Ted Humphreys, 29–40. Indianapolis, Ind.: Hackett, 1983.

Kant, Immanuel. 1785. *Grounding for the Metaphysics of Morals.* Trans. James W. Ellington. Indianapolis, Ind.: Hackett, 1993.

Kant, Immanuel. 1795. *"To Perpetual Peace: A Philosophical Sketch,"* In *Perpetual Peace and Other Essays*, trans. Ted Humphreys, 107–143. Indianapolis, Ind.: Hackett, 1983.

Kant, Immanuel. 1798a. *Anthropologie du point de vue pragmatique.* Trans. Michel Foucault. Paris: Vrin, 1964.

Kant, Immanuel. 1798b. *Anthropology from a Pragmatic Point of View.* Trans. Victor Lyle Dowdell. Carbondale: Southern Illinois University Press, 1978.

Kant, Immanuel. 1983. *Perpetual Peace and Other Essays.* Trans. Ted Humphreys. Indianapolis, Ind.: Hackett.

Kant, Immanuel. 1991. *Political Writings.* 2nd enlarged ed. Ed. Hans Reiss. Trans. H. B. Nisbet. Cambridge: Cambridge University Press.

Kantorowicz, Ernst H. 1957. *The King's Two Bodies: A Study in Mediaeval Political Theology.* Princeton, N.J.: Princeton University Press, 1997.

Koopman, Colin. 2013. *Genealogy as Critique: Foucault and the Problems of Modernity.* Bloomington: Indiana University Press.

Le Guin, Ursula K. 1974. *The Dispossessed.* New York: HarperPrism, 1994.

Lynch, Richard A. 1993. *"Bakhtin's Ethical Vision."* *Philosophy and Literature* 17, no. 1 (April 1993): 98–109.

Lynch, Richard A. 1998. *"Is Power All There Is? Michel Foucault and the 'Omnipresence' of Power Relations."* *Philosophy Today* 42, no. 1 (Spring 1998): 65–70.

Lynch, Richard A. 2001. *"Mutual Recognition: Reading Hegel Against Kojève."* *International Philosophical Quarterly* 41, no. 1 (March 2001): 33–48.

Lynch, Richard A. 2013. *"Michel Foucault's Shorter Works in English: Bibliography and Concordance."* In *A Companion to Foucault*, ed. Christopher Falzon, Timothy O'Leary, and Jana Sawicki, 562–592. Oxford: Wiley-Blackwell, 2013.

Macey, David. 1993. *The Lives of Michel Foucault.* New York: Vintage, 1995.

Machiavelli, Niccolò. 1532. *The Prince.* Trans. Harvey C. Mansfield Jr. Chicago: University of Chicago Press, 1985.

Mann, Thomas. 1924. *The Magic Mountain.* Trans. John E. Woods. New York: Vintage, 1996.

Manuel, Frank E., ed. 1965. *Utopias and Utopian Thought.* Boston: Beacon.

Marx, Karl. 1843a. *"Letters from the Franco-German Yearbooks."* In *Early Writings*, 200–209. New York: Vintage, 1975.

Marx, Karl. 1843b. *"For a Ruthless Criticism of Everything Existing."* In *The Marx-Engels Reader*, 2nd ed., ed. Robert C. Tucker, 12–15. New York: Norton, 1978.

Marx, Karl. 1845 *"Theses on Feuerbach."* In *The Marx-Engels Reader*, 2nd ed., ed. Robert C. Tucker, 143–145. New York: Norton, 1978.

Marx, Karl. 1859. *"Marx on the History of His Opinions"* [preface to *A Contribution to the Critique of Political Economy*]. In *The Marx-Engels Reader*, 2nd ed., ed. Robert C. Tucker, 3–6. New York: Norton, 1978.

Marx, Karl. 1975. *Early Writings*. New York: Vintage.

Marx, Karl. 1978. *The Marx-Engels Reader*. 2nd ed. Ed. Robert C. Tucker. New York: Norton.

McCarthy, Thomas. 1990. *"The Critique of Impure Reason: Foucault and the Frankfurt School."* In *Ideals and Illusions: On Reconstruction and Deconstruction in Contemporary Critical Theory*, 43–75. Cambridge, Mass.: MIT Press, 1991.

McCarthy, Thomas. 1991. *Ideals and Illusions: On Reconstruction and Deconstruction in Contemporary Critical Theory.* Cambridge, Mass.: MIT Press.

McDowell, John. 1996. *Mind and World.* Cambridge, Mass.: Harvard University Press.

McNay, Lois. 1992. *Foucault and Feminism: Power, Gender, and the Self.* Boston: Northeastern University Press.

McWhorter, LaDelle. 1999. *Bodies and Pleasures: Foucault and the Politics of Sexual Normalization.* Bloomington: Indiana University Press.

McWhorter, LaDelle. 2003. *"Foucault's Political Spirituality."* *Philosophy Today* 47, no. 5 (SPEP Supplement 2003): 39–44.

Meinecke, Friedrich. 1924. *Machiavellism: The Doctrine of Raison d'État and Its Place in Modern History.* Trans. Douglas Scott. New Brunswick, N.J.: Transaction, 1998.

Menand, Louis. 2001. *The Metaphysical Club.* New York: Farrar, Straus and Giroux.

Merrick, Jeffrey, and Bryant T. Ragan Jr., eds. 1996. *Homosexuality in Modern France.* New York: Oxford University Press.

Mill, John Stuart. 1859. *On Liberty.* Cambridge: Cambridge University Press, 1989.

Miller, James. 1993. *The Passion of Michel Foucault.* New York: Simon & Schuster.

Millett, Kate. 1970. *Sexual Politics.* New York: Doubleday.

Nagel, Thomas. 1977. "*The Fragmentation of Value*." In *Mortal Questions,* 128–141. Cambridge: Cambridge University Press, 1979.

Nagel, Thomas. 1979. *Mortal Questions.* Cambridge: Cambridge University Press.

Narayan, Uma. 1995. "*Colonialism and Its Others: Considerations on Rights and Care Discourses*." *Hypatia* 10, no. 2 (Spring 1995): 133–140.

Nehamas, Alexander. 1998. *The Art of Living: Socratic Reflections from Plato to Foucault.* Berkeley: University of California Press.

Neurath, Otto. 1913. "*The Lost Wanderers of Descartes and the Auxiliary Motive*." In *Philosophical Papers, 1913–1946,* ed. and trans. Robert S. Cohen and Marie Neurath, 1–12. Dordrecht: D. Reidel, 1983.

Neurath, Otto. 1932. "*Protocol Sentences*." In *Philosophical Papers, 1913–1946,* ed. and trans. Robert S. Cohen and Marie Neurath, 91–99. Dordrecht: D. Reidel, 1983.

Neurath, Otto. 1935. "*The Unity of Science as a Task*." In *Philosophical Papers, 1913–1946,* ed. and trans. Robert S. Cohen and Marie Neurath, 115–120. Dordrecht: D. Reidel, 1983.

Neurath, Otto. 1983. *Philosophical Papers, 1913–1946.* Ed. and trans. Robert S. Cohen and Marie Neurath. Dordrecht: D. Reidel.

Noddings, Nel. 1984. *Caring: A Feminine Approach to Ethics and Moral Education.* Berkeley: University of California Press, 2003.

Noddings, Nel. 2002. *Starting at Home: Caring and Social Policy.* Berkeley: University of California Press, 2002.

Nussbaum, Martha C. 1986. *The Fragility of Goodness: Luck and Ethics in Greek Tragedy and Philosophy.* New York: Continuum.

Nye, Robert A. 1996. "*Michel Foucault's Sexuality and the History of Homosexuality in France*," In *Homosexuality in Modern France, ed.* J. Merrick and B. T. Ragan Jr., 225–241. New York: Oxford University Press, 1996.

O'Leary, Timothy. 2002. *Foucault and the Art of Ethics.* Cambridge: Cambridge University Press.

O'Leary, Timothy, and Christopher Falzon, eds. 2010. *Foucault and Philosophy.* Oxford: Wiley-Blackwell.

Quart, Alissa. 2012. "*The Milk Wars*." *New York Times* (July 15 2012): SR9.

Roach, Tom. 2012. *Friendship as a Way of Life: Foucault, AIDS, and the Politics of Shared Estrangement.* Albany: SUNY Press.

Robbins, Jim. 2012. "*Manmade Epidemics*." *New York Times* (July 15 2012): SR1.

Rousseau, Jean-Jacques. 1755. *Discourse on the Origin of Inequality.* Trans. Donald. A. Cress. Indianapolis, Ind.: Hackett, 1992.

Sawicki, Jana. 1991. *Disciplining Foucault: Feminism, Power, and the Body.* New York: Routledge.

Schuld, J. Joyce. 2003. *Foucault and Augustine: Reconsidering Power and Love.* Notre Dame, Ind.: University of Notre Dame Press.

Scott, Charles E. 1990. *The Question of Ethics: Nietzsche, Foucault, Heidegger.* Bloomington: Indiana University Press.

Senellart, Michel. 2004. "*Course Context.*" In CdF78ET, 369–401.

Shilts, Randy. 1988/2007. *And the Band Played On: Politics, People, and the AIDS Epidemic.* 20th anniversary ed. New York: St. Martin's Griffin.

Stampp, Kenneth M. 1956. *The Peculiar Institution: Slavery in the Antebellum South.* New York: Vintage, 1989.

Sullivan, Andrew. 1998. *Love Undetectable: Notes on Friendship, Sex, and Survival.* New York: Knopf.

Taylor, Charles. 1977. "*Self-Interpreting Animals.*" In *Human Agency and Language: Philosophical Papers 1*, 45–76. Cambridge: Cambridge University Press, 1985.

Taylor, Charles. 1984. "*Foucault on Freedom and Truth.*" In *Philosophy and the Human Sciences: Philosophical Papers 2*, 152–184. Cambridge: Cambridge University Press, 1985b.

Taylor, Charles. 1985a. *Human Agency and Language: Philosophical Papers 1.* Cambridge: Cambridge University Press.

Taylor, Charles. 1985b. *Philosophy and the Human Sciences: Philosophical Papers 2.* Cambridge: Cambridge University Press.

Taylor, Dianna, and Karen Vintges. 2004. *Feminism and the Final Foucault.* Urbana: University of Illinois Press.

Tillich, Paul. 1951. "*Critique and Justification of Utopia.*" In *Utopias and Utopian Thought*, ed. Frank E. Manuel, 296–309. Boston: Beacon, 1965.

Tocqueville, Alexis de. 1835. *Democracy in America.* Trans. Frederick Lawrence. New York: Harper Perennial, 2006.

Tronto, Joan. 1993. *Moral Boundaries: A Political Argument for an Ethics of Care.* New York: Routledge.

Tygiel, Jules. 1997. *Baseball's Great Experiment: Jackie Robinson and His Legacy.* Expanded ed. New York: Oxford University Press.

West, Cornel. 1982. *Prophesy Deliverance! An Afro-American Revolutionary Christianity.* Louisville, Ky.: Westminster John Knox.

White, Richard. 1999. "*Friendship: Ancient and Modern.*" *International Philosophical Quarterly* 39, no. 1 (no. 153) (March 1999): 19–34.

White, Stephen K. 1986. "*Foucault's Challenge to Critical Theory.*" *American Political Science Review* 80, no. 2 (June 1986): 419–432.

Index

active self-transformation, 135; homosexual relationships and, 136
ACT-UP (AIDS Coalition to Unleash Power), 2, 163–165
Adorno, Theodor, *Dialectic of Enlightenment*, 10, 85
aesthetic *versus* ethical, 143–144
aesthetico activity, 141
The Age of Ruptures (Daniel), 184
AIDS epidemic, Foucauldian political model and, 163–165
analytics of power *versus* theory of power, 21–22
anarchism, 173–174
anatomo-politics, 96; sex and, 146–147
aporias, 185–186
apparatuses of security. *See* security
archeological period, 12
Aristotle: on friendship, 157–158; *phronesis*, 183
art of government, 118–120, 200–201; Christianity and, 119. *See also* pastoral power
arts of existence, 144–145
attitude: to existence, 172; modernity as, 169–171; non-necessity of power, 173–174; self-fashioning and, 143. *See also* critical attitude
autocritique process, 54
axiological approach to Foucault, 12–13

Baptist, Edward E., *The Half Has Never Been Told,* 211n15
Beauvoir, Simone de, *The Ethics of Ambiguity,* 94, 137, 189
Benhabib, Seyla, on critical theory, 5–6

Bentham, Jeremy, *Panopticon Writings,* 55, 58, 73
binary relationships, 34–35
biopolitics, 95; medicine, 107; modulation, 107; pastoral power and, 122; risks and, 200; sex and, 146–147
biopower, 21; definitions, 106; description, 90; disciplinary power and, 124; global reach, 212n7; governmentality and, 123–126; introduction of term, 62; macro forms of power, 90; pastoral power and, 119–120; population and, 108–109; security and, 107
bodies and pleasures, 213n5; deployments of power, 148; disciplinary power and, 148–149; homosexuality and, 148; modern power and, 150; resistance to power and, 149–150; utopian vision and, 149–150
bootstrapping freedom, 187–195
Butler, Judith, on theory of power, 24–25

carceral archipelago, 78–79
carceral society, 114
care: ethics of care, 159–160; as practice, 159–160
care of the self, 159–160; benefit to others, 162–163; *epimeleia heautou,* 162; homosexual friendship, 163–164; parrhesia and, 179
"The Care of the Self as a Practice of Freedom" (Foucault), 137
Caring (Nodding), 159
censorship, 27–28
Christianity, governing and, 119
codes: morality and, 139–140; penitence and, 140; subjectivity and, 140

Jimmy Casas Klausen, *Fugitive Rousseau: Slavery, Primitivism, and Political Freedom*

Drucilla Cornell, *Law and Revolution in South Africa: uBuntu, Dignity, and the Struggle for Constitutional Transformation*

Abraham Acosta, *Thresholds of Illiteracy: Theory, Latin America, and the Crisis of Resistance*

Andrew Dilts, *Punishment and Inclusion: Race, Membership, and the Limits of American Liberalism*

Lewis R. Gordon, *What Fanon Said: A Philosophical Introduction to His Life and Thought*. Foreword by Sonia Dayan-Herzbrun, Afterword by Drucilla Cornell

Gaymon Bennett, *Technicians of Human Dignity: On the Politics of Intrinsic Worth*

Drucilla Cornell and Nick Friedman, *The Mandate of Dignity: Ronald Dworkin, Revolutionary Constitutionalism, and the Claims of Justice*

Richard A. Lynch, *Foucault's Critical Ethics*